The Real Ike

The Real Ike

Eisenhower Fact and Fiction

MARTIN MACK TEASLEY

UNIVERSITY PRESS OF KANSAS

Published by the University Press of Kansas (Lawrence, Kansas 66045), which was organized by the Kansas Board of Regents and is operated and funded by Emporia State University, Fort Hays State University, Kansas State University, Pittsburg State University, the University of Kansas, and Wichita State University.

Cover design by Karl Janssen
Cover art: White House portrait of Dwight D. Eisenhower painted by James Anthony Wills, 1967. White House Historical Association/White House Collection.

Library of Congress Cataloging-in-Publication Data
Names: Teasley, Martin Mack, author
Title: The real Ike : Eisenhower fact and fiction / Martin Mack Teasley.
Description: Lawrence, Kansas : University Press of Kansas, [2025] | Includes bibliographical references and index
Identifiers: LCCN 2025008535 (print) | LCCN 2025008536 (ebook) | ISBN 9780700640690 paperback | ISBN 9780700640706 epub
Subjects: LCSH: Eisenhower, Dwight D. (Dwight David), 1890–1969 | United States. Army—Officers—Biogra phy | Dwight D. Eisenhower Library | Generals— Texas—Biography | Presidents—United States—Biog raphy | United States—Politics and government— 1953–1961 | BISAC: BIOGRAPHY & AUTOBIOGRA PHY / Presidents & Heads of State | HISTORY / United States / General | LCGFT: Biographies Classifi cation: LCC E745.E35 T43 2025 (print) | LCC E745.E35 (ebook) | DDC 973.921092 [B]—dc23/eng/20250813
LC record available at https://lccn.loc.gov/2025008535
LC ebook record available at https://lccn.loc.gov/2025008536

British Library Cataloguing-in-Publication Data is available.
Authorised Representative Details: Easy Access System Europe
Mustamäe tee 50, 10621 Tallinn, Estonia | gpsr.requests@easproject.com

For Ingeborg

CONTENTS

I remember so well that time in 1966 when Dwight D. Eisenhower told me that I had a duty to my country as a young citizen of America. Ike praised me, saying I was a member of the finest generation this nation had produced, despite "the kooks, misguided people, Beatles and beatniks" who took up so much space in the media.

To be fair, Eisenhower's high praise was not directed at me personally. In actuality, the former president and five-star general was speaking to me and the other 1,871 college graduates receiving their degrees from Kansas State University in Manhattan, Kansas, on that hot June day in 1966. The elder statesman gave us our patriotic marching orders, after which he was awarded an honorary doctorate from the university. In retrospect, Eisenhower's presence in Ahearn Fieldhouse that day was a harbinger of my future career path, which became three decades of service with the National Archives helping promote and preserve Ike's place in history. I was destined to serve as deputy director of the Eisenhower Presidential Library and Museum (1979–2005) and executive director of the non-profit Eisenhower Foundation (2005–2013).

As it would turn out, my formal education and military service were the perfect preparation. Immediately after college, I spent five years on active duty as an air force intelligence officer with assignments in Germany and Vietnam. At the US Air Forces in Europe headquarters in Wiesbaden, Germany, I was the North Atlantic Treaty Organization (NATO) target materials release officer, sending US-produced, classified, tactical, intelligence-targeting materials to NATO flying units at bases throughout western Europe. Eisenhower had served as the first military Supreme Allied Commander of NATO. I was exposed to NATO military lingo in addition to the usual US military terminology—a very helpful skill set for my work at the Eisenhower Library.

From Germany, I was assigned to the Seventh Air Force headquarters on Tan Son Nhut Air Base near Saigon, Vietnam. I worked behind the fence in the SCIF, which, as many people have learned recently in the news, means a sensitive compartmented information facility. During my time with the Eisenhower Presidential Library, the archives included almost a half-million pages of classified material in its historical holdings.

My "need to know" continued; I was destined to hold a top secret security clearance in the civil service for over thirty years.

After active military duty, I spent twenty-five years in the Air Force Intelligence Reserve program. My assignment the last dozen years was as a mobilization augmentee for the US Defense/Air Attache at the American embassy in London, England. The US embassy, located in Grosvenor Square, was across the street from the building that served as General Eisenhower's World War II headquarters. I walked by a statue of Eisenhower (and saluted) each time I entered the embassy during my tours there.

My formal education includes a BA in German, MA in International Relations, and ML in Librarianship. Each of these degrees were very apropos for my work at the Eisenhower Library. I joined the US National Archives in 1972 and served with that agency until 2005. My initial assignment was in Washington, DC, in the Office of Presidential Papers in the Nixon White House. This was on the fourth floor of the Old Executive Office Building in the White House compound—later renamed the Eisenhower Office Building. Richard M. Nixon, of course, had been Eisenhower's vice president from 1953–1961. Another of my connections to Eisenhower.

After assuming the position as deputy director at the Eisenhower Presidential Library and Museum in Abilene, Kansas, in 1979, my focus became Ike. My knowledge about his life and times grew quickly as I oversaw research and reference service in the twenty-six million pages of historical material in the archives. I also solicited additional personal papers for the library collection from former Eisenhower administration officials, conducted oral history interviews with those who knew and worked with Ike, and organized academic conferences at the library. I presented formal papers and gave speeches about Ike at numerous venues across the state and around the country, at university symposia, the Smithsonian Institute, Eisenhower Library conferences, Elderhostels, historical societies, and community service clubs.

No doubt one of the most beneficial experiences for this writing project came from the thousands of reference inquiries about Eisenhower that crossed my desk and were assigned by me to the library's archives staff for research and reply. I had my pulse on the major, minor, little-known, and even very strange issues and questions that arose about Ike from scholars, journalists, and, often most interestingly, from the public. One of my staff archivists once complained in frustration, "What are we, the

Ike Trivia Center?!" I told him, "Yes, as a matter of fact we own that role as well as carrying out our usual work with academic researchers." I oversaw the library's studied and professional response to all these queries, large and small.

General and President Eisenhower may have saved the free world a couple of times—World War II and during the Cold War—and that story has already been well-covered (and rightly continues to be studied) by historians. Myriad books have been published about General Eisenhower and his role in leading the Allies to wartime victory in Europe. Numerous titles also document his two terms in the White House: ending the Korean War, creating the Interstate Highway System, balancing the budget, signing the first civil rights legislation since Reconstruction, sending troops to integrate Little Rock Central High School, putting America into outer space with the creation of NASA and first launch of US satellites, handling the Suez Crisis, and waging the Cold War. New books about Ike are published each year as he continues to grow in stature in the eyes of historians and the public. Eisenhower has recently been ranked as high as the fifth best in the pantheon of US presidents, and, dare I say, he is worthy of Mount Rushmore. Still, there is much more to learn about this American hero.

A different focus is what I intend to give my readers. Rather than the usual chronological account of the major events in the general and president's military and political careers, each of my twenty-five chapters stands alone and focuses on a lesser-known facet of Eisenhower. That said, these chapters are as well-documented as those found in any other book about Ike. The footnote citations in *The Real Ike: Eisenhower Fact and Fiction* make that evident. I have referenced existing scholarship on the life and times of Dwight D. Eisenhower, but there are citations for new material from the rich archives of the Eisenhower Presidential Library, as well as from many other sources.

You will learn personal things about Ike that may surprise. There are accomplishments as president that have gone unrecognized in the published books about Eisenhower, and where credit is long overdue. There are even things that could be viewed upon initial blush as negative, which may give the reader pause, but that need to be placed in proper perspective for complete understanding. And there are various myths about Ike that are often most unusual and intriguing. Ike was a complicated man.

A final word. After researching and writing this book, my admiration for Dwight D. Eisenhower has only grown. *The Real Ike: Eisenhower Fact and Fiction* aims to not only enlighten but occasionally help set the historical record straight. My hope is that it will also be an enjoyable read. You will see why we still like Ike.

Martin Mack Teasley
Abilene, Kansas
2025

CHAPTER ONE

THE DWIGHT D. EISENHOWER PRESIDENTIAL LIBRARY IN ABILENE
FROM IVORY TOWER TO PEOPLE'S LIBRARY

Question: "From Abilene? Isn't someone famous from there?"
Answer: "Yeah, there's an Eisenhower Museum, but I haven't
been down there since Fifth Grade. He was a famous general."
—*Anonymous Abilene High School Student*

I asked for directions to the Eisenhower Presidential Library when I
showed up in Abilene to report as deputy director in February 1979. A
helpful citizen said, "Go south on Buckeye Avenue to the fourth traffic
light, then cross the railroad tracks, and the Ivory Tower will be on your
left." Well, not really, but it might as well have happened this way. The
Eisenhower Library was indeed, for all intents and purposes, the "ivory
tower" on the edge of the village, even if it was on the wrong side of the
tracks in southside Abilene.

Dr. John E. Wickman, the director of the library at that time (who would
serve for the next twenty years), was a very smart man with a doctorate
degree in history and, as a result, a very academic perspective on the mission of the institution. Research into the millions of pages of historical
manuscripts was for serious scholars. The university researchers were
very well-served, and the historical assessment of Eisenhower was on the
rise during Wickman's administration of the library.

The few public programs held were academic conferences similar in
nature to those found on a university campus. Security guards ensured
there was no walking on the grass by those visiting the twenty-two-acre Eisenhower Center grounds. It was idyllic and quiet. Most people in Abilene
were proud to have the Eisenhower Library, Museum, and Boyhood Home
in their town, even if they had not been there since their fifth-grade school
field trip to the museum. It was a major tourist attraction that certainly
helped the local economy, but the citizenry knew very little about what
went on behind the marble walls inside the library building. And rarely
did they set foot on the hallowed grounds of the ivory tower. But things
were about to change.

As deputy director, I was soon charged with planning and implementing public programs. During the 1980s, I worked closely with the Kansas Committee for the Humanities and area universities in organizing a series of exciting conferences at the Eisenhower Library. Our approach was to invite not only traditional academic historians, but also famous authors and individuals who had played a role in the historical events of the Eisenhower era.

We began in 1980 with a three-day conference entitled "America in the 1950s." Playwright Robert E. Lee (1918–1994) discussed how his plays of the era reflected the cultural values being debated in society at the time. His works *Inherit the Wind* and *Auntie Mame* were both important period pieces that were made into motion pictures. The issue of race in America in the 1950s was discussed by Arthur S. Flemming, chairman of the US Civil Right Commission and attorney Charles S. Scott, who had represented the plaintiffs in *Brown v. Board of Education*. The opening keynote address was given by John Henry Faulk (1913–1990), a radio star and humorist who was blacklisted by Senator Joseph McCarthy in the 1950s.

Most unusual, no doubt, was a conference session entitled "The Schizophrenic Fifties: Affluence, Conformity & Alienation," which featured beatnik poet Allen Ginsberg (1926–1997) reading excerpts of his famous poem "Howl" to a captivated, if mildly embarrassed, audience. The poem is full of not-so-subtle word pictures of gay erotica and drug use—not as shocking in Greenwich Village but not the normal fare in Abilene, Kansas. And no doubt for the benefit of his Eisenhower Library audience, Ginsberg added an extra stanza that does not appear in the original version of "Howl." This involved Ike and his secretary of state, John Foster Dulles. The beatnik from New York City more than lived up to his image. Toto, we weren't in Kansas anymore; except we were.

For a 1982 Conference on the North Atlantic Treaty Organization (NATO), we had two early NATO Supreme Allied Commanders, as well as the current supreme commander, all the way from NATO headquarters in Brussels. These four-star generals were the successors to General Eisenhower, who served as the first Supreme Allied Commander Europe (SACEUR), between 1951 and 1952.

"The American Dream" was examined in 1983. The keynote address was by Richard Reeves, *New Yorker* magazine writer and author of *American Journey: Traveling with Tocqueville in Search of Democracy in America*. Author Merle Miller spoke on "Ike and the American Dream." Miller was just finishing research at the Eisenhower Presidential Library on his 859-page epic work *Ike the Soldier: As They Knew Him* (1987). Other speakers included Joanna Stratton (*Pioneer Women*), Richard Rodriguez (*Hunger of Memory*), Marie Winn (*The Plug-In Drug: Television, Children, and the Family*), and space shuttle *Columbia* astronaut Colonel Joe Engle.

In 1988, "In the Service of their Country: Women During the Eisenhower Era" included: two of the first female general officers in the US military; one of the original Women Airforce Service Pilots (WASPs) who ferried aircraft across the Atlantic during World War II; and female US ambassadors.

The 1980s was an exciting decade of public programming at the Eisenhower Presidential Library that culminated in a year-long series of events throughout 1990 commemorating the centennial of Dwight D. Eisenhower. Today, the library continues to provide excellent public programming, with a wide variety of events; everything from lectures, book talks, and monthly "lunch and learn" presentations by Eisenhower scholars on a wide array of historical topics. On the first Saturday in June, the anniversary of D-Day is commemorated. Military reenactors bivouac on the Eisenhower Center grounds, museum admission is free, the Fort Riley commanding general's mounted color guard performs on their magnificent horses, and the day ends with an outdoor concert at sunset performed by a symphony orchestra from the steps of the majestic library building. People by the thousands come from miles around with their lawn chairs and blankets to listen and celebrate and enjoy the food vendors. Very different from the days when the security guards kept people off the grass.

Each year, hundreds of scholars from across the country and around the world conduct research in the rich archival holdings at the Eisenhower Library. The holdings of this presidential library are unrivaled in scope and depth and total over twenty-six million pages. To provide a concept of the volume of the historical materials, if the 33,000 archive boxes were lined up, they would extend two and a half miles. This detailed documentation of the Eisenhower Era covers World War II, the Cold War, and almost anything else that was happening in the 1940s and 1950s. It is not just Ike's papers. The library holdings include the personal papers of more than five hundred other important individuals—generals, cabinet officials, secretaries and under-secretaries of government agencies, White House staff, personal friends—people who worked with Eisenhower in the service of their country. These personal papers collections document their entire careers, extending before and well beyond their time in the Eisenhower administration. The richness of this vast archival collection is the source of Ike's elevation by historians to the near-great echelon of American presidents.

The research room is typically visited by those looking for original source material for their MA thesis or PhD dissertation in history or political science. The average research stay is five days and about one-quarter of the scholars are from universities overseas. These academic users are the *raison d'etre* of the research room at the Eisenhower Library. Read the acknowledgments and examine the footnotes of any serious book about the European Theater during World War II or about international and domestic events in the 1950s in which America played a role, and you will see that the published work was very likely researched at least in part at the Eisenhower Presidential Library. Interestingly, overseas scholars come to this library to study their own country's foreign policy vis-à-vis the United States, because our holdings are normally open for research and are much more complete than the records in their own home country archives.

While serious scholarship remains the mainstay of the Eisenhower Presidential Library, in the earlier days there were other audiences that were not being served. Prior to the Eisenhower Centennial 1990, when an Abilene youth went out of town, he or she might be asked by someone, "You're from Abilene? Isn't someone famous from there?" The Abilene student would often respond, "Yeah, there's an Eisenhower Museum and stuff, but I haven't been down there since Fifth Grade. He was a famous general." This unfortunate lack of familiarity with their hometown hero had to change.

The first step was narrowly focused on foreign language students at Abilene High School (AHS). My spouse, Ingeborg Teasley, the German language teacher at AHS, ask me to devise a program whereby her students could visit the Eisenhower Library research room to examine original historical documents in the German language. With the library's rich holdings on World War II, NATO, the Cold War, and US relations with Germany, it was not difficult to identify archives boxes full of material that would allow the students to see the practical side of their foreign language study. We could offer correspondence to President Eisenhower from West German Chancellor Konrad Adenauer or World War II propaganda leaflets in German language dropped by the Allies on enemy soldiers, or even a fascinating copy of the last will and testament of Adolf Hitler. After the initial visit in 1985, this research activity became an annual field trip experience for the German II, III, and IV students at Abilene High. The project was innovative enough that an article entitled "German Language Study at the Dwight D. Eisenhower Library" was published in *Foreign Language Annals*.[1] Soon thereafter, the library developed foreign language guides to holdings for Spanish- and French-language high school students as well. *Sehr gut, tres bon, muy bueno!*

In 2001, the Abilene High School sophomore English class research projects began. Mitzi Gose, an English teacher at AHS, initiated this concept and collaborated with archivists at the Eisenhower Library to prepare small research files on a wide variety of historical topics from the Eisenhower era. The packets contain copies of original documents from the rich manuscript collections in the holdings of the library. Students are each asked to select a subject of interest, and they then make four to five one-hour visits to the library to conduct research using these original sources and become an "expert" on their Ike-related topic. The exercise culminates back in the classroom, where the teacher has them each give a short oral presentation to the class on their research. The wide-ranging subjects include D-Day, Little Rock school integration, the Holocaust, the Interstate Highway Act, the polio vaccine, the execution of spies Julius and Ethel Rosenberg, the shooting down of the U-2 reconnaissance plane over the Soviet Union, the role of First Lady Mamie Eisenhower, and many other topics. Now when these sophomores graduate and head off to college or go out into the workforce, they have an answer when asked by friends, "Hey, tell me something about Eisenhower." They have become Ike experts in one narrow facet of his life.

For several years in the 1990s, always on a sunny fall day in October, the entire K-12 student body (some 1,500 students) of Unified School District 435 marched down on foot or rode a bus from every Abilene school to the grounds of the Eisenhower Center for an hour-long outdoor commemoration as part of Eisenhower legacy week. The students and faculty would enjoy patriotic music and presentations about their hometown hero to remember and honor Ike on the anniversary of his October 14 birthday. The logistics of this mass event eventually proved too cumbersome to continue, but for several years, the youth of Abilene were learning more and more about Eisenhower.

Kim Barbieri, the first education specialist at the Eisenhower Library, developed a wonderful program entitled Five Star Leaders (FSL) for students primarily at the high school and college level. The curriculum has even been used by army officers at nearby Fort Riley and Fort

Leavenworth as part of their continuing professional military education. Participants in Five Star Leaders role-play and examine original historical documents in recreating the decision-making that went into two historic Eisenhower-related events. These involve the preparation and planning for the General Eisenhower–led Normandy invasion on June 6, 1944 (D-Day), and his presidential decision to send the 101st Airborne Division paratroopers to Arkansas to enforce the court-ordered integration of Little Rock Central High School in 1957. The new education staff at the Eisenhower Foundation has further extended the reach of the program by developing an FSL version for middle-school-age students. By now, several thousand students of all ages have graduated from Five Star Leaders.

The Eisenhower Library was limited to the work of a single education staff member for two decades. The library did its best with few resources. Reinforcements arrived in 2012 with the hiring of two education specialists by the library's non-profit partner, the Eisenhower Foundation. Within a year, supported by grants and fundraising, a new and dynamic education program was initiated. Known as "IKEducation," it was geared primarily at school-age children (K-12), with the goal of educating a new generation about the important legacy of Kansas hero and national figure Dwight D. Eisenhower. Over the last several years, the foundation's education staff has grown, and tens of thousands of young students have made field trips to the Eisenhower Library and Museum and participated in enrichment exercises in conjunction with their visits. There are now online options for use by teachers in classrooms beyond commuting distance. There is something for students of all ages, including such varied topics as:

Little Ike Artifacts
Dogs for Defense
Rosie the Riveter
Constitution Day
Paint Like Ike (recreate an Eisenhower original oil painting)
Navajo Code Talkers
Space Race
Spies Among Us: The Red Scare
Desegregation of Little Rock High School
Holocaust: From a Name to a Number
Omaha Beach on D-Day

For enthusiasm you could not match a group at the other end of the age spectrum, namely participants in the library's annual Elderhostel program. Each year from 1988–1999, a class of twenty-five to fifty senior citizens spent a week at the library studying the Eisenhower era. The program consisted of lectures, field trips, behind-the-scenes tours, and actual research using original manuscript materials. The Eisenhower Library was the first presidential library to host a week-long, on-site Elderhostel. The exciting thing was the fact the six-day program was not simply a series of formal lectures, but rather a fluid seminar with the "teachers" often becoming the "students" as the hostelers shared with library staff and guest faculty "how it really was back in those days."[2]

Another sea change at the library was a new approach to the official "public use" of the government facilities of the Eisenhower Center complex. The center has increased the opportunity for organizations of a non-political and non-commercial nature to use the facilities. The Community Foundation of Dickinson County has held their annual recognition banquet in the library courtyard. A "dining out" was held by one of the army units at nearby Fort Riley.

For twenty-two years, from 1983–2005, the library hosted the Kansas state finals of the National History Day contest. The first weekend in May, some three hundred junior high and senior high school students from across the entire state converged on the library to compete for the right to participate in the National History Day finals held each June at the University of Maryland. This was a perfect program to be hosted as part of the library's expanding public use of buildings. After two decades, History Day eventually outgrew the Eisenhower Library and moved to the state historical society museum in Topeka. But History Day has now been replaced by another great student program, namely the finals of the Kansas State Geography Bee.

A one-time event of an entirely different nature was the Abilene High School junior-senior prom held at the library in the spring of 1993. The students from Ike's alma mater had a truly memorable evening dancing to the DJ in the library's grand lobby, with its Italian marble walls. The library had even installed a temporary disco ball overhead. The students enjoyed refreshments in the adjacent interior courtyard of the Eisenhower Library building. The only "ill effect" of this event was finding miniature silver and blue decorative stars around the building floors for several weeks thereafter, but that brought smiles to the faces of the maintenance staff.

The rich and growing archival holdings of the Eisenhower Library have played an integral role in Ike's recent, impressive rise to the upper reaches of presidential rankings by historians. It can also be argued that the enhanced public programs of the Eisenhower Library have raised his esteem among the general population. So, change has indeed come to the Eisenhower Presidential Library over its sixty-year existence. No angry peasants stormed the ivory tower walls with torches and pitchforks. Instead, the institution extended its hand and opened the doors to Abilene and the entire state of Kansas. The citizens of Ike's hometown now have a definite sense of ownership in this true gem on the Great Plains.

CHAPTER TWO

THE IKE NICKNAME

Ike—"a fellow, especially if uncouth or rustic."
—*Random House Historical Dictionary of American Slang*

It seems perhaps a simple question, but it is one with no easy answer. When reference archivists at the Eisenhower Presidential Library answer the telephone, the inquiring voice on the other end occasionally has just one question: "Why was he called Ike?"

Even Dwight Eisenhower himself did not know the origin of his now world-famous nickname. He did not address this issue in any of his four books, including *At Ease: Stories I Tell to Friends*, the anecdotal autobiography of his early years. That would have been the logical opportunity to lay to rest this question for future generations. Eisenhower wrote that while growing up in Abilene, he had always been called Ike by his friends and it was as simple as that. Furthermore, he also noted, "Maybe I let it slip, but shortly after arriving at West Point soon all were calling me Ike."[1] The moniker followed him for the rest of his life.

Ike was not an uncommon nickname for Abilene boys growing up at the turn of the twentieth century. When boyhood friend Benjamin Reese wrote the now famous General Eisenhower during the war and addressed him more formally as "Dwight," Ike admonished Reese by writing back, "While amongst the old Woodbine gang I had no monopoly on the name 'Ike,' I still expect to be called that by my friends."[2] Eisenhower was referring to the gang of boys who used to while away the summer weekends camping south of Abilene, along banks of the Smoky Hill River. Dwight Eisenhower was not the only Ike among his youthful friends, but the handle stuck with him.

Eisenhower's biographers have attempted to provide an explanation for the nickname, but their conclusions leave one wanting. In one of the earliest works about Eisenhower, Alden Hatch wrote in *General Ike* (1944) that the "Ike" designation originated with Dwight's playmates and that Ike seemed the logical match for the Eisenhower name.

Edgar and Ike were known as Big Ike and Little Ike. Something about the name of Eisenhower seemed to the Abilene boys and girls to demand that nickname. Nearly all the boys were called by it while they were in school, but it stuck to Dwight.[3]

If the Eisenhower surname "demanded" the Ike nickname, why? Historian Kenneth S. Davis in his biography *General Eisenhower, Soldier of Democracy* (1945), again made this claim of the nickname being somehow preordained, writing that it was "perfect and inevitable." Davis, however, provided no further rationale or explanation of why this was the case, simply settling for calling it inevitable.

The inevitable nickname for an Eisenhower is "Ike," and when Edgar and Dwight went to school it was applied to both of them. Edgar became "Big Ike" and Dwight "Little Ike," and the same names were applied later on to their two younger brothers, Earl and Milton.[4]

Edgar said that the nickname was natural because "the name Eisenhower was entirely too long for anybody to put up with." When Edgar left Abilene, he left the name Ike behind.

Another theory was proffered by famous military historian and biographer Stephen Ambrose. He wrote, in *Eisenhower: Soldier, General of the Army, President-Elect, 1890–1952* (1983), that Ike was a natural transformation of the first syllable of Eisenhower's last name.[5] Kudos to Professor Ambrose for this attempt at a logical phonetic explanation. But the answer is more complicated than that.

Ike grew up in a different America; an America where immigrants or those with foreign-sounding names were often the target of ethnic slurs. The *Random House Historical Dictionary of American Slang* defines Ike as a term originating around 1896 meaning "a fellow, especially if uncouth or rustic."[6] A second source, the *Dictionary of American Slang*, cites the same turn-of-the-century period for the use of Ike as a term meaning "an uncouth or stupid person"; a rube.

Ike is also a teasing nickname for Isaac, a common Jewish name. Eisenhower's childhood years coincided with a great influx of immigrants to America from Eastern Europe, with strange sounding family names, such as Eisenhower's own, many of them Jewish. The *American Dictionary of Slang* includes this as a definition of Ike: "To cheat, to lower the price by haggling, to 'Jew down.'"[7] "Ikey"—derived from Ike—is defined in *A Dictionary of Slang and Unconventional English* as: "(1) A Jew, esp. a Jewish receiver of stolen goods; (2) a pawnbroker of any nationality; (3) the 'inevitable nickname of men with Jewish surnames or features.'"[8]

Boyhood buddies calling the Eisenhower boys Ike in the early 1900s was not viewed as an insult. Growing up in rural America, their friends on the rough-and-tumble playgrounds of south-side Abilene would not have gotten away with it if it had been. This innocent ethnic slur was in fact more a term of respectful teasing and even endearment. You can understand why the boys in the Woodbine gang at that time would like to call each other Ike. It was the "Bubba" or "doofus" of its era. Just the right, affectionate put-down nickname for a youth with a foreign-sounding last name like Eisenhower, who was cocky, a natural leader, and a bit rough around the edges.

There is more in another chapter about the later aftereffects of the innocent use of the Ike ethnic slur. In the 1915 West Point yearbook, graduating cadet Dwight D. Eisenhower is humorously labeled as "Ike the terrible Swedish-Jew, as big as life and twice as natural." Antisemitism was acceptable in polite society during this era.

Nevertheless, the endearing Ike label stuck with him and, in the end, it became the world-renowned nickname for a war hero and part of the most famous presidential campaign slogan in modern American history—"I Like Ike."

Everybody liked Ike.

CHAPTER THREE

IKE THE ATHLETE
AN NCAA RULES VIOLATOR?

"Athletes take a certain amount of kidding, especially from those who think it is always brawn versus brains."
—*Dwight D. Eisenhower,* At Ease

If Dwight D. Eisenhower's dreams had been fulfilled, he would be enshrined today in the National Baseball Hall of Fame in Cooperstown. Instead, Kansas honors its most famous native son with an internationally known, five-building presidential library complex in his Abilene hometown. This twenty-two-acre campus includes a museum, the library/archives, the Eisenhower boyhood home on its original site, his final resting place in the chapel, and a visitors center. Rather than hitting home runs and sliding into home plate for a career, Ike the athlete grew up to become a five-star general, serve as Supreme Allied Commander in World War II, and be elected the thirty-fourth president of the United States. Not bad.

Athletics were to play a central role throughout Eisenhower's life. Young Ike was one of six brothers growing up in turn-of-the-century Abilene. The Eisenhower boys could field half a baseball team themselves, and they were always up for a game at the Lincoln School playground across the street when chores were finished around the family home. Dwight dreamed of becoming either a locomotive engineer (the train tracks are only stone's throw from the boyhood home) or a professional baseball player.

Eisenhower played both football and baseball in school and was elected president of the letterman's club after he single-handedly re-established it as an active organization at Abilene High School. As a senior in 1909, his baseball team lost only one game—to the Kansas University freshmen.

After high school, Eisenhower worked two years at the Belle Springs Creamery in Abilene before going off to the US Military Academy (West Point) in 1911 at the age of twenty. At West Point, Cadet Eisenhower showed great promise on the gridiron. He was a good-sized young man for the time, standing 5'10" tall and weighing 170 pounds. During his sophomore year at the military academy, he was cited by the eastern media as a promising running back and given the nickname "the Kansas Cyclone."

Unfortunately for Ike, he injured his knee in a game against Tufts University and his playing career was over. Eisenhower, for whom sports were paramount, became disheartened and his academic grades fell. He strongly considered dropping out of the military academy and going south to Argentina to become a cowboy (another of his boyhood dreams from growing up in the one-time Wild West town of Abilene). Fortunately for history, Ike's classmates discouraged him from this rash decision, and he went on to graduate and have a distinguished military and political career.

No longer able to play football, Eisenhower as a third-year student was asked to take over coaching duties for the lackluster West Point junior varsity team. This was an honor never bestowed on a cadet; it was always handled by one of the officers on the academy staff. Ike took the assignment very seriously and immediately developed a winning football team with a large following. It was here that Eisenhower developed many of the motivational and teaching skills that would make him a leader among men. To his chagrin, after graduation from the military academy this reputation as a great coach was to "haunt" him throughout his early military career. As a young officer, he found himself at each new assignment having been recruited by the post commander not necessarily because he had great potential as an infantry officer, but rather for his skill as a winning coach for the post football team. That said, what better motivator of men than a coach, whether on the gridiron or on the battlefield?

Many years later, during World War II, General Eisenhower quickly learned that former football players were often his best generals. In his memoirs he noted that while athletes take a certain amount of kidding about "brawn versus brain," he took great personal satisfaction in how well ex-footballers seemed to do in wartime leadership positions. This was more than coincidence in Ike's view. He cited names like Omar Bradley, George Patton, and James Van Fleet to make his point. Eisenhower said: "I believed that football, perhaps more than any other sport, tends to instill in men the feeling that victory comes through hard—almost slavish—work, team play, self-confidence, and an enthusiasm that amounts to dedication."[1]

In October 1958, President Eisenhower received the first annual gold medal presented by the Football Hall of Fame. The award was instituted to recognize individuals dedicated to propagating the concept of amateur football. At the presentation banquet in New York City's Hotel Astor ballroom, Eisenhower, the former player and coach, was honored for his "lifetime devotion to American college football."

But was Dwight D. Eisenhower always just an "amateur athlete" worthy of recognition by the Football Hal of Fame? Stories have persisted that Ike may have had a brush with professional baseball before going to West Point in 1911 or during summer leaves from the military academy while back in Kansas. There was a story of him playing as a center fielder in a few games during the summer of 1913 on a Great Bend baseball team that played in the old semi-pro Kansas State League. There has been much confusion and misinformation about this interesting tidbit from Eisenhower's early days.

Noted biographer Merle Miller wrote in *Ike the Soldier* that young Dwight played semi-pro summer ball under the assumed name "Sweeney" to keep his collegiate athletic eligibility intact for his return to West Point in the fall of his third year at the military academy. Mr. Miller gleaned this information from a film in the Eisenhower Library audiovisual collection that he viewed while researching his book. Unfortunately, Merle did not hear very clearly because in the film—*The Young Mr. Eisenhower*—the president recalls that when playing ball out of town, the opposing crowd would sometimes shout, "Get that Swede out of there!" Swede, not Sweeney. The blond-headed Ike was often mistaken for a big, bruising Scandinavian farm boy. Ike's West Point yearbook also refers to Eisenhower as a Swede. To further discredit Miller's conclusion, Ike in the film referred to high school football games, not post–high school baseball games.[2]

The most serious research and writing on this issue appeared more recently by a professor at Fort Hays State University (FHSU) in Hays, Kansas. Mark E. Eberle is in the Biology Sciences Department at FHSU. He is an avid baseball fan and as such conducted extensive research on the history of semi-pro baseball in Kansas during the time when Eisenhower would have played. Eberle has produced an impressive and perhaps seminal work entitled "Eisenhower, Wilson, and Professional Baseball in Kansas."[3]

The question: Did Dwight D. Eisenhower commit an infraction of the National Collegiate Athletic Association (NCAA) rules by playing professional ball in Kansas and then participating in amateur athletics on the West Point football team? Should Army forfeit those games in which he played in the 1912–13 season? (Army played five games before the Tufts game in which Ike was injured.) Eisenhower would probably have signed the "eligibility card" at West Point, completed by all college student athletes, although no record survives. The card included the following two questions for the student athlete:

> Have you ever at any time competed for a money prize, or against a professional for any kind of prize?
>
> Have you ever received money or any other compensation or concession for your athletic services, directly or indirectly, either as a player or in any other capacity?

In applying these strictures, the NCAA rules committee could discriminate between the deliberate use of athletic skill as a means to a livelihood versus technical, unintentional, or youthful infractions of the rule. Since Cadet Eisenhower earned more than his share of demerits at the military academy, perhaps these violations were simply "youthful infractions."

Eberle concludes that Eisenhower may indeed have played baseball professionally, even allowing for "the lapses in specific aspects of the memory" of the president. Eberle accepts the fact he cannot document the specific circumstances under which Ike might have played professionally. He is, however, reasonably confident that Eisenhower's playing time did not include regular season games.

Interestingly, included in Ike's post-presidential files in the Eisenhower Library is the following typed note sent to those handling his public correspondence for guidance on how to answer questions about this issue.[4]

> As of August 1961, DDE indicated inquiries should not be answered concerning his participation in professional baseball—as it would necessarily become too complicated.
>
> The following are Mrs. Whitman's remarks to Colonel Schulz regarding the above subject.
>
> "DDE did play professional baseball one season to make money, he did make one trip under an assumed name (did not say whether Wilson or not). But, he says not to answer this because it gets "too complicated."
> Per RLS 8/5/61

In a very insightful and almost poignant comment, Eberle speculates that General Eisenhower was perhaps embellishing his amateur baseball experiences in conversations with two major league managers many years later in 1945, which gave the story legs. Ike did, after all, want to grow up to be a professional baseball player, not the president of the United States.

Any supposed Eisenhower infractions adversely impacting West Point athletic football records would have occurred over a century ago, hopefully well beyond the statute of limitations, if any exist. That said, if we do consider continuing any further investigation of this controversy, one should also perhaps determine whether the "Kansas Cyclone" is owed any retroactive payment of Name, Image, and Likeness (NIL) compensation from the army for the half-season of varsity ball he played in 1912. Just saying.

One more anecdote. Do you remember reading about the time Dwight D. Eisenhower boxed the legendary Notre Dame football coach Knute Rockne (1888–1931) in Abilene in 1907, when both were young men, and they fought to a draw? I hope not, because it did not happen. According to the lore, Knute was supposed to have come to town with the carnival and the fight was arranged with Eisenhower, who was himself a pretty good boxer in his youth. Rockne apparently did do some boxing to raise funds in order to afford to go to college, and he enrolled at Notre Dame in 1910. The Rockne vs. Ike saga was not true, but nevertheless, the story persisted during the years Ike was in the White House. The editors of a ninth-grade reader to be published by Boston-based D. C. Heath and Company wrote the President in 1956 asking him to verify the authenticity of the story, which appeared originally under the title "As the Twig is Bent" in *Esquire* magazine in September 1944 (shortly after General Eisenhower became famous for D-Day) and then again in 1950 in a tenth-grade anthology.[5]

The president told his secretary Ann Whitman there was not a word of truth in the story and that he never met Knute Rockne until he was grown up. There was some concern about how to handle the reply to D. C. Heath and Company without causing trouble for the other publishers who had run the story earlier. The White House finessed the issue in Ann Whitman's reply to Heath.[6]

August 4, 1956
Dear Miss Welsh:
Thank you for your courtesy in submitting to the President the story entitled "As the Twig is Bent." I am sorry that I cannot authenticate the incident, although it is, of course, a fairly well-known tale that seems to interest many people.
With best wishes,
Sincerely,
Ann C. Whiteman
Personal Secretary to the President

This became the standard answer to all queries about the Knute Rockne and Ike boxing episode. The story was well-known and of interest to many people, but regretfully the White House could not authenticate the incident.

Although Rockne did not come to Abilene in 1907 to box against Dwight, as fate would have it, the famed Notre Dame football coach died in a 1931 plane crash in a cornfield in Bazaar, Kansas, just eighty miles from Ike's hometown.

Later in life, Eisenhower remained active by hunting and fishing, but his biggest sports passion was golf. Ike was a very serious golfer, and, with his brute strength, he could drive the ball 225 yards, even well past his sixtieth birthday. In his time at West Point he could do one-armed chin-ups. Ike writes that after his football injury ended his athletic career, he worked in the gym to sustain and increase his arm strength and shoulder muscles.[7] Even in Dwight's forties and fifties, Eisenhower's military aid Harry Butcher recalled witnessing Ike's favorite "parlor game," which consisted of standing stiff and erect without moving a muscle and then slowly falling forward and at the very last instant, when it looked as if he would break his nose on the floor, using his strong hands and muscular arms to quickly break the fall.[8] No wonder that, while in the White House, he created the President's Council on Youth Fitness (1956) over his concerns about the physical condition of America's youth.

Ike had a 14–18 handicap but broke eighty on four occasions at the Augusta National golf course. Eisenhower exercised some presidential prerogatives. If you played with him you were required to make your short putts, while he picked up his "gimmies!" About a year before his death, at the age of seventy-seven, Ike achieved the golfer's dream of a hole in one at the 104-yard thirteenth hole at Seven Lakes Country Club in Palm Springs.[9]

During his retirement years while living on his Gettysburg farm, Eisenhower continued to exercise. Gettysburg College history professor Michael Birkner conducted an oral history interview in 2024 with the long-time athletic trainer at the college, Gareth "Lefty" Biser. Lefty told Birkner that Ike came regularly to the college gym (up to three times a week) to ride a stationary bike. Physical fitness continued to be important to the elder statesman.[10] Another motivation was of course the importance of exercise after having experienced heart issues.

There is no doubt that sport was a significant part of Eisenhower's life. His presidential speeches, press conferences, and even personal conversations were often punctuated by sports metaphors. He chided congress for handling his budget as a "political football."

President Eisenhower's speech to the Republican National Committee in 1957 sounded more like a locker-room pep talk. He urged the badly divided GOP leaders to be more unified and to work as a "team" in achieving party goals. Eisenhower asked them whether an offensive football player would decide not to throw a crucial block just because he disagreed with the play called in the huddle. Eisenhower, ever the coach, answered the question himself: "Of course not. He does his part, and the team goes on to score. . . . It's this simple: We've [Republicans] got a good team. Let's look like one!"[11]

Dwight D. Eisenhower will be remembered by history quite properly as the World War II hero who led the Allied landings at Normandy on D-Day and as the thirty-fourth president of the United States, presiding over eight years of peace and national prosperity. But we should not forget his other legacy—Eisenhower the athlete.

In Ike's case it was certainly brawn and brain.

CHAPTER FOUR

"HAIL TO THE CHEF"
IKE THE COOK

"In the history of man, no military commissary has raised envy. Due to a combination of efficiency, disinterest, and the lack of a feminine touch, all of the food in an army kitchen is boiled until the tops rattle off the pots."
—*Amor Towles,* A Gentleman in Moscow

Born in 1896, Mamie Geneva Doud grew up in a wealthy family with servants. "Do not learn to cook, lest you be condemned to a life in the kitchen." Mamie Geneva Doud's mother had warned her daughter of this potential calamity. Mamie obviously took that lesson to heart as she was a self-proclaimed "cooking school dropout." It is indeed fortuitous that Dwight Eisenhower was pretty darn good in the kitchen. At the time they got married, the young nineteen-year-old bride had only learned to prepare mayonnaise and fudge. Miss Alcott's Finishing School in Denver had taught Mamie wonderful table manners, calligraphy, and the art of small talk, but she and Ike were destined to subsist on love alone if it was not for Ike's culinary skills coming to the rescue.

Mamie had grown up in a household with a family cook, and when she wandered into the kitchen it was probably to ask for a cookie.[1] On the other hand, Ike as a child learned there was no such thing as "women's work." Ida had six sons and no daughters. All her boys mopped and waxed the floors, did the laundry, sewed, and, yes, even cooked. The boys took turns preparing the big Sunday meal to be ready when the rest of the family came home from church.

Eisenhower got his real baptism by fire as a cook when he was compelled to take over the kitchen chores for the family when his youngest brother, Milton, was quarantined with scarlet fever. The older Eisenhower brothers and their father went off to work each morning, and mother stayed upstairs in the sickroom with the four-year-old child. Ike was downstairs in the kitchen, charged with cooking the big noon meal for the entire family. Ida would shout down instructions for Ike, who had just turned thirteen years old. He would later say:

I don't think the family lived too well during those weeks but I learned something about the preparation of simple dishes for the table. My principal contribution was hearty vegetable soup, always a family favorite. . . . I got together soup meat and big joints and vegetables, well seasoned, which produced a really passable dish. By starting out each meal with a bowl of vegetable soup, it was no disaster if the main courses that I prepared did not come off too well.[2]

Ike pestered his mother for additional cooking lessons, and he soon learned how to prepare potatoes in a variety of manners—boiled, baked, or roasted—and also how to pan-grill steaks and finish a meal off by making a good peach, apple, or cherry pie. Young Ike's growing culinary skills were paying other dividends as well. He was appointed by his gang of boyhood friends as permanent chef for their camping trips down by the Smoky Hill River. Being the cook had its perks, as Ike and his co-chef were exempt from clean-up duty, gathering firewood, and other tedious camp chores. The cooks also got first dibs on the servings when the amount of food in question was limited.[3]

As a boy, he had been taught to be discerning when buying meat, even to take the trouble of getting to know the butcher and insisting on the proper cuts and treatment of beef. Grandson David shared that the elder Ike continued to be a "meat snob" in later life, even into his post-presidential years. When staying at their retirement home in Palm Desert, California, the former president enjoyed visiting the large grocery stores in the area and always lingered by the butcher's counter looking over the fresh meat choices and, above all, taking note of the quality being offered.[4]

As it turned out, Eisenhower's boyhood interest in food and cooking greatly benefited the men he later commanded in the army after his graduation from West Point. Ike felt that since soldiers were paid so little, the very least they deserved was decent food. After inspecting a few mess halls during his first assignment at Fort Sam Houston, he noted, "I learned that even good food could be quickly ruined by bad preparation." Lieutenant Eisenhower did the unusual thing of volunteering for the Army Cooks and Bakers School to learn more about cooking for large groups of men. As a result, in future years, any young officer serving under Eisenhower's command was well-advised to take seriously their charge to feed their troops well. Eisenhower later reflected:

I didn't learn enough at the Fort Sam Houston school to qualify as a cook. But I did learn about the problem of trying to bring four-star cuisine out of recipes which use hundreds of pounds of ingredients and gallons of water. I knew enough so that I could discover what was wrong with food that men in my command were getting. I have made things miserable on occasion for young captains or lieutenants, responsible for messes, who limited their inspection to questioning whether pots and pans were shined brightly enough. Some had no idea whatsoever about a balanced meal and others cared not at all whether food not only tasted properly but looked appealing. I insisted that officers learn enough about their business, including the kitchen, to oversee it intelligently.[5]

At one point during his second year in the army, Lieutenant Eisenhower was temporarily appointed as a mess officer by a fussy colonel who had been dissatisfied with the previous kitchen bosses. Ike knew that if the colonel were happy, everyone's life on the post would be better. He took the initiative by rising early every morning to go dove hunting. He would then prepare a variety of breakfast dishes, to the colonel's delight. One day there would be dove stew with carrots and potatoes; the next day might feature doves cooked with bacon strips across the breast; then perhaps Ike's own concoction of dove pot pies. Going above and beyond was no doubt reflected in the lieutenant's efficiency reports.[6]

Sergeant Mickey McKeogh was General Eisenhower's orderly during World War II and had firsthand knowledge of how food and its preparation was indeed a high priority for "the boss." Ike was always interested in the kitchen of any of the many houses he used as temporary quarters in England, North Africa, France, and Germany. "He likes to taste things cooking in the kitchen, and sometimes he will take the lid off a pot on the stove and taste what is in it and talk to the cook about whether to put anything else in whatever is cooking."[7]

McKeogh noted that Eisenhower was especially interested in the kitchens that prepared the food for the men under his command.

His inspections of the kitchens, incidentally, were always very thorough. He'd examine the pots and pans and the tables and knives. Sometimes he'd have the ice boxes opened and if he saw some beef there he'd sometimes pull off a piece and eat it, raw. And once, one of the G.I.'s in the kitchen saw him and yelled: "My God, he eats raw meat!" He did eat raw hamburger sandwiches, with an onion, when he could get them, but he didn't usually go around eating raw meat in chunks.[8]

John Eisenhower said of his father, "The Old Man, a gourmet, loved to cook, and he went about this hobby with the same concentration he brought to bear on everything else." Cooking had an almost therapeutic effect on Ike and whenever something important was on his mind or troubling him, he headed for the kitchen. Mamie noted that when her husband heard the news about the attack on Pearl Harbor, he went straight to the kitchen and began making vegetable soup. In 1960 the Paris Summit meeting with the Soviet Union collapsed after the U-2 incident. That same evening, a very disappointed President Eisenhower hosted a cookout dinner at the US embassy residence and was quickly hard at work charcoal-broiling steaks for the American delegation. "As always, when the steaks were about ready, he gave a sharp announcement—command is more accurate—for the guests to drop what they were doing and head for the dining room." The perfectly cooked steaks were served, and the guests were the beneficiaries of the president's therapy session.[9]

Charles M. Harger, editor of the *Abilene Reflector-Chronicle* newspaper, described an event that occurred during the post–VE Day homecoming visit by the victorious five-star general on June 4, 1945. After the parade proceeded down Buckeye Avenue and then west onto Third Street, Eisenhower went to the private home of a boyhood friend for a luncheon. With old-time familiarity, Ike insisted on going to the kitchen to see what the waitresses had for the table. The cooks and servers were delighted by the general's interest and praise. Harger noted these are the things that men with "swank" do not do. "He (Ike) does these things naturally and unconsciously, and that is why he is loved wherever he is."[10]

Ike was a real fan of cornmeal and used it for breading the trout he loved to catch and cook during his Colorado fishing trips. Another of his specialties was cornmeal pancakes. He told anyone who asked for the recipe to always prepare the batter the night before, with the added instruction to flip them only once while cooking. Another tip he shared with army mess sergeants was adding melted butter to the cornmeal batter. The flapjacks would not only taste better, but they would also not stick to the griddle. Sage advice.[11]

It was in 1948 that Dwight D. Eisenhower's cooking prowess became well-known nationwide. The retired five-star general was now serving as president of Columbia University in New York City. A few years earlier, in 1942, a committee of faculty wives at Columbia had decided to

Colonel Eisenhower adorned in his cooking apron stands next to Mamie seated in an Adirondack chair in the backyard of their quarters on Fort Lewis, Washington in 1941. Mamie, never a culinarian, was delighted with her husband's skill with a spatula. The couple treated some of their army friends to barbecue at this gathering during the summer prior to the attack on Pearl Harbor. (Courtesy Eisenhower Library)

compile a cookbook to raise money for the University Committee for War Relief. The school newspaper, the *Columbia Spectator*, noted that all proceeds from *What's Cooking at Columbia: A Recipe Book* went "to help cook Hitler's goose." The recipes were mostly from faculty members and administrators and their spouses. Due to its popularity, the cookbook was updated in 1948. The very first recipe in the new edition was for vegetable soup. The contributor? None other than the former Supreme Allied Commander of Allied Forces in Europe, now university president Dwight D. Eisenhower.[12]

Ike's recipe created a sensation across the campus and, later, the country. When soliciting the university president's office for an entry in this updated edition, the committee publishing the cookbook had no doubt anticipated receiving a recipe from the university's first lady, Mamie Eisenhower. Instead, they were surprised with a 900-word missive on vegetable soup that included detailed planning, logistics, and food preparation from the former Normandy invasion planner himself. General Eisenhower spared no details in helping ensure preparation of the best vegetable soup ever.[13]

Word about the soup spread quickly across the Columbia campus. What caught everyone's attention was Ike's last instruction: "As a final touch, in the springtime when nasturtiums are green and tender, you can take a few nasturtium stems, cut them up in small pieces, boil them separately as you did the barley, and add them to your soup. (About one tablespoonful after cooking.)"[14]

The Associated Press noticed this unusual detail and sent news of Ike's unique soup across the wires. Eisenhower said later that his vegetable soup recipe generated more attention from the press and public that any other announcement he released in his years as university president. He was bombarded with inquiries about where one could purchase nasturtium flower stems. There is no record of his responses, but his most likely advice to those who asked was to visit their local nursery in the spring to get some bedding plants. For young Ike growing up, he only had to step out the backdoor into the family garden. He was very familiar with the peppery flavor the stems added to dishes. In a recent article, the National Gardening Association's Learning Library says that nasturtiums are among the best-known edible flowers and are very popular with chefs. Perhaps they were channeling Ike the cook.[15]

One of President Eisenhower's good friends was Freeman Gosden, a

In July 1952, presidential candidate Eisenhower cooks a breakfast of flapjacks and bacon at a mountain retreat near Frazer, Colorado. Ike no doubt used his special corn meal pancake recipe. (Courtesy Associated Press)

radio star famous for his role as Amos in the *Amos and Andy* show. The two often played golf together at Augusta National and in Palm Desert, California. Gosden once described Ike's unconventional method of grilling steaks. "The first-time friends would see him put the steaks directly on the coals, they would think he possibly had gone berserk." The general preferred a three-inch-thick New York cut (also known as a Kansas City strip). Ike first filled a small pan with salt and pepper and dipped the steaks, covering them completely with the spices (including the sides of the steaks). After the fire was burning hot, he placed the steaks directly on top of the coals, for a few minutes on each side, and then they were taken off and laid on a board. Ike then used a wire brush or stiff bristle brush to rub the meat hard to take off the ashes and excess salt. The meat was then moved to a clean board and cut diagonally across the grain into slices about one-quarter inches thick. According to his grandson David, Ike, the "griller-in-chief," expected his guests to already be seated and ready to enjoy the delicious steak cooked to perfection.[16]

Barbecuing the perfect steak was always a nice respite for Dwight D Eisenhower. Here Ike is shown sharing the grilling duties with former President Herbert Hoover while on a working vacation in Fraser, Colorado, August–September 1954. The traveling White House was set up at Lowry AFB in nearby Denver and Eisenhower remained busy signing legislation, pushing a button to dedicate America's first atomic power plant in Shippingport, Pennsylvania and giving a nationwide radio and television address to the American People on the achievements of the 83rd Congress, which had just adjourned. (Courtesy Eisenhower Library)

As president, Eisenhower even grilled inside the White House. He would fire up the grill in the Solarium, his favorite room on the residence's top floor. The Solarium's floor-to-ceiling windows provided spectacular views of the Washington Monument and the National Mall while you ate your steaks. When a reporter asked how they got the smoke out of the glass room, the White House press secretary said, "By opening the windows. You can't stop the President from cooking." Eisenhower was the perfect president to be serving in office during any "Eat Beef" promotion campaign by the national cattleman's association or other such organization. His diet called for beef every day, sometimes twice a day.[17]

It was no secret that President Eisenhower and Mamie often had their evening meal sent upstairs on trays to the White House residence, where they enjoyed watching the evening news on television. The gossip in Washington was that they ate frozen TV dinners, which the C.A. Swanson company had introduced to America in 1953. In fact, the First Family did not eat frozen dinners, but they did enjoy the convenience of occasionally carrying in Chinese food from the Sun Chop Suey Restaurant in Washington. The Eisenhowers had been ordering food from this restaurant since 1930, starting with their earlier assignment in Washington. This was no doubt a nice honor for the restaurant, but the proprietor Mr. Wong noted that now the Secret Service also wanted to investigate every one of his employees. In 1956, Wong shared with a reporter the details of one large Eisenhower order delivered to the White House: five orders of chicken chop suey, six orders of fried rice, four orders of egg foo yung, and egg rolls. Ike and Mamie must have had some guests in the White House residence based on the size of this carryout banquet.[18]

Ike was always up for trying new foods. When getting away from the White House and spending time at their farm in Gettysburg, the president would slip into town to browse in food stores. For him a supermarket was like an oriental bazaar, packed with delicacies that he felt compelled to purchase. He brought home items to try out in the kitchen, often with no idea of how they were to be prepared or even how they would taste. It was Ike's and Mamie's cook in Gettysburg, Delores Moaney, who was faced with the challenge of tackling the exotic cans and strange-smelling packages.[19]

The American public was used to presidents like Ike who were avid sportsmen and outdoorsmen. But Eisenhower the cook was something different. No other president sported an apron that proclaimed "Hail to the Chef," and no other occupant of the White House was so confident of their cooking skills to offer advice such as "I find that self-rising flour makes my baking much easier. . . . I mix my batter at night and let it stand until morning."[20]

Ike was obviously a Renaissance man.

CHAPTER FIVE

THE FIRST PREPPY PRESIDENT

"President Eisenhower turned up in a white Lacoste shirt . . . the
alligator really took on an aura of prestige and mystique."
—*Genevieve Buck*, Chicago Tribune, *January 24, 1982*

The evidence is overwhelming. Dwight D. Eisenhower was the first
"preppy president." We have photographic proof and there is written documentation that he owned multiple Lacoste polo shirts. Ike can be seen
wearing the alligator-adorned shirts on the golf course and looking very
suave. And remember, *The Official Preppy Handbook* is on record recommending the Lacoste shirt: "The sport shirt of choice is the Lacoste. Only
the all-cotton model will do, the one with the cap sleeves with the ribbed
edging, narrow collar and two button placket (never buttoned) . . . Velour
is not Preppy, and should never appear anywhere in the Prep wardrobe."[1]

This fashion statement was very unintentional on Ike's part, but nevertheless it happened. President Eisenhower valued his reputation and
assiduously discouraged any use of his name or image for commercial
promotion of products. But that policy did not prevent Ike as president
from accepting the gift of several unique and comfortable imported golf
shirts from Mr. Vincent Draddy of the David Crystal Company in New
York City. And so, the preppy saga began.

In 1950, Mr. Draddy purchased a few thousand French-made Lacoste
sports shirts as a favor to a tennis-player friend, Billy Talbert. Draddy owned
the Izod line of clothing in New York City and thought he would add some
prestige to his American line of sportswear with this avant-garde product
from Europe. Unfortunately, after the purchase, sales did not materialize.
The shirts were expensive for the time at $8 each. They also had a strange
crocodile emblem embroidered on the left breast.[2]

In explaining the crocodile emblem on the Lacoste shirt, the first thing
to note is that—despite what the American audience may have believed—
the reptile depicted is not an alligator. The original designer was a dash-
ing and popular French tennis player named René Lacoste (1904–1996),
whose nickname was "Crocodile." During his illustrious career in the late
1920s, Lacoste was a champion at Wimbledon and at the US Open tennis
tournament.

Once he retired in the 1930s, he started a knitwear company called *La Chemise Lacoste* (The Lacoste Shirt). René was seeking a shirt to add to his inventory that was more accommodating to the upper-body moves of tennis players on the court. He had noticed his friend the Marquis of Cholmondeley—a well-known polo player—wearing his polo shirt during a tennis game because of the comfort and the freedom of movement it provided. (It is believed that the polo shirt was invented in the nineteenth century to meet the needs of British polo players in the hot climate of colonial India.) René Lacoste commissioned an English tailor to make similar shirts for the game of tennis and his new product line was invented.

But why the alligator, or should we say crocodile, on the Lacoste shirt? There are two theories about the French tennis player's nickname. The first was Lacoste's athletic boldness on the court and the size and shape of his distinctive nose, which indeed could be likened to the snout of a crocodile. The second theory concerned an alleged wager he made during a tennis tournament in which the winner was to receive a crocodile-skin suitcase. In any event, the media dubbed him the crocodile and he embraced the nickname.[3]

Interestingly, in the United States the Lacoste shirts eventually became widely known for their unique "alligator" emblem. To those in the know, it was still a crocodile. As one publication wrote: "In a case of mistaken identity, the Lacoste crocodile became known as the alligator when upper-middle class 'prepsters' mistook the French reptile for its American cousin."[4]

With non-existent sales in New York City, Vincent Draddy and the David Crystal Company cleverly began giving the Lacoste shirts away to prominent individuals to promote interest in the unique garment. John Wayne, Bing Crosby, Bob Hope, golfer Sam Snead, and other high-profile types began wearing their new polo shirts to tournaments and sporting events. Also included among the famous group was another well-known golfer: the sitting president of the United States, Dwight D. Eisenhower. White House files at the Eisenhower Presidential Library show that Ike indeed received as gifts some seventy-five *Chemise Lacoste* shirts between 1956 and 1960.[5]

What was priceless was the free advertising the David Crystal Company received when Ike and other notables were seen in public wearing their preppy shirts. Crystal wrote to one of his senior staff, David Gottlieb, in January 1956 of how pleased he was to see a photograph in the newspaper of President Eisenhower "wearing our famous Lacoste shirt" while playing golf with his White House chief of staff, Sherman Adams. "This, of course, tickled my vanity to no end," Crystal continued. Crystal asked Gottlieb to send Ike more of the Lacoste shirts, and soon thereafter the president received an additional supply. In his thank you letter, Eisenhower told Crystal he anticipated an immediate improvement in his golf game while wearing the new Lacoste shirts. Ike said that donning the shirts was "practically a gilt-edge guarantee that they will improve my golf game. After my performance of yesterday, I assure you that I appreciate the gift and need the guarantee. Please accept my warm thanks for your thoughtful kindness."[6]

Ike responded with a written note of thanks each time he received a supply of the Lacoste shirts at the White House. The president signed each of these letters personally, which was not always the case when the White House acknowledged gifts. Often it was Ike's personal secretary Ann Whiteman whose signature block would be on routine thank-you letters. The Lacoste gift acknowledgments always included Eisenhower's signature, a testimony to how much he enjoyed receiving them.

But it was not just wearing the famous shirts that elevated Eisenhower to full preppy status. There are other conditions that must be met. For one, the *Handbook* recognizes the significance of earning a nickname as an important factor in achieving preppydom. Ike Eisenhower certainly qualifies for membership on that account. From *The Official Preppy Handbook*: "A nickname is a gift. Whether given deliberately by the family or unintentionally by a peer it bespeaks of a certain In-ness and inaccessibility to outsiders It's like being tapped for a secret society, minus the degrading rituals. It's tangible proof that you've gained entrance into an exclusive camaraderie."[7]

Eisenhower's academic performance and behavior at West Point clearly meet one additional qualification for preppy membership. The *Handbook* features a chapter entitled "Breaking the Rules: The importance of getting kicked out." It notes, tongue in cheek, only those who continually fail to strive and succeed are rewarded with the respect reserved for the upper crust. But it is not just underachieving academically that earns recognition; "behavioral antics" will also give you credibility as a preppy. While Cadet Ike was never dismissed from the military academy, he strongly considered quiting after his sophomore year when he could no longer participate in athletics. His dreams of a sports career were dashed. Fellow cadets dissuaded Ike from resigning and fulfilling a far-fetched fream of heading south to Argentina to become a *gaucho* (cowboy). He stayed at

Eisenhower between rounds of golf at the Newport Country Club (Rhode Island) sports an Izod shirt on August 30, 1958. While not his intent, Ike was one of the famous individuals who helped the alligator logo–adorned shirt take off in popularity. (Courtesy Eisenhower Library)

West Point, but upon graduation demanded to be assigned to the infantry branch despite his football injury, which was against army policy. If the assignment was not granted, he would decline his commision as a second lieutenant and resign from the army. His wish was granted with a waiver. While not quite meeting the preppy qualification of "the importamce of getting kicked out," it was close.

Ike's grades were unimpressive, another qualifier for full preppy status. He ranked a mediocre 64th out of 164 cadets in his graduating class. Furthermore, Cadet Eisenhower most famously earned more than his share of demerits for comportment, finishing in the lower part of his graduating class when measuring for discipline. He ranked 125th out of 164. In the behavior antics department, Ike was well ahead of schedule on his way to preppydom.

Ironically, Mamie Eisenhower unwittingly played her own small role in her husband's qualification for membership in the preppy club. The

First Lady's favorite colors were pink and green and the *Handbook* states quite clearly that the wearing of pink and green is the surest and quickest way to group identification within the preppy set. "There is little room for doubt or confusion when you see these colors together—no one else in his right mind would sport such a chromatically improbable justaposition."[8] Of course Ike did not wear those colors himself, but he slept in a bedroom decorated by Mamie in pink and green for most of his married life.

So, Dwight D. Eisenhower, known famously by his classic nickname Ike, indeed underachieved at West Point in academics and military discipline, but he rose to the highest levels of fame and prestige in American history, and then later rocked the Lacoste shirt in official White House photographs—he even had his collar up!

Case closed on Ike being the first "preppy president."

CHAPTER SIX
OY VEY! IKE THE TERRIBLE SWEDISH-JEW

"This is Señor Dwight David Eisenhower, gentlemen, the terrible
Swedish-Jew, as big as life and twice as natural."
—The Howitzer, 1915

Little did they know it, but the witty cadet editors of the 1915 West Point
yearbook became the unlikely perpetrators of the much later rumors
that Dwight D. Eisenhower was a Jew. And, indeed, stories that Ike was
Jewish surfaced both during World War II and in his later presidential
campaign.

In their attempt at humor, the yearbook writers were merely following
the logic that the Ike nickname was short for Isaac, a name associated with
nineteenth-century Jewish immigrants. And, in Eisenhower's case, it was
not merely that he was a Jew but a "terrible Swedish-Jew." Ike was quite
a physical specimen and had blond hair in his early years. Swede was another name thrown occasionally at Eisenhower by opposing fans during
his football-playing days in Abilene. "Stop that Swede" was yelled from the
bleachers. Those taunts, along with the Ike nickname, followed him to the
military academy. Eisenhower most likely felt flattered by this affectionate
"name-calling" and wore it as the badge of honor it was intended to be.

In 1942, General Eisenhower was visited at his London wartime headquarters by Quentin Reynolds, associate editor and writer at *Collier's* magazine. During the visit, Ike's staff brought in a letter just received from his
brother Milton Eisenhower, who was a senior official with the Office of
War Information in Washington. Reynolds reports that Eisenhower read
it and snorted. The general then showed the letter to his office visitor. It
read as follows:

I was at a cocktail party here in Washington, given by one of those old
dowagers. She said very nicely to me, "You must come from a fine
family, young man. You have an important job here and your brother
is leading our troops abroad and I understand another brother is a
banker. What a pity it is that you Eisenhowers are Jewish." . . . I looked
at her, sighed unhappily, and said, Ah, madam, what a pity we aren't.

DWIGHT DAVID EISENHOWER

ABILENE, KANSAS

Senatorial Appointee, Kansas
"Ike"

Corporal, Sergeant, Color Sergeant; A.B.,
B.A., Sharpshooter; Football Squad (3, 2),
"A" in Football; Baseball Squad (4); Cheer
Leader; Indoor Meet (4, 3).

*"Now, fellers, it's just like this. I've been asked
to say a few words this evening about this business.
Now, me and Walter Camp, we think—"*
—*Himself*

THIS is Señor Dwight David Eisenhower, gentlemen, the terrible Swedish-Jew, as big as life and twice as natural. He claims to have the best authority for the statement that he is the handsomest man in the Corps and is ready to back up his claim at any time. At any rate you'll have to give it to him that he's well-developed abdominally—and more graceful in pushing it around than Charles Calvert Benedict. In common with most fat men, he is an enthusiastic and sonorous devotee of the King of Indoor Sports, and roars homage at the shrine of Morpheus on every possible occasion.

However, the memory of man runneth back to the time when the little Dwight was but a slender lad of some 'steen years, full of joy and energy and craving for life and movement and change. 'Twas then that the romantic appeal of West Point's glamour grabbed him by the scruff of the neck and dragged him to his doom. Three weeks of Beast gave him his fill of life and movement and as all the change was locked up at the Cadet Store out of reach, poor Dwight merely consents to exist until graduation shall set him free.

At one time he threatened to get interested in life and won his "A" by being the most promising back in Eastern football—but the Tufts game broke his knee and the promise. Now Ike must content himself with tea, tiddledywinks and talk, at all of which he excels. Said prodigy will now lead us in a long, loud yell for— Dare Devil Dwight, the Dauntless Don.

Military academy cadet Dwight David Eisenhower's senior page in the 1915 West Point *Howitzer* yearbook became the source of an unusual myth about him. The yearbook's cadet writers poked fun at each graduating cadet on their full-page entry, which included a photograph and a humorous narrative. Eisenhower was referred to as Ike "the Swedish-Jew." (Courtesy Eisenhower Library)

General Eisenhower put the letter down, laughed, and said to Reynolds, "Wasn't that a wonderful answer to give the old battle axe? I'd forgotten that there were people like that still in the world."[1]

Shortly thereafter, in 1943, Allied Supreme Commander General Eisenhower came face-to-face with "Ike the Jew" allegations made during the North African military campaign. North Africa was under Vichy French rule at the time, a regime that shared Nazi views on the Jews and had effectively eliminated Jewish rights in the region. Arabs outnumbered Jews forty to one in the area. As part of a disinformation campaign, the Germans were anxious to foment an Arab uprising against the Allied forces and spread the rumor in Morocco that Eisenhower was a Jew sent to their country by "Jewish President" Roosevelt to "grind down the Arabs and turn over North Africa to Jewish rule." Any resulting Arab unrest or open rebellion would have been disastrous for the war effort in North Africa. The political staff at Allied headquarters was so concerned by the rumors that they reacted quickly by publishing material on Eisenhower in local newspapers and in special leaflets to establish evidence of his real ancestry.[2]

In *Crusade in Europe*, Ike illustrated the delicate nature of the situation Allies faced by describing his astonishment when he was shown a letter signed by a man who was identified as the "Rabbi of Constantine," who implored him to go very slowly in relaxation of anti-Jewish practices or else, the letter said, "the Arabs would undoubtedly stage a pogrom." Eisenhower cited this as but one minor example of "the confused nature of the racial and political relationships" he faced. Nevertheless, Eisenhower was forceful in his demand that Vichy French authorities ameliorate anti-Jewish laws and practices in North Africa, and appropriate proclamations providing relief were indeed issued.[3]

A decade later in 1952, anti-Semitic groups hoped to block his selection as the Republican Party's presidential nominee by conducting a vicious whispering campaign. The Patriotic Tract Society printed millions of leaflets entitled "Eisenhower, the Swedish Jew" based on his entry in the 1915 *Howitzer* yearbook. A Star of David appeared next to "Ikie" Eisenhower's photo on the front of the leaflet and on the reverse it cited candidate Eisenhower as the choice of a veritable "Who's Who" listing of American Jews.[4]

Eisenhower was not Jewish, but in 1952 he told Mr. Maxwell Abbell, "The Jewish people couldn't have a better friend than me." Abbell was a lawyer, businessman, and philanthropist serving as president of the

United Synagogue of America. Ike shared with Abbell that he and his brothers were raised in Abilene on the teachings of the Old Testament. "I grew up believing that the Jews were the chosen people; that they gave us the high ethical and moral principles of our civilization." Abbell held Eisenhower in great esteem for his care and treatment of the Jewish displaced persons whom his armies had liberated from the Nazi concentration camps at war's end. "His friendship for the Jews left no room for doubt," said Abbell.[5]

The respect was mutual, and Maxwell Abbell was appointed chairman of a new US presidential committee Eisenhower created in January 1955. The President's Committee on Government Employment Policy was charged with advising the chief executive on employment practices throughout the federal government to help ensure equal opportunity for those applying for federal government positions and prohibit discrimination against any current employee because of race, color, religion, or national origin.[6] Eisenhower felt Abbell was a perfect fit to lead this presidential committee.

An examination of Jewish American voting patterns in presidential elections shows that in 1956, Ike received the highest percentage of Jewish votes of any Republican candidate in the past one hundred years (Calvin Coolidge to Donald Trump). Forty percent of the Jewish voters pulled the lever for Eisenhower in his 1956 reelection whereas the average percentage for all Republican candidates in the twenty-five presidential elections during this ten-decade period was 23 percent. Eisenhower was not Jewish, but the campaign slogan "I Like Ike" appealed to an exceptionally large minority of Jewish voters.[7]

Ike no doubt earned and appreciated the strong political support he was receiving from American Jews, but that did not affect his actions in the Suez Canal Crisis that unfolded in the weeks preceding the 1956 election. US intelligence revealed that Israel was preparing to invade Egypt, so Eisenhower demanded a pledge from Israeli Prime Minister David Ben-Gurion that he would keep the peace. Four days prior to the November 6th election, Ike wrote his friend Edward "Swede" Hazlett noting the Israeli prime minister may have assumed he could "take advantage of this country" because of the approaching election and the importance so many US politicians attached to winning the Jewish vote. That was not to be the case with Eisenhower. It was principle above politics. In his words: "I gave strict orders to the State Department that they should inform Israel that we would handle our affairs exactly as though we didn't have a Jew in America. The welfare and best interests of our own country were to be the sole criteria on which we operated."[8]

The hundreds of thousands of annual visitors to the world-renowned US Holocaust Memorial Museum in Washington, DC, may enter the building by crossing the Eisenhower Plaza. The plaza honors General Eisenhower for his prescience and determination in helping document for posterity the horrors of the Holocaust at the end of World War II. His forward-thinking in 1945 ensured there was eye-witness testimony and press coverage of the existence of concentration camps, and this evidence has played an essential role in combating Holocaust deniers ever since. The following quotation is carved on the granite wall facing the Eisenhower Plaza.

> The things I saw beggar description. . . . The visual evidence and the verbal testimony of starvation, cruelty and bestiality were so overpowering. . . . I made the visit deliberately, in order to be in a position to give first-hand evidence of these things if ever, in the future, there develops a tendency to charge these allegations to propaganda.
> Gen. Dwight David Eisenhower
> Supreme Commander of the Allied Forces
> Ohrdruf Concentration Camp
> April 15, 1945

As outlined in the chapter on "Ike and God" in this book, Eisenhower's religious upbringing as a youth in Abilene was not Jewish, but rather in the River Brethren sect. Family Bible time and Sunday school were part of his early life. After leaving home for West Point in 1911, Eisenhower did not join or attend church with any regularity for the next forty years (except mandatory chapel at the military academy). After his election as president in 1952, Ike quietly joined the Presbyterian Church, of which his wife was a member.

One final bit of evidence might be of interest to readers. As is the standard practice with all presidents of the United States, a thorough autopsy was performed after Eisenhower passed away on March 28, 1969. This autopsy was conducted by the medical staff at the Walter Reed Medical Center in Bethesda, Maryland. The eighty-four-page report includes a pathologic diagnosis, external examination, microscopic examination, photographs, and a narrative summary. A complete copy of the autopsy is in the archives at the Eisenhower Presidential Library.[9] What the medical report clearly confirms is that David and Ida Eisenhower did not have a rabbi visit their home eight days after the birth of their son Dwight to perform a bris ceremony. If the Eisenhower family were indeed Jewish, this significant religious ritual (circumcision) certainly would have been performed.

Thus ends the veracity of any "allegations" about the Jewish heritage of Dwight D. Eisenhower.

CHAPTER SEVEN

IKE'S RUMORED BLACK ANCESTRY

"Brothers have always considered Ike one of our own."
Elderhostel participant, Eisenhower Library

"That would be neat!" Ike's granddaughter Susan said that with a surprised smile on her face, many years ago while we walked through a gallery in the Eisenhower Presidential Museum in Abilene. The occasion was the opening of a new museum exhibit honoring General Eisenhower's role in winning World War II. Susan Eisenhower and I were having a private conversation that evening as we walked among the exhibits, and for some reason I asked if she had heard the stories about Dwight D. Eisenhower's alleged Black ancestry. Susan was surprised. She said, "no," that was news to her. But then, without even a moment's pause, she added, "That would be neat!"

Questions about Ike's ancestry were familiar to the staff at his presidential library. During my many years as deputy director, overseeing the archives at the Eisenhower Presidential Library, our reference desk would receive an occasional inquiry asking whether the thirty-fourth president was of African American decent. This email from a college student in Ohio was a typical example: "I need to know for one of my papers if Dwight had african american blood. . . . Specifically I am asking as to weather [*sic*] or not he had an african american mother." Our polite reply to such reference requests was always in the negative—we had no evidence in our twenty-six-million-page archives confirming this theory. The Eisenhower family genealogy also indicates otherwise.

For several years, the Eisenhower Presidential Library in Abilene hosted an annual Elderhostel for senior citizens with themes such as "World War II," the "Fabulous Fifties," or simply "The Eisenhower Era." During one of these week-long educational seminars, we had an African American gentleman among the attendees. In a private conversation during coffee break, I asked him if he had heard the stories of Ike's Black ancestry. He told me, "Oh yes, the 'Brothers' have always considered Ike one of our own."

The genesis of these theories and questions was inevitably the background of Ike's mother, Ida Stover. She was born on May 1, 1862, in Mount

Wedding photograph of David Jacob Eisenhower and Ida Elizabeth Stover. They married in Lecompton, Kansas, on September 23, 1885, and after the wedding set up household in Hope, Kansas, a small town twenty-five miles south of Abilene. Decades later, the wedding photograph became the source of rumors of Ida's African American ancestry. (Courtesy Eisenhower Library)

Sidney, Virginia, in the heart of the Shenandoah Valley during the Civil War. Her family had lived in Virginia for several generations and before that in Pennsylvania from early colonial times. She was the youngest child and only daughter of elderly parents, and when her mother died, Ida was sent to live with an aunt and uncle who lived in the same Virginia county. When she turned twenty-one years of age in 1883, Ida took her inheritance and emigrated to Kansas to join her brother in Lecompton and attend Lane University. She soon met fellow student David Eisenhower and the two were married after just two semesters of study. David's and Ida's wedding photograph taken in 1885 would become the default "evidence" offered for all the Black heritage theories. According to Ida's great niece, Ida fell from a galloping horse as a young girl and broke her nose.[1] This injury may well explain in part the flat nose bridge she had. Ida's skin was also more of a slight olive color and she had full lips.

During a two-year period in the second decade after the Civil War,

1879–1880, there was a lively migration of African American freedmen from the Lower Mississippi Valley (e.g., Louisiana and Mississippi) to Kansas. There was such enthusiasm among those participating in the move north that newsmen of the day nicknamed the exodus the "Kansas Fever." Fast-forward over a hundred years and one finds this Kansas Fever Committee notice in the *Topeka Capital-Journal* on October 8, 1996, announcing plans to celebrate not only Eisenhower's birthday but also his "African heritage" on the state capitol grounds:

CELEBRATE IKE'S BIRTHDAY
The Kansas Fever Committee will have a brief ceremony at noon Oct. 14 to celebrate the 106th birthday and African heritage of former president Dwight D. Eisenhower. The event will be at the Amy Biehl Tree on the south side of the Capitol. The public is invited. Birthday cake will be served.

Ike's "African heritage" was in question on the East Coast around the same time. In 1993, Dianne Wilkerson became the first African American female to serve in the Massachusetts state senate. Her political career got off to a shaky start when, just before taking office, she publicly blasted the US media and educational system for conspiring to keep important cultural achievements of minorities concealed. Wilkerson is an attorney, and her controversial remarks were made before the Bench-Bar Committee of the Massachusetts Bar Association. Wilkerson cited as an example of this "cultural cover-up" the fact that President Dwight D. Eisenhower's mother was Black. "She had darker skin than I do," Wilkerson was quoted as saying in the *Massachusetts Lawyers Weekly*. Senator Wilkerson noted she should have figured this out earlier but was not tipped off until she saw a photograph in an old 1968 edition of either *Time* or *Life* magazine that showed clearly that Eisenhower's mother was Black. The "incriminating photo" was a cropped copy of the 1885 wedding portrait. Wilkerson then claimed the national magazine was quickly yanked from the newsstands to stop the story from spreading. An archivist at the Eisenhower Library responded to a media inquiry about this Wilkerson saga by saying the library's records show Ida Eisenhower was of Germanic decent and there was no evidence of Black lineage. Subsequently, when Senator Wilkerson was asked by the press to respond to the Eisenhower Library disclaimer, she replied to the reporter, "You don't think there is any such thing as black Germans?"[2]

There is also printed literature promoting the theory Eisenhower was African American—suspect as the publications may be. In 1965 an eighteen-page self-published pamphlet appeared, entitled *The Five Negro Presidents: According to What White People Said They Were.* The author, Joel Augustus Rogers (1880–1966), was a Jamaican American journalist, author, and historian; a prolific writer who focused on the history of Africa and the African diaspora. (Rogers was from mixed-race parents and his own wife was German born.) In *The Five Negro Presidents,* Rogers named four of the earlier US presidents he maintained had a Black heritage: Thomas Jefferson, Andrew Jackson, Abraham Lincoln, and Warren G. Harding. He was hesitant to name the fifth president mixed-race because there was "no published research on his ancestry." As far as Rogers knew, the allegation was based on a photograph of this president's mother, who was Virginia born, and some photographs of the president himself. That Rogers did not identify Dwight D. Eisenhower by name as the fifth president in his pamphlet was likely in deference to the fact the former president was still alive in 1965 when the tract was published. But his major "evidence" was, once again, the famous Ida Stover Eisenhower wedding portrait.[3]

Then there is *The Six Black Presidents: Black Blood, White Masks* by Auset BaKhufu, published in 1993. This was no pamphlet; rather a full-length book of some 350 pages. The author is described as a social/counseling psychologist, educator, writer, certified teacher, and crisis intervention counselor. BaKhufu devoted almost ninety pages to her rambling chapter on Ike. She maintained the Ida Stover wedding photograph was not the only evidence, but that the president himself "had ethnic features" as a youth, "although he looked essentially White during his elder years." BaKhufu maintained no one was going to convince her that during Ike's entire life he had not been asked if he or his mother was "colored or Negro." His racial denial would have been a serious self-imposed burden he carried throughout his life. "Not understanding the beauty of blackness, Ike could only hold the trauma and hurt inside."[4]

BaKhufu speculates that young Eisenhower's decision to attend West Point may have been race related. Did Ike resent the fact his mother claimed white, although he surely understood the societal necessity? Or did he subconsciously resent the truth—that he too was of color? By choosing a military profession so abhorrent to Ida, was this a way to strike back and rid himself of the anger he would never be able to express openly?[5]

BaKhufu even pointed to a medical theory she believed added scientific credence to her view that Ike was African American. It was no wonder

Eisenhower had several heart attacks during his life. She said case studies showed Black people suffer from a much higher incidence of hypertension than white people. Hypertension causes heart attacks. Furthermore, Eisenhower was under the additional stress of living two lives. For a Black person pretending to be white, and in fear of being discovered, the stress level could be tremendous.[6] Add to that the pressure of being president of the United States.

My conclusion is that the theories about Eisenhower's African American ancestry remain unconvincing. Credit for Ike's history of heart problems stems much more logically from the fact he was a heavy smoker of unfiltered cigarettes for some thirty-five years (four to five packs a day during the war). He held two of the most stressful jobs in the twentieth century; Supreme Allied Commander during World War II and two terms as president during the height of the Cold War. He was fortunate to live to the age of seventy-eight years.

As a young man from the south side of the tracks in Abilene, Ike applied to West Point simply to obtain a "free" college education, not out of resentment of a hidden racial secret. With his appointment to the military academy, little did he realize he would be signing up to serve his country for the next fifty years in uniform and in the White House.

US census records for the decades preceding the Civil War show no slaves listed for Ida's Stover ancestors in Augusta County, Virginia, or earlier in Pennsylvania. In addition, Eisenhower descendants have done extensive genealogical study on Ike's ancestry, with no surprising results to report.

Apparently, Barack Obama's official place in history as the first African American US president is not threatened by Dwight D. Eisenhower. Oh well. As Susan Eisenhower said about her grandfather's reported Black heritage, that would have been neat.

CHAPTER EIGHT

IKE THE PILOT

"I'll bet that if I had started a little younger, I could be a crack
pilot by this time."
—*Lt. Colonel Dwight D. Eisenhower*[1]

History owes Mr. John Sheldon Doud a debt of gratitude for denying Lieutenant Dwight D. Eisenhower permission to marry his nineteen-year-old
daughter, Mamie Geneva Doud, in 1916. Read on to understand.

Mr. Doud was very fond of Ike and had initially given the marriage
proposal his blessing, but upon learning the ambitious (and adventurous)
infantry officer had applied for a transfer to the fledgling Army Aviation
Section, the concerned father changed his mind. Military flying was a
dangerous occupation, and Mr. Doud did not want Mamie returning to
her parents' home as a young widow. After a day or two of deliberation, Eisenhower wisely decided to marry the woman he loved and forgo the lure
of the aviation branch with its adventure and the appealing 50 percent increase in pay, earned for hazardous duty. As a natural leader, Eisenhower
would doubtless have risen in the ranks and become a general officer in
the Army Air Corps by the time of World War II. He would not, however,
have been the overall Supreme Allied Commander and would have been
denied the opportunity to lead Allied forces in the liberation of Europe on
D-Day. That assignment was destined for an army infantry general officer.
Even as a three-star or four-star air corps general, Ike would not have been
the war hero and world figure he was. And more significantly, Eisenhower
certainly would not have been elected as US president in 1952. Ike's decision in 1916 was destiny.

As it turned out, Ike's dream of flying was not denied forever, but only
deferred. Nineteen years after he turned down his chance to join the
Army Air Corps, Lt. Colonel Eisenhower found himself in the Philippines
(1935–1939) as a US military advisor helping train the Philippine army.
As fortune would have it, a certain Captain Lewis and Lieutenant William
Lee were army pilots and fellow advisors assigned to help train Philippine
flight cadets for their own nation's air corps. Lewis and Lee soon agreed to
give Ike private flying lessons early in the morning before he went into the

office and during frequent official trips he made with them while flying to visit Philippine Army units scattered throughout the islands.

Lieutenant Lee noted in a later oral history that Eisenhower was a confident student. When he had the flying controls, Eisenhower "was light and relaxed; he had good coordination. . . . We pounded that into his head, because he was a golf player and he knew that in playing golf you've got to be relaxed."[2]

Eisenhower soloed on May 19, 1937, and during the next two years accumulated a total of 180 flying hours in the Stearman PT-17 and Stinson Reliant airplanes. The Bureau of Aeronautics in Manila issued Ike his private pilot's license on July 5, 1939. The Philippine certificate met US standards and Eisenhower was issued his pilot's license by the US Civil Aeronautics Authority on July 15, 1940.

Eisenhower had achieved his dream of flying, but with the advent of World War II he rose quickly in military rank and responsibility and found little opportunity to pursue it. After the war, as army chief of staff, NATO commander, and president of the United States, he became the VIP passenger aboard the aircraft, and it became even more complicated, as he explained in his memoir At Ease:

> After World War II, I had ceased to fly altogether, except that once in a while, on a long trip, to relieve my boredom (and demolish the pilot's), I would move into the co-polit's seat and take over the controls. But as the Jet age arrived, I realized that I had come out of a horse-and-buggy background, recognized my limitations, and kept to a seat in the back.[3]

Trivia question: How many US presidents were pilots? The answer is three: George H. W. Bush, George W. Bush, and Dwight D. Eisenhower. There were significant differences in their flying experiences. George H. W. Bush served as a torpedo bomber pilot in the US Navy during World War II. He flew the TBM Avenger off the aircraft carrier USS *San Jacinto* in the Pacific Theater. The elder Bush flew combat bombing missions for several months in 1944 and logged over 1,200 hours, with 126 carrier landings. Bush 41 was shot down by the Japanese on one mission and rescued in the ocean by a US submarine. He finished his wartime service stateside as an instructor pilot in 1945.

George W. Bush was in the Texas Air National Guard from 1969 to 1972. He served two years of full-time active duty for pilot training, followed by four years flying in the national guard. Bush 43 logged 576 flying

A personal dream deferred. Ike earned his private pilot's license at the age of forty-eight in the Philippines in July 1939. (Courtesy Eisenhower Library)

hours, over half of which were in the supersonic F-102 Delta Dagger jet fighter interceptor. While in the National Guard, Bush inquired about being assigned with a unit in Vietnam but did not have the requisite number of flying hours to qualify.

We will never know exactly how important Eisenhower's flying experience in the Philippines was in making him a strong advocate for airpower. We can well imagine that his 180 hours behind the stick gave him an appreciation of its potential. In any event, Ike became a true believer in airpower in his role as Supreme Allied Commander during World War II. In planning D-Day, Eisenhower demanded and received the total dedication of Allied flying resources for the landings. The soundness of his faith in airpower was substantiated by none other than German Field Marshall Erwin Rommel, who stated that Allied air superiority had been the primary reason for his enemy's success and his own failure.[4]

On June 17, 1945, at the end of the war in Europe, a large study group made up of the most experienced and progressive officers, known as the General Board, was established to prepare a factual analysis of the strategy and tactics employed by US forces in the European Theater of Operations. Ike wrote in *Crusade in Europe* that foremost of the lessons learned by

Table 1. Piloting Experience of US Presidents

	Years	Age	Flying Hours	Of Note
Eisenhower	1935–39	45–49	180	+140 hrs as observer
Bush 41	1943–45	19–21	1228	126 carrier landings
Bush 43	1969–72	23–25	576	278 hrs in jet fighter

the board was "the extraordinary and growing influence of the airplane in the waging of war."[5] Just two years later, as army chief of staff in 1947, Eisenhower played a major role transforming the US Army Air Corps into a new branch of service: the US Air Force.

As president, Eisenhower brought new aircraft into the presidential fleet; two Lockheed VC-121 Constellations. These state-of-the-art commercial aircraft had a cruising speed of 300 mph, and the Constellations are considered today by aviation historians to be the last of the great American propellor-driven airliners. The White House christened these two new presidential aircraft *Columbine II* and *Columbine III*, named for the official flower of First Lady Mamie Eisenhower's home state of Colorado.

Ike participated in one accidental but inevitable and important contribution to US aviation history. In 1953, *Columbine II* while carrying President Eisenhower became the first plane given the call sign "Air Force One." This new designation was the result of a near collision that had occurred earlier that same year between the president's aircraft and an Eastern Airlines commercial flight over the East Coast. Air traffic controllers were confused during that incident because the two planes carried the same flight number. As a result, to this day "Air Force One" remains the official designation for any aircraft carrying the president of the United States, guaranteeing that plane a wide berth in the sky.

A more substantial contribution to US aviation safety occurred when President Eisenhower sent a message to Congress on June 13, 1958, urging the establishment of a new aviation management organization to support the needs of both civil and military aviation. Planes were becoming faster and much more plentiful across the nation's skies. Air traffic had doubled in the decade after the end of the war. Jet aircraft were growing in number, as was helicopter traffic in urban areas. This serious congestion was occurring at the same time aviation facilities were becoming inadequate for efficient and safe management of air traffic. Ike as a student pilot in the 1930s had relied on visual flying, but times were changing. In his message to Congress, President Eisenhower referred to a recent deadly collision of two civil airliners over the Grand Canyon. Ike said, "This tragedy gave dramatic support to the view that even in the less congested portions of our nation's airspace the separation of aircraft should not be left to chance or to the visual ability of pilots."[6]

Eisenhower recommended that Congress enact legislation establishing a Federal Aviation Administration (FAA) at the earliest possible date. The senators and representatives heeded his urging and only ten weeks later, on August 23, 1958, Ike was able to sign legislation into law creating the FAA.

In Eisenhower's "New Look" defense strategy, the president gave budgetary preference to the youngest military branch, the US Air Force. The army was his life for fifty years but maintaining a large peacetime army during a drawn-out Cold War was too financially burdensome and strategically unnecessary. The Soviets had 175 army divisions in Europe. In Ike's view, the only practical—and budgetarily sound—way to counter this imbalance was a deterrent threat of massive nuclear retaliation that would be carried out in large part by a superior US bomber force in case of war. Airpower was the answer.[7]

There were other firsts. Eisenhower became the first president to fly in a jet (a Boeing 707) in August 1959 during an overseas trip to visit Chancellor Konrad Adenauer in West Germany. He was also the first president to ride in a helicopter. Ike had an amazing life's journey. He was born in 1890, the year historians say the American frontier officially closed, and he died in 1969, the year the US put a man on the moon and a new frontier was opened.

Most gratifying to Ike, he fulfilled many a young man's dream of one day poking holes in clouds, piloting his own magic flying machine.

CHAPTER NINE

"TAKE ME TO YOUR LEADER"
IKE AND THE EXTRATERRESTRIALS

"The evidence presented on UFOs shows no indications that these phenomena constitute a direct physical threat to national security."
—*CIA Report on UFOs, January 17, 1953*

It was a dark and stormy night when Ike viewed the remains of the Roswell space aliens . . . okay, not really. It was a clear, cool Saturday evening in Palm Springs, California, on February 20, 1954. President Eisenhower was on a well-deserved golfing vacation from the White House. After golfing that Saturday, the president allegedly used the cover story of a dental emergency—namely breaking a crown on a tooth—to slip away from public view and make a secret trip under evening darkness from Palm Springs to Edwards Air Force Base (AFB). Why? According to UFO true believers, Eisenhower's real purpose was to view the bodies of aliens kept in cold storage since the crash of their spaceship in the desert near Roswell, New Mexico, in 1947. To them, this scandalous revelation must prove that Ike was just another player in the cabal that has for decades been hiding the truth about the famous Roswell incident and unidentified flying objects in general.

Sorry, UFOers, but the president really did break a crown and have a night visit with a Palm Springs dentist rather than a hushed trip to Edwards AFB. Dr. James Mixson, a professor in the School of Dentistry at the University of Missouri, Kansas City, has studied Ike's dental history extensively and wrote to the Eisenhower Library in 1995 to debunk the story. Professor Mixson pointed out that Eisenhower had a history of problems with the crown on his upper left central incisor and, in fact, it had fractured three times before.[1]

After Sunday morning church services on February 21 at Palm Springs Community Church, reporters were briefed that Ike had required emergency dental treatment the previous evening and had visited a local dentist, Dr. Frank Purcell. Later that same Sunday evening, there was a reception for Eisenhower at the Smoke Tree Ranch in Palm Springs and among the over four hundred guests attending were Dr. and Mrs. Purcell. The UFO crowd claims this was part of the cover-up story. However, White House appointment book records at the Eisenhower Library document that Dr. and Mrs. Purcell were indeed among the attendees and that Ike had a dental appointment the prior evening sometime after 8 p.m.[2] The president's press secretary, James Hagerty, kept a diary and noted, "Saturday, February 20, 1954, at Palm Springs—Pres broke cap off tooth—had it fixed at local dentist—Dr. C. A. Purcell."[3]

Another fact to consider—Edwards AFB is located over 130 miles from Palm Springs and would have required six hours of driving time for the round trip. Construction on the Eisenhower Interstate Highway system did not start until the following year. Plus, you always need a good hour or two to examine the remains of aliens from outer space. The president thus would have returned in the early hours of the next morning if he had made that arduous trip and barely had time to shower before the 9:30 a.m. church service in Palm Springs. There were no press reports of him having fallen asleep during the sermon.

But wait, there's more. Conspiracy buffs believe this was not Eisenhower's first introduction to the "true story" regarding the existence of UFOs. On November 18, 1952, President-elect Ike reportedly made a forty-five-minute visit to the Pentagon to be briefed on something called the Majestic-12 (MJ-12) program, established by President Truman. MJ-12 was allegedly the US government's secret operation on UFOs. In the mid-1980s, the Eisenhower Library was sent a copy of a "briefing document" stamped TOP SECRET/MAJIC that was quickly determined by the library to be fake due to dubious formatting and markings. The Majestic-12 hoax is described later in this chapter.

Do not stop reading! Before you head outside to look up at the sky with new fear and trepidation (or just plain excitement), perhaps a few more salient facts are in order to help set the record straight. The documentation in the historical holdings of the Eisenhower Presidential Library discounts and disproves the above UFO stories.

A reporter asked President Eisenhower about UFOs at a press conference on December 15, 1954:

Question: Mr. President . . . recent news reports indicate that some European governments are investigating quite seriously the flying saucer problem. And not too long ago there was a book published in this country that purported to show that our Air Force thought that some of these flying objects, at least might come to be extraterrestrial in origin.

I wonder if you could tell us if our authorities really do suspect something of that kind or, if not, what is the form of the things?

The President: Well, with regard to these recent reports, nothing has come to me at all, either verbally or in written form. And I must say, when I go back far enough, the last time that I heard this talked to me, a man whom I trust from the Air Forces said that it was, as far as he knew, completely inaccurate to believe that they came from any outside planet or otherwise.[4]

I think we can all agree that when the air force says there is nothing to worry about, we should relax. Or perhaps not.

In early 1953 the US government was concerned enough with the growing UFO phenomenon that the Central Intelligence Agency (CIA) convened a four-day panel of scientific experts to study the issue. Their task was "to evaluate any possible threat to national security posed by Unidentified Flying Objects ('Flying Saucers') and to make recommendation thereon." From January 14–17, 1953, the distinguished group of academic consultants—physicists, geophysicists, and astronomers—met, studied evidence, and interviewed other experts before submitting their report to the CIA.[5]

In their final report, dated January 17, 1953, the scientific panel concluded (1) "the evidence presented on UFOs shows no indications that these phenomena constitute a direct physical threat to national security" and (2) "the continued emphasis on the reporting of these phenomena does, in these parlous times, result in a threat to the orderly functioning of the protective organs of the body politic."

In other words, the experts neither confirmed nor denied the existence of UFOs but said they were not a national security threat. However, what was a threat to the "orderly functioning" of the country was the unreasonable publicity and concern about flying saucers. The report concluded that the only danger to the nation was the continued false alarms about UFOs that might cause the country to be distracted and ignore real indications of hostile threats from enemies. There could develop a harmful distrust by the citizenry of duly constituted authority. In modern parlance, we would call this a "credibility gap."

The panel recommended that the national security agencies take immediate steps to strip the UFOs of the "special status" they were being given and remove the aura of mystery they had unfortunately acquired.

The 1950s were indeed the heyday of science fiction writing and movies. I loved to read science fiction as a youth during this time. In the summer of 1952, the frequency of reports of flying saucer sightings reached a peak, no doubt stimulated by articles on UFOs in leading popular magazines.

The CIA's scientific panel urged implementation of an integrated program designed to reassure the public of the total lack of evidence of inimical forces behind the phenomena. They also recommended training for official personnel to better recognize and reject false UFO reports quickly and effectively, thus reducing public overreaction. At the same time, the report recommended the government strengthen regular channels for the evaluation of and prompt reaction to indications of true hostile measures. In other words, put the kibosh on false reports but at the same time be better prepared to recognize when the real enemy was at the door.

Why did President Eisenhower trust what an air force official told him about UFOs? Perhaps because of Project Blue Book—the official study of the paranormal sightings prepared by none other than the US Air Force. Was the fox guarding the hen house?

Project Blue Book was the culmination of a two-year study by the air force on the subject of "Unidentified Aerial Objects," to use their official term. Conducted by the Air Technical Intelligence Center at Wright-Patterson AFB, Ohio, the detailed examination was in response to the ever-increasing number of reports of unexplained sightings since mid-1947 (in other words, since the Roswell incident). In the summary of their Blue Book findings, the air force concluded that there was no threat to the security of the US presented by these UFOs. Nevertheless, the sightings were important to investigate and evaluate if "flying saucers represented technological developments not known to this country." In other words, let us make sure these unexplained flying wonders are our own.[6]

The challenge for the air force was that reports of UFOs were usually personal "impressions and interpretation" of unexplainable events. Authorities had only these very subjective reports, making it difficult to apply scientific methods of study. The air force computerized the available data by using IBM punch cards (for anyone out there old enough to remember those Hollerith cards), and then it was analyzed objectively. Blue Book looked for distinguishing characteristics in the data, seeking trends or patterns. The goal was to determine the probability that any of the reported "Unknowns" represented observations of technological developments not familiar to the air force. From the unscientific data available, the study determined the following identification breakdown of the 854 official UFO reports received from 1953 and 1954:

Balloons	16%
Aircraft	20%
Astronomical	25%
Other	13%
Insufficient Info	17%
Unknown	9%

It was clear to the air force that improved reporting and investigating procedures were needed. The key to a higher percentage of solutions was a rapid on-the-spot investigation by trained personnel. In late 1954, the 4602nd Air Intelligence Service Squadron was created to conduct quick-response field investigations. Beginning in 1955, investigators from the 4602nd made a significant difference in determining the cause of UFO sightings. For the first six months of 1955, there were 131 reports of UFO sightings and of these the number categorized as "Insufficient Info" or "Unknown" dropped from a combined 26 percent in 1953–1954 to only 10 percent of the total sightings.

Balloons	26%
Aircraft	21%
Astronomical	23%
Other	20%
Insufficient Info	7%
Unknown	3%

While there were still a significant number of unexplained UFOs in 1955, the air force believed that all UFOs could have been explained if more complete observational data had been available rather than simple "impressions" and "interpretations" provided by the eyewitnesses. Project Blue Book made the strong point that there had been a complete lack of valid evidence of the discovery of physical matter in any case of a reported unidentified aerial object. There was no record of flying-saucer wreckage having been found and certainly no trace of space aliens.

When the Project Blue Book report was released to the public on

October 25, 1955, Secretary of the Air Force Donald A. Quarles made the following statement:

> On the basis of this study we believe that no objects such as those popularly described as flying saucers have overflown the United States. . . . However, we are now entering a period of aviation technology in which aircraft of unusual configuration and flight characteristics will begin to appear. . . . Some of these may take novel forms . . . we expect to develop airplanes that will fly faster, higher and perhaps farther than present designs, but they will still obey natural laws and if manned, they will still be manned by normal terrestrial airmen. . . . The Department of Defense will make every effort within bounds of security to keep the public informed of these developments so they can be recognized for what they are.[7]

The interest in UFOs has experienced a resurgence in recent years. No doubt partly in response, a new office has been created in the Department of Defense to explore and help explain these events. In July 2022, the All-domain Anomaly Resolution Office (AARO) was established to allow a team of experts to use "a rigorous scientific framework and data driven approach" in addressing these incidents. For credibility, the office's vision statement indicates that transparency is also important. Furthermore, there is new terminology. We no longer spot unidentified flying objects (UFOs) but rather are witnessing unidentified anomalous phenomena (UAP). The AARO's mission statement also makes clear that the paramount concern is national security:

> MISSION: Minimize technical and intelligence surprise by synchronizing scientific, intelligence, and operational detection identification, attribution, and mitigation of unidentified anomalous phenomena in the vicinity of national security areas.[8]

The secretary of the air force said in his 1955 statement, "We are now entering a period of aviation technology where aircraft of unusual configuration and flight characteristics may start appearing." The mysterious, mythical, top secret Area 51 north of Las Vegas was no doubt the home base for many of the alleged flying saucers witnessed by skygazing Americans and commercial pilots. Area 51 is indeed a real operating base where our spy planes and secret stealth aircraft, such as the SR-71 Blackbird reconnaissance aircraft (fastest plane in the world) and B-2 flying wing, were developed and test flown over the years. Development work continues on other platforms even to the present time. Most flights are at night and the new technology is kept in underground hangers. The message is: "Nothing to see here, move along!"

In my role as an intelligence officer in the US Air Force Reserve during the 1980s, I had oversight of an intelligence reserve detachment that drilled on weekends at Nellis AFB, just outside Las Vegas. These reservists were men and women who otherwise had full-time jobs as civilians. One of the reserve officers under my command at Nellis AFB was a Department of Defense civilian, an engineer who worked in the underground facility at Area 51. He could not tell me any details about his work, even though I had a top secret security clearance; I had "no need to know." But I did learn that he, along with many of his co-workers, commuted via a daily, thirty-minute roundtrip flight on a government-chartered passenger jet every Monday through Friday from the Las Vegas commercial airport to Area 51. Rush hour traffic was not a problem.

In June 2019 there was a post by a college student named Matty Roberts that went viral on Facebook, challenging American citizens to "Storm Area 51, They Can't Stop All of Us!" It was initially meant as a joke, but by September 2019 over two million people had indicated they would participate. Due to the overwhelming response, Roberts then changed the nature of the event to a music festival that he dubbed "Alienstock," to be held in downtown Las Vegas. As it turned out, only about one hundred revelers showed up at the actual back gate of Area 51. The UFO faithful had indeed heeded the serious air force warnings that trespassers would be arrested. However, there were enough partygoers at "Alienstock" in Vegas that Roberts declared it a success and vowed to make it an annual event.[9]

Since 2015, an annual Contact in the Desert conference has taken place in Indian Wells, California. According to the website (contactinthedesert. com), the four-day program provides intensive course training for UFO investigators. Basic registration for the 2023 conference was $325 for an individual and $550 for a couple. The Interstellar Pass and Galactic Pass (meals not included) were much more. The website's face page cites the 2023 theme as "Science + Future—What's Next?" USA Today called the event "The Woodstock of UFO Conferences," while Forbes in more detail noted, "The Woodstock of UFOlogy is a weekend of education into the Science of UFOs & Extraterrestrial Life."[10]

These types of UFO conferences have been annual events for at least seventy years. In April 1954, President Eisenhower received a telegram informing him there had been a space craft convention to investigate UFOs at Giant Rock Airport in California. Organizer George Van Tassel reported that the 6,000 convention attendees had voted unanimously that the job of investigating UFOs should be transferred from the military to our elected branch of government. "The people are rapidly losing faith in the military after 7 years of confusing answers from Air Force Intelligence," the telegram said. They recommended creation of a study group composed of representatives from civilian, scientific, military, and even theological organizations. (Note: The CIA Scientific UFO Panel in 1953 had included such experts, except for a theologian, but the findings were not declassified until 1982.) Ike's White House respectfully referred the space craft convention telegram to the Department of Defense for consideration and acknowledgement. There is no record of a response from the Pentagon.[11]

Herbert Pankratz was one of our fine archivists at the Eisenhower Presidential Library in Abilene. For efficiency, we assigned our archives staff certain areas of specialization in responding to telephonic or written queries from the public and also when assisting on-site visitors to the library's research room. The rest of the staff jokingly referred to Herb's area of expertise as "Planes, Trains and Automobiles" from the title of the popular 1987 film starring Steve Martin and John Candy. And indeed, Herb could quickly tell you if the old Chrysler sedan you bought at an auction had indeed been previously owned by Eisenhower as promised by the car dealer. Ditto for people wondering about the true historical nature of railroad passenger cars or airplanes in which Ike might have traveled.

But Herb had another more unusual specialty. He was the Eisenhower Library's go-to UFO specialist. As Herb explained to the Kansas City Star newspaper in a 1996 telephone interview, "I got the job by default. Nobody else wanted to take those calls," he said laughing. "But we also wanted consistency in our responses." When someone on the staff gave Herb a little, green, plastic Martian figure in jest, Herb proudly placed it in plain sight, sitting on top of the computer monitor at his desk. He was always most polite and professional when dealing with the "UFO true believers." It was also fortunate that Herb usually wore cowboy boots to work because it sometimes got pretty deep.

Now on to Majestic 12 or Project MJ-12, which was an alleged secret federal panel created by President Harry Truman to investigate the Roswell incident. MJ-12 then continued into the Eisenhower administration, according to "ufology" experts. (Note: Ufology is the study of reports, visual records, physical evidence, and other phenomena related to unidentified flying objects (UFOs).)

Things got interesting in the mid-1980s when reports surfaced of the discovery of a key document: a formerly top secret memorandum dated July 14, 1954, from President Eisenhower's national security advisor Bobby Cutler informing General Nathan Twining, chairman of the US Air Force, about a meeting on the subject of Majestic 12 scheduled to take place on July 16, 1954, at the White House National Security Council. Finally, this appeared to be the evidence, which had been heretofore lacking, to prove that there was a secret government cabal intent on keeping the lid on the truth about the existence of UFOs.

There was indeed a document found in the records at the National Archives in Washington, DC. But alas, there appeared to be issues with its authenticity. A thorough joint investigation was done by the National Archives in Washington, DC, and the Truman and Eisenhower Presidential Libraries, which concluded the document was a fake.[12] First, there was a missing water mark on the pages of the memo. Then, the classification stamped on the document—"Top Secret Restricted Information"—was a marking that did not exist in 1954 and was not used at the National Security Council until fifteen years later during the Nixon administration. There was also no record at the Eisenhower Library or at the National Security Council (NSC) of such a top secret document being declassified and opened for viewing by researchers. Government records keepers meticulously keep such documentation to avoid security violations.

In addition, President Eisenhower's appointment books contain no entry for a special meeting on July 16, 1954, the date of the alleged NSC meeting. Even when the president had an "off-the-record" meeting, the White House appointment books always contained entries indicating the participants and the time of the meeting. "Off-the-record" meant not announced to the media or public, but the meeting was still documented in the administrative records for history. Another problem was the fact that Bobby Cutler, the alleged author of the document, was on an overseas trip at the time the suspicious memo was written.

In the research room at the National Archives, there is always an attendant on duty to (1) assist researchers, (2) answer questions, and (3) call other staff to have boxes of records pulled from the closed stack areas for the researchers to examine. The attendant has one other important responsibility: (4) to make certain no original historical documents are mutilated or stolen from the nation's archives. There is another equally important duty we had not recognized; namely, to ensure no fake documents are inserted into the records in an effort to rewrite history. That is what happened in this case.

Advice to history collectors—do not pay for any Majestic 12 documents you find for sale online or at manuscript auctions. They would be of no true historical value, even if they might prove to be an interesting collectible for other reasons.

It is easy to be very dismissive about the existence of extraterrestrials, but many people have seen things in the sky that cannot be explained. My own parents were convinced they were eyewitnesses to one of these unexplained phenomena years ago. On their weekday thirty-mile commute from the small town of Alma, Kansas, to Topeka, they spotted three very bright lights one morning. The strange lights hung in the air without moving for a long time and then exited quickly. They were not the army helicopters from neighboring Fort Riley that one saw occasionally. Mom and Dad were not superstitious people, and they were well-read and well-traveled. My father was a radar technician in his early military career before moving on to his specialty as a nuclear weapons officer. No technical slouch was he. My mother was a legal secretary. These were not people to be easily deceived. They never made a big deal out of their unexplainable sighting and rarely if ever brought it up.

I must confess I am still very much a skeptic. What we know for certain is that Dwight D. Eisenhower did not view the remains of space aliens allegedly kept in secret cold storage after the Roswell incident and that Project Majestic 12 was a hoax. This assessment may disappoint the true believers. What is important is that we remember Ike was the president who brought America into outer space with the creation of the National Aeronautics and Space Administration. He launched the first US satellites, and his *Explorer 1* discovered the Van Allen radiation belt. Eisenhower established Project Mercury with John Glenn and the original team of astronauts.

Hopefully, this will suffice as "close encounters" for most of us.

CHAPTER TEN

"OTHER LOSSES"
GENERAL EISENHOWER'S ONE MILLION MISSING GERMAN POWS

"God I hate the Germans!"
—*General Eisenhower letter to Mamie, September 19, 1944*

You will be pleased to learn that, upon due reflection, the statue of Dwight D. Eisenhower was not torn down and removed from the Eisenhower Presidential Library grounds in 1989. Okay, the magnificent fifteen-foot bronze sculpture of General Ike—the centerpiece of the twenty-two-acre campus in Abilene, Kansas—was not seriously at risk of being sent to the dustbin of history. Nevertheless, the demand was being made by a few angry people. And it was not only the bronze Ike edifice that was to be removed. Eisenhower's portraits were to be banned from the walls of the Eisenhower Museum as well. As it turns out, General Ike was accused of being an alleged war criminal. Who would have thought?

What lousy timing for this controversy. In the fall of 1989, the Eisenhower Library was deep into planning for the grand commemoration of Ike's 100th birthday (1890–1990). The Eisenhower Centennial was set to begin a year-long celebration the following January with events in Abilene and across the nation. It was unfortunate that Canadian author James Bacque published his provocative book at this same time, entitled *Other Losses: An Investigation into the Mass Deaths of German Prisoners at the Hands of French and Americans After World War II*. Unbeknownst to the Eisenhower Library—and the rest of the world for that matter—General Eisenhower was now accused of being a mass murderer.

Bacque maintained in *Other Losses* that in the cold, wet spring of 1945, as many as one million German POWs died of disease and starvation through intentional neglect at the hands of their American and French captors. "Their deaths were knowingly caused by army officers who had sufficient resources to keep the prisoners alive." According to Bacque, General Eisenhower as Allied commander was not only aware of this situation, but in fact helped create it with the result in mind.

Plans for the Dwight D. Eisenhower Centennial Celebration in 1990 called for a year-long series of programs, events, and VIP visits to Abilene to commemorate the important contributions to history made by the wartime Supreme Allied Commander and thirty-fourth president of the United States. It seemed Mr. Bacque's *Other Losses* was in danger of becoming the proverbial skunk at the dinner party.

In late April 1945, the Germans continued to fight hard against the advancing Russians in the east. By contrast, the war on the western front was winding down. There were mass surrenders of German troops. The Germans hoped this strategy would deliver as many Wehrmacht troops as possible into the merciful hands of the Western allies rather than the Russians. According to Bacque, this strategy was a gamble that proved to be a bad one.[1]

Five million German troops thus were put under the control of Supreme Allied Commander Dwight D. Eisenhower. This was most unfortunate for the surrendered enemy soldiers because Eisenhower—at least according to Bacque—held a fierce and obsessive hatred not only of the Nazi regime, but of all things German. Eisenhower's hatred, combined with a compliant and indifferent military bureaucracy, produced an alleged horror of "death camp" magnitude in France beginning in the spring of 1945, in which Bacque claimed more German soldiers died from disease and starvation in just a few months than had been killed in actual combat during the entire four years on the western front.

James Bacque was making these shocking accusations:

(1) The alleged "food shortage" in postwar Europe has been exaggerated by historians to cover up the German POW deaths, which should not have happened.[2]

(2) The US Army circumvented the 1929 Geneva Convention on prisoners of war status by inventing the new category "disarmed enemy forces" (DEFs) for German POWs. This allowed General Eisenhower to withhold adequate food and shelter from the DEFs.[3]

(3) The motive for all of this? Quite simply, revenge. Eisenhower hated the Germans for starting World War II and causing all the death and destruction that ensued.

By May 8, 1945—VE Day—Allied armies were swamped with some 7 million displaced persons (DPs) in Germany and 1.6 million in Austria. These included Nazi slave laborers from all over Europe and German concentration camp inmates. Added to this was a flood of some 12 to 14.5 million ethnic German refugees who arrived in the war-torn country after having been expelled from their homes in central and eastern Europe.

Overnight, postwar Germany experienced a 15–25 percent population growth due to this dramatic influx of DPs and refugees.[4]

Eisenhower had forewarned the German population of the impending food shortage in a proclamation issued on March 31, 1945. He urged the German people to continue all agricultural work and to put refugees to work on farms. He admonished farm workers not to join the *Volksturm* (the German home guard made up of young and old men not serving in the regular military) as the war was ending but to continue in their critical agricultural work. He urged German civilians to resist with force all attempts of the Nazi Party to carry away food stocks and to prevent the slaughter of cattle, pigs, and fowl. He reminded the German people that during the war they had lived on food stuffs robbed from occupied territories, but that in 1945 they would "have to eat only that which they themselves produce."[5]

Even if General Eisenhower had not found himself with millions of additional mouths to feed at war's end, there would have been a serious food shortage. In 1945 the German civilian population subsisted on a near-starvation diet of 1,550 calories per day, the same caloric number that was to be provided the POWs. German agriculture was faced with greatly decreased production in 1945. Due to war priorities, German farmers had little or no access to fertilizer for their crops and no fuel for tractors. With the release of eastern European slave laborers and Russian POWs, there was also a serious shortage of farm workers at the war's end. Most German men of working age had served in the military and were still prisoners of war and unavailable to help with farming. The real end to the food shortage did not happen until the summer of 1948 with the revival of the European economies.[6]

Then there was the Russia problem. The eastern portion of occupied Germany, the "breadbasket" of the defeated nation, was now under Soviet control. The US and its Western allies could not look in that direction for any support. Russia was sending those food stuffs eastward to its own struggling homeland. US Army unit records from World War II show another unique food problem involving Russians. The US 180th Infantry Regiment, situated near Munich in occupied Germany, reported the following incidents in June 1945. On June 2 five Russian displaced persons were "accosted and handled" by American troops for shooting at sheep herds in the area. Two days later, a signal corps unit reported, "We are to have patrols continually check zoo south of town as Russian DPs are stealing animals for nutrition purposes." Everyone was hungry.[7]

The war against Japan aggravated the problem. General Eisenhower's pleas to his superiors in Washington for additional food supplies were competing with an even more compelling logistical demand—namely the need for all available shipping to be relocated to the Pacific Theater for the unfinished business with the Japanese. Food stuffs may have been available in America, but the shipping conduit to Europe could not be enlarged to meet the sudden increase in demand.

It was not just the German population and German POWs who were hungry as the war ended. In May 1945, the US Army's chief quartermaster of the COMZ (communications zone/rear echelon) reduced rations by 10 percent for all US officers and enlisted men still in Europe.[8] In addition, General Eisenhower was asked by the War Department to investigate press reports circulating in the US that some 50,000 US service men repatriated from German prisoner of war camps were being held in a temporary American camp in France, under conditions worse than they had experienced while prisoners of the Germans. Ike did visit Camp Lucky Strike, where GIs were waiting for transportation home, and he offered the men quicker trips stateside if they were willing to double up and sleep in shifts on the ships, using the "hot bunk" concept. The GIs eagerly agreed and the lengthy wait for the trip home was reduced.[9]

The Allied governments were also looking ahead and rightly fearful of the threat of famine in the winter of 1945–1946. They were stockpiling food in preparation for the worst. Indeed, the existing supply barely got those in Europe through that initial postwar winter, and the food shortage lasted three more years.

Why the designation Disarmed Enemy Forces (DEFs)? Bacque's conspiracy thesis rests in large part on the Allied decision to have German prisoners of war redesignated as DEFs. The number of POWs was the problem, along with the food shortage. Eisenhower had anticipated capturing three million German soldiers in the closing months of the war. Instead, the actual figure ended up being around five million—one million of whom were German soldiers who had fled from the Russians in the east. The British Allies had agreed at the end of the war to take one-half of the captured German soldiers but soon reneged, arguing that they did not have a place to keep them or men to guard them on the Continent and that moving them to England would arouse public resentment and adversely affect British morale.[10]

The US forces were overwhelmed by the sheer numbers of POWs. In some camps, one thousand prisoners shared a single water faucet. The dire food situation in most German cities and villages also delayed the release of the prisoners back into the civilian population. In addition, the destroyed German transportation system disrupted shipments of much-needed food and supplies intended for the POWs.

The Geneva Accords required that POWs be provided 2,000 calories of food a day. Working prisoners should receive 2,900 calories. Eisenhower cabled George Marshall that if captured German soldiers were given the formal POW status, it would necessitate the provision of rations "far beyond the capacity of the Allies even if all German sources were tapped." In any event, Eisenhower emphasized that "it would be undesirable to place the German Armed Forces upon a scale of rations far in excess of that available to the civil population." In effect, this would be punishing the civilians more than the former members of the Wehrmacht. Ike recommended the Disarmed Enemy Forces designation, and the final decision for DEF status was made by the allied European Advisory Commission (1943–1945), which was made up of senior diplomatic representatives from the governments of the American, British, and Soviet wartime allies. The commission helped plan the occupation of postwar Germany.[11]

By summer's end in 1945, there were many ex-soldiers who were willing POWs, as they were better fed than they would have been on the outside. An anecdote is in order. My German-born wife's Uncle Gerhard, who was drafted in Germany as a young teenager in the waning months of the war, arrived home in the late summer of 1945 after release from an American camp. He shocked his waiting family by proceeding to sit down to lunch with them and casually spreading their entire weekly ration of butter onto a single slice of bread and eating it. For years thereafter, they never let "Onkel Gerd" forget how good he had had it as an American POW.

As the war was ending, the US Army theatre provost marshal prepared a weekly report giving the status of Disarmed Enemy Forces. The reports include the following four categories:

- Number of DEFs GAINED
- Number of DEFs DISCHARGED
- Number of DEFs TRANSFERRED
- OTHER LOSSES

It is this latter disposition, "OTHER LOSSES," that caught Mr. Bacque's attention and gave him the title for his book. The category "DISCHARGED" seemed to cover those DEFs released from captivity. He therefore mistakenly concluded "OTHER LOSSES" could only mean those who died. Examination of army records from the time shows that "OTHER LOSSES" included primarily the release of several hundred thousand members of the *Volksturm*—youngsters and oldsters drafted near the end of the war—who were set free by the Allies without formal discharge and told to go home to their mothers or grandchildren.[12]

Discharging the Disarmed Enemy Forces was not a simple matter. Many American camp commanders sought permission from headquarters for the "blanket release" of many of these soldiers, but this could not be authorized for two reasons.

First, the sudden release of massive numbers of DEFs would have inflicted even greater shortages, disorder, and wanton behavior on the suffering civilian population. Second, it was imperative that all DEFs be screened prior to release. Supreme Headquarters Allied Expeditionary Force (SHAEF) directives stipulated that a general discharge was permitted for all DEFs after screening, except those in automatic arrest categories such as senior SS men and war criminals, or the sick and disabled who were unable to travel to their hometowns. Those who were from towns and villages located in the east, in the newly created Soviet zone of occupation, were also to be held. Many German prisoners suffered during this internment, but this screening was an important part of the Allies' "Denazification process." Those released received a half loaf of black bread and a pound of lard for the journey home.

Shortly after the war, West German Chancellor Adenauer spoke to the Bundestag concerning the fate of 1.4 million missing German soldiers. The chancellor's speech is cited by Bacque from a German book, and he claims that those POWs who US authorities listed as "Other Losses" are among the missing. Closer examination shows that Bacque's footnote misleadingly cites the source of the quote as a publication entitled *One Great Prison* (1951). It is important to note that the complete title of the cited work is *One Great Prison: The Story Behind Russia's Unreleased POWs*. Russian handling of German POWs: that was a true scandal.

In 1957, the West German government began an extensive official history of German POWs in World War II. It took sixteen years and twenty-two volumes to complete the job. The so-called Maschke Commission concluded that the German prisoner mortality rate in US camps was 1 percent as compared to a 20–25 percent death rate in Russian camps. The commission stated, "There were no mass deaths in the West."[13]

Did Eisenhower hate the Germans? By the last months of the war, General Eisenhower certainly did hate the enemy. He not only blamed them for starting the war and the death and destruction he saw all around but also detested them for continuing the conflict long after any reasonable people would have quit. He personally signed thousands of condolence letters to mothers and fathers and wives of fallen American soldiers and grew more bitter as the war progressed. In his World War II memoir *Crusade in Europe*, Ike wrote: "I know of no more effective means of developing an undying hatred of those responsible for aggressive war than to assume the obligation of attempting to express sympathy to families bereaved by it."[14]

In two letters to Mamie written in September 1944, as the tough fighting continued in Europe, General Eisenhower made well-known references about his angry feelings toward the Germans. Ike wrote, "The German is a beast," and then, a week later, "God, I hate the Germans!"[15] Eisenhower's anger grew even more when he saw firsthand the concentration camps at the war's end. The myth is that Ike reportedly said he was ashamed of his German name, but historians have been unable to confirm this quote in any of their extensive research.

One inflammatory statement by Eisenhower is used by Bacque to show his alleged intent to eliminate as many German soldiers as possible. As the campaign in North Africa was winding down, Ike wrote, from Tunisia, to General George Marshall on May 25, 1943, about several concerns he faced. He closed his letter with a postscript complaining about the burdens of guarding a quarter-million POWs taken in recent battles in the North Africa campaign. An entire US division was being diverted from combat and placed on guard duty, meaning US forces were shorthanded in protecting their rear flank. Eisenhower noted that in all the military schools he had attended during his career, none anticipated the headache that could come out of a quarter-million POWs. Transportation systems were clogged, and Ike could only evacuate 30,000 POWs per month out of the theater. At that rate it would take eight months to send them all to POW camps being prepared in many states across the US. In the last sentence of the postscript, a frustrated Ike wrote: "It's a pity we could not have killed more."[16]

Unfortunately, conspiracy buffs can take delight in the fact that this sentence was deleted from the letter, which was sanitized in its published form in the official Eisenhower Papers volume printed in 1970. The

Department of Defense official historian advised the Eisenhower Papers Project at Johns Hopkins University that it was obviously a "facetious statement," but that he doubted "based on lengthy experience in Washington—that even an explanatory footnote (would) protect the General against quotation out-of-context." The historian recommended deleting the sentence, which was done by the Hopkins Papers Project.[17] It should be noted that the letter in unedited form—with the inflammatory postscript included—has been available to all researchers visiting the Eisenhower Presidential Library since 1967—over twenty years before Bacque cited it in his book. The moral of the story for all writers, editors, and journalists is that censorship will always backfire eventually.

As the war was ending in April 1945, General Eisenhower drove to visit General Bradley and General Patton at their forward headquarters in Germany. Ike was struck by the surreal nature of watching the peaceful countryside of Germany as he and Sgt. McKeogh (aka Mickey) traveled along the autobahn. It was among the most beautiful scenery they had seen in Europe. Mickey wrote:

> The Boss looked at it and shook his head. He said it was hard to understand why with a country as beautiful as that, the Germans didn't stay in it. "In their own yards," he said. He shook his head as if puzzled . . . they could have stayed in their country and they didn't; they had gone out and asked for trouble. And they were getting it. He looked at the fields and quit smiling, "They're sure getting it," he said.[18]

If Eisenhower harbored ill will toward the Germans during World War II, it was short-lived. A mere five years after the war's end, he returned to Europe as the first Supreme Allied Commander of the newly formed North Atlantic Treaty Organization (NATO) and immediately began taking steps for the rearmament of West Germany and bringing it into NATO as a full partner in the military alliance. Ike was able to make a distinction between the German people and the Nazis.

Apparently, the Germans were in a very forgiving mindset as well. In 1955, President Eisenhower told his press secretary that immediately after the war ended, one of the most amazing things he saw in postwar Germany during the Allied occupation was the way in which the people were greatly relieved to be free of the Nazis and Hitler. Ike said, "Maybe it was because my name was Eisenhower and they liked the German sounds of it, but they used to cheer me everywhere I went."[19]

In December 1990, the Eisenhower Center at the University of New Orleans sponsored an international conference to examine the allegations made by Bacque in *Other Losses*. A group of historians from the US, Canada, Germany, and Austria met at the Eisenhower Center and presented papers that were published in a book in November 1992 entitled: *Eisenhower and the German POWs: Facts Against Falsehood*. The group of historians acknowledge there were indeed thousands of deaths in the prisoner camps and that this was a very under-researched issue in existing scholarship about World War II. Bacque deserved credit for exploring this tragic history. However, that concession to Bacque was followed by a very damning second statement noting that while many German POWs did indeed die in the months immediately after the war's end, it was certainly not in the exaggerated numbers maintained by Bacque. The Canadian journalist's conclusions were very wrong:

> When scholars do the necessary research, they will find Mr. Bacque's work to be worse than worthless. It is seriously—nay spectacularly—flawed in its most fundamental aspects. Mr. Bacque misuses documents; he misreads documents; he ignores contrary evidence; his statistical methodology is hopelessly compromised; he makes no attempt to look at comparative contexts; he puts words into the mouth of his principal source; he ignores a readily available and absolutely critical source that decisively deals with his central accusation; and, as a consequence of these and other shortcoming, he reaches conclusions and makes charges that are demonstrably absurd.[20]

Bacque wrote that Red Cross food shipments to German POWs were blocked by the US military. In fact, that food was diverted to feed other Germans, namely the two million displaced civilian refugees facing the threat of starvation in that country.[21]

In the cold spring weather of 1945, German POWs were certainly exposed to the elements in camps without shelter, but new prisoner enclosures were being constructed as fast as possible. Bacque partially quotes a cable from Eisenhower to General Marshall saying the new enclosures "will provide no shelter or other comforts."[22] The implication was an intentional effort to leave the prisoners exposed to the elements. However, Ike's cable read in full stated that the new enclosures "will provide no shelter or other comforts *initially but will be improved as far as practicable by the Prisoners of War themselves utilizing local materials* (emphasis added)."[23]

Mr. Bacque deserved credit for shedding light on the widespread mistreatment of German POWs in the spring and summer of 1945. Prisoners were beaten, denied water, often lived in open camps without shelter, and did not have adequate medical care. Their mail was often withheld. Men did die needlessly and inexcusably. But the estimated number of deaths totaled around 56,000, about 1 percent of the five million POWs; not the one million alleged by Bacque.

The Eisenhower Center team concluded overwhelmingly that Bacque was wrong on every major and nearly all his minor charges against Eisenhower. To sum up, they wrote: General Eisenhower did not run death camps, German prisoners did not die by the hundreds of thousands, there was a real food shortage in 1945 postwar Europe, and there was nothing sinister about the designation "Other Losses." Bacque's missing millions of POWs were largely old men and young boys in the militia who were dismissed early and sent home from the American camps. Some were also POWs transferred from camp to camp for assorted reasons.[24]

Dr. Albert E. Cowdrey, chief of the Conventional War Studies Branch, under the chief of military history for the Department of the Army, wrote a chapter entitled "A Question of Numbers" in the New Orleans conference book. When reading *Other Losses*, Cowdrey was reminded of the old saw, "Lies, Damn Lies, and Statistics." Cowdrey blamed "mathematical illiteracy" (innumeracy is today's term) by many scholars and journalists for not seeing through the false theses presented by *Other Losses*.[25] A year earlier, in his report to the US Army chief of military history, Cowdrey wrote the following overall assessment of Bacque's work:

> Summing up, I would say that Mr. Bacque has misinterpreted a tragedy that was caused in part by errors in planning, in part by the conditions of 1945, and in part by the place of a defeated people at the bottom of every totem pole. He has invented numbers suggesting a deliberate crime of enormous scope with the aim of creating a sensation and selling books. Neo-Nazis, however, will love his thesis anyway. The really unfortunate thing about it is that a good book might have been written on the subject.[26]

What is the lay reader to do when confronted with the outrageous allegations made in *Other Losses*? Stephen Ambrose said, "I suggest that he or she trust common sense." Ask the obvious questions: "Where are the one million bodies?" and "Is this book consistent with our picture of Eisenhower's character as we know it from innumerable other sources?" The answers to those two questions brings one closest to the truth.[27]

The cold, wet spring of 1945 in western Europe, combined with the overwhelming number of surrendering POWs, did indeed present the Allies with an almost insurmountable challenge. There were deaths. But Dwight D. Eisenhower was not a mass murderer, he did not run death camps, and prisoners did not die by the hundreds of thousands.

The Eisenhower statue will stay.

CHAPTER ELEVEN

KAY SUMMERSBY

"I trust she pulls herself together, but she is Irish and tragic."
—*General Eisenhower, 1947*

If you are someone who has not heard of General Eisenhower's alleged affair with his wartime driver, Kay Summersby, you are either (1) fairly young, (2) not well-read in the popular history of recent US presidents, or (3) not into sensationalism and rumor. That said, your luck is about to change, or at least your knowledge about the veracity of the Summersby-Eisenhower saga.

Who was Kay Summersby? Born Kathleen MacCarthy-Morrogh on November 23, 1908, in County Cork, Ireland, Kay was eighteen years younger than Eisenhower. Her father was Donald Florence MacCarthy-Morrogh (1869–1932), a retired British army officer. Kay led a somewhat pampered life as a young girl. She was the oldest of four children: Kay (born 1908), Elizabeth Evelyn (known as Evie) (born 1910), James Clement (known as Seamus) (born 1912), and Mary Sheila (known as Pik) (born 1918).

Kay and her siblings grew up on a ninety-seven-acre estate named *Inish Beg* (which means Small Island). As the name implies, the family estate was on a small but lovely emerald island on the River Ilen, in the south of Ireland, just four miles from where the river empties into the Atlantic Ocean. According to Kay, her years on the estate included governesses, hunts, spatting parents, and riding in the fields. In her own words, she was prepared "only to sit a horse properly and pour tea correctly."[1]

I asked her good friend Anthea Gordon Saxe, who also was executor of Kay's estate, about any family photographs that might exist. Anthea said Kay did not have a good childhood—there was a lot of fighting—and she speculated that taking photographs was probably not a priority. In fact, Kay's mother once left her husband and took the children to London; Kay's father eventually brought them back. Kay indicates there were indeed childhood photographs taken. She writes in her second book that she lost dozens of family photographs that were in her luggage, now at the bottom of the Mediterranean Sea. She was aboard the troop ship SS *Strathallan*, which was torpedoed in 1942 on her way to North Africa to join the Supreme Headquarters Allied Expeditionary Force (SHAEF) team.[2] (More about that wartime adventure to follow.)

I managed to obtain an early photo of Kay and two of her siblings from Kay's nephew, Michael MacCarthy-Morrogh, the son of Seamus. Michael was a history teacher at a boarding school in Shrewsbury, England, now retired, and is the well-published author of several books relating to Irish history.

Inish Beg is no longer in the MacCarthy-Morrogh family, but a visit to inishbeg.com shows that one can rent luxury accommodations on the very estate where Kay Summersby grew up. One may book a so-called self-catering holiday in Ireland at the estate.

In 1932, Kay left her home in Ireland at the age of twenty-three and, with London as home base, traveled around Europe. She then settled in London and took business school classes in the mornings and art classes in the afternoon. She admits her social life led to neglect of her studies. Kay had a chance to work as an extra in a film and stopped going to class altogether. She was flirting with the idea of becoming an actress when she met Gordon Summersby, a young publisher, who later became an officer in the British army. They married in 1936, and she then worked as a fashion model. Her husband was later shipped out to India when World War II began. By 1939, Kay was a mannequin for House of Worth, a fashion house near Grosvenor Square in the ritzy Mayfair section of London. However, in September 1939, England had declared war on Germany and, in the patriotic fervor of the time, she left that fashion work behind and joined her sister Evie as an ambulance driver for the British Motor Transport Corps. Kay quickly learned her way around the maze of city streets as she drove through London during the Blitz, a skill that would make her invaluable.

In 1942, Kay met a handsome thirty-one-year-old American army officer stationed in London: Lt. Colonel Richard R. Arnold. He was an army engineer who graduated from West Point in 1932. Summersby and Arnold were both already married but fell in love and agreed to seek divorces. It was this same year that Major General Dwight D. Eisenhower came into her life. Kay was detailed as Ike's driver from the British Motor Transport Corps when he made his first visit to London with Major General Mark Clark in May 1942. The generals were on temporary duty to make plans for the buildup of US forces in England. During this short fact-finding trip, she drove the two generals to countless military facilities

Kay and siblings circa 1914. This may be the only
surviving photograph of Kay Summersby as a child.
Her family heirlooms, including photographs, lie at
the bottom of the Mediterranean Sea after her military
transport ship was torpedoed on the way from England
to North Africa in December 1942. *Left to Right*: Kay
(age 6), Seamus (age 2), and Evie (age 4). (Courtesy
Eisenhower Library)

and various headquarters around London and made an impression on
Ike with her knowledge of London and her dedication and engaging personality.

Eisenhower returned to Washington after the quick planning tour, but
Army Chief of Staff General George Marshall gave Eisenhower formal
command of US Forces in the European Theater and Ike returned to London the following month, in June 1942. He would remain in Europe and

North Africa for the next three-and-a-half years, leading the Allied war effort. At Eisenhower's request, Kay Summersby got a permanent assignment from the Motor Transport Corps as his driver.

Eisenhower's headquarters moved around Europe and North Africa, while Kay served on his personal staff from 1942–1945. During these war years, Kay led a most interesting life, driving Ike throughout England, North Africa, and France (not Gibraltar or Germany).

SHAEF headquarters locations

London	June 25, 1942
Gibraltar	Nov. 6, 1942
Algiers	Nov. 24, 1942
Sidi Athmann (Tunisia)	July 7, 1942
Amilcar (Tunisia)	July 16, 1942
Algiers	July 21, 1942
London	January 17, 1944
Granville, France	September 1, 1944
Versailles	September 16, 1944
Reims	February 24, 1945
Frankfurt	May 26, 1945

Kay's journey from London to the new SHAEF headquarters in Algiers turned out to be very eventful. She had already survived the Blitz in London and now got a firsthand taste of the war at sea. General Eisenhower and his key staff had relocated from England to Gibraltar on November 5, 1942, and two or three weeks thereafter to Algiers, where the North African campaign was underway. On December 11, Kay departed Glasgow, Scotland, for Algiers on a troop transport named *Strathallan* to rejoin the SHAEF team. The vessel carried around 250 nurses and 4,400 British and American troops destined for duty in North Africa. On December 21, the tenth day of an uneventful voyage, the *Strathallan* was in the Mediterranean Sea about forty miles north of Oran, Algeria, when she was torpedoed at 2:30 a.m. by U-562, a German submarine.[3] Kay spent a night in a lifeboat and was then rescued by a British destroyer the next day. All her personal effects and clothing were lost, but she was safe. She came ashore in Oran, some 250 miles from Ike's Algiers headquarters, and after a day or two, she and another female SHAEF staff member who had been on the ship were picked up by Eisenhower's B-17. Kay arrived in Algiers in

Kay Summersby is shown driving General Eisenhower in North Africa in 1943. Ike, wearing four stars, sits in the rear seat and an unidentified person rides in the front passenger seat. During the war, there was an entire motor pool of army staff cars and this vehicle appears to be a Buick. A Cadillac version of the type of staff car also used by Ike is now on display in the Eisenhower Museum in Abilene, Kansas. (Courtesy Eisenhower Library)

time to celebrate Christmas with the staff and then get to work, very glad to be alive.

Colonel Richard Arnold (since promoted from lieutenant colonel) was now also serving in North Africa, in Tunisia, some five hundred miles from Algiers. Colonel Arnold requested permission to marry Kay Summersby in a formal memorandum dated March 11, 1943, sent up through proper military channels and approved with signatures by General George Patton as II Corps commander and Eisenhower as the overall US Army commander in the North African Theater. In his memo, "Subject: Marriage," Arnold gave a tentative date for the planned nuptials with Kay as June 22, 1943, or at the conclusion of the ongoing Tunisian campaign, if that were to cause a delay.[4] The request was readily approved but, very sadly, Dick Arnold died in a landmine explosion on June 6, 1943, barely two weeks prior to the planned wedding. He was one of seven officers and nineteen men who died as the army engineers removed over 200,000 German mines from the Tunisian battlefields.[5] Summersby was devastated by losing her fiancée. In the weeks that followed Colonel Arnold's death, Eisenhower wrote Kay's mother, Mrs. Vera McCarthy-Morrogh, to let her know that Kay was not coping well with the tragedy. "Basically, none of us can do much. She is crushed and hurt to the point where nothing seems important and where she does not even realize that her best friends are trying to help."

To take her mind off the grieving, General Eisenhower gave his Irish driver the additional responsibility of answering his ever-increasing volume of public mail, the "fan mail" as it was known. Kay was very efficient and quickly earned the general's complete trust in handling this correspondence. She could draft routine letters for Ike's signature that needed very little editing, if any. She soon took her place sitting in a nearby office and became an important administrative member of the headquarters team. In addition, Kay was vivacious and an excellent hostess for visiting dignitaries, and she quickly became a valuable member of Ike's immediate staff—known affectionately as "the family." The family included US Navy aide Captain Harry Butcher, Eisenhower's British aide Colonel Jimmy Gault, US Army Aide Major Ernest "Tex" Lee, and US Army Sergeant Nana Rae.

The family was not only international, inter-service, and inclusive of both genders—there was even another species involved: Telek the Scottie. Earlier, while still in London, General Eisenhower had put pressure on his staffer Major Tex Lee to get a dog for the office and a male Scottie pup was indeed presented to Ike on his fifty-second birthday—October 14th, 1942. Sitting around the fire that night, Eisenhower picked a name for his dog—Telek—being something of a contraction of Telegraph Cottage, which was the name of the general's residence on ten acres in the outskirts of London. During the war, Telek went everywhere and led an exciting life with the rest of the staff. A mate was even found—named Caacie (pronounced Khaki like the army's well-known color)—and over twenty pups were born during the next three years. Telek did spend six months as a "POW" in mandated quarantine after returning to England from North Africa, but that was the only time he was not underfoot in the headquarters. Kay was destined to be Telek's major caregiver during most of this period and, in fact, after the war took the dog back to the United States. Telek lived until 1959 and was Kay's last connection with the SHAEF family.

When she joined Ike's staff, Kay herself was concerned about the appearance of having an attractive woman just outside the supreme commander's office. She later noted in her first book, *Eisenhower Was My Boss* (1948):

In Algiers, the General once walked into his office to find one of the stenographers filing her fingernails. Puffing away at a cigarette like a woman in her boudoir. The resultant storm was such that I never smoked in my office from that day on. It was an order, if not a direct order, and I never disobeyed it. Nor did I smoke while on duty in the staff car. Likewise, I once heard the General remark that he disliked red fingernail polish. He never mentioned it to me, but I adopted natural, clear polish thereafter.

There was no resentment on my part in sticking to both these rather unusual ideas. General Eisenhower was a militant champion of women in war and I had no wish to let him down by presenting the picture of a night-club woman at the very door of his office.[6]

Having Kay around provided Ike an occasional respite from the generals, colonels, politicians, newsmen, and myriad worries he encountered every day. General Eisenhower believed very strongly that his leadership role meant never appearing downcast or disheartened by the war news or stressed by difficult decisions he was required to make. According to Kay, one day while in a low mood he paid her a high compliment when he told her, "You're the one person who ever sees me with my hair down. I don't have to keep up pretenses—because you're not after rank, you don't blab to the press, and you don't gossip with staff members."[7] Kay does contradict this in her second book, *Past Forgetting* (1976), when describing General Eisenhower returning to the headquarters one day in Tunisia and being in a dismal state of mind over the lack of opportunity to attack the enemy because of the torrential rain and mud that immobilized tanks and even jeeps. Kay wrote "only the inner circle was allowed to see how depressed he really was. To the rest of the world, he was his usual brisk, charming and confident self—just a bit weary, that was all."[8] Apparently, it was not just Kay, but others in the inner circle, i.e., "the SHAEF family," who on rare occasions witnessed Ike's real mood.

Susan Eisenhower writes in *How Ike Led* that she came to realize that her grandfather's leadership abilities consisted of more than just the obvious. In a chapter entitled "The Loneliness of Power," Susan maintains that in addition to command of one's inner self, there is a level of acting required. In both his roles as Supreme Allied Commander during the war and later as president, Ike could not be optimistic all the time, but the need to project a positive outlook was paramount as a leader. "He understood,

Kay Summersby is shown in the administrative area outside General Eisenhower's office in late 1943 or 1944. After her US officer fiancé died in the line of duty, Summersby was relieved of driving responsibilities and given reception and correspondence duties in Ike's headquarters office. (Courtesy Eisenhower Library)

perhaps better than anyone else, pessimism's corrosive impact and the negativity it can produce in an organization and those associated with it." Power brought with it a certain kind of loneliness, even in the company of friends and trusted family.[9]

Kay and other staff members flew to Washington, DC, in the summer of 1944 when a group from General Eisenhower's headquarters made a visit back to the United States from London. During her time in DC, she met many wives of the senior US officers she knew in Europe and brought them news and greetings from the war zone. Kay confessed in *Eisenhower Was My Boss* that some of the army spouses left a bad taste in her memory. These military wives were extremely rank conscious and calculating, and Kay was also hurt and angered at their slander of Women's Army Corps (WACs) serving overseas. Her female colleagues on Ike's staff had warned her in advance about this, but she was nevertheless surprised and disappointed at the "selfish venom" that she experienced firsthand. "Some of the most social Army wives made it quite clear—crystal clear—they regarded any uniformed female overseas as a mere 'camp follower.'"[10]

Rumors of a romantic relationship between Eisenhower and Summersby surfaced during the war and persist to this day. The attractive Miss Summersby was almost always there in the traveling group with Eisenhower, wherever the general went. When he visited troops in the field or near the front, she was usually the one who drove him in the commanding general's official vehicle. During rare moments of leisure, Kay even went horseback riding with Ike. But as Kay pointed out, Eisenhower lived in a goldfish bowl. Time alone riding horses would have been nearly impossible.

> The Army had cleared the area and there were guards posted—it seemed as if they were behind every bush—so we felt quite safe. We also felt as if we were on parade. There was always a security man riding discreetly behind us, in addition to the sharpshooter guards. It is an eerie feeling, knowing that your every more is being watched. Ike often complained about it, not only while riding but as it affected every phase of his life.[11]

The rumors were further fueled after a very public appearance at the end of the war by Ike and Kay at the Prince of Wales Theatre in London on May 14, 1945. It was more innocent than it sounded. The Eisenhower party sat in two boxes and the group included not only Ike and Kay but also Ike's son Second Lieutenant John Eisenhower, whose escort was a British friend of Kay's serving in the Women's Royal Naval Service (WRNS) (popularly known as the "Wrens"). Also in the theater boxes right behind Ike were Kay Summersby's mother, General Omar Bradley, and Eisenhower's British aide Colonel Jimmy Gault. The party saw a musical revue entitled *Strike It Again*. War hero General Eisenhower received a long and thunderous standing ovation from the London audience before and after the performance.[12]

Although still a British citizen, Kay had received a commission as a lieutenant in the US Army on November 20, 1944, and, as an officer, she could no longer serve as a driver. Her army military occupation specialty (MOS) was administrative officer. At the end of the war in Europe, Eisenhower served several more months as commander of the military occupation force headquartered in Frankfurt, Germany. In November 1945, he traveled to Washington, DC, at General Marshall's request and did not return to Germany. He instead immediately assumed a new position, replacing Marshall as army chief of staff. Kay Summersby was transferred from Frankfurt to Berlin to work for General Lucius D. Clay, who was the deputy military occupation governor.

Ike wrote Kay a letter on November 22, 1945, apologizing for not being able to bring her as part of his new staff in Washington, which included several individuals from the wartime headquarters staff. Her non-citizen status was an issue preventing her from being eligible for a job in the Pentagon. On a more personal level, he said:

> In this letter I shall not attempt to express the depth of my appreciation for the unexcelled loyalty and faithfulness with which you have worked for me the past three and a half years, under my personal direction. I will try to do this in a more formal letter when I get out of the hospital, to which I am going tonight. (Note: Eisenhower had bronchial pneumonia and was hospitalized for nearly two weeks.) I am sure you understand that I am personally much distressed that an association which has been so valuable to me has to be terminated in this particular fashion but it is by reasons over which I have no control. I shall watch your future with the greatest interest and I particularly request that at any time you believe I can be of any help you will let me know instantly, either by a letter or by cable. After you come to this country I would be more than glad to do my best in helping you get a job in any place where anyone would have need for a person of your particular qualifications.[13]

In a handwritten postscript note, Ike added, "This is dictated because I'm in bed—taking medicine constantly. Nana (Rae) wrote it up for me. Take care of yourself—and retain your optimism. D."

In January 1946, General Eisenhower wrote a letter of recommendation for Kay to use in finding future positions. He described her outstanding characteristic as "reliability," saying she had knowledge of operational secrets during the war of the gravest type. Eisenhower said Kay had an "engaging personality" and was particularly capable as a receptionist and in managing appointments. He concluded by writing, "Lt. Summersby is definitely a superior type."[14]

In late 1946, Kay had finished her tour in Berlin and was transferred stateside to Hamilton Field in California as assistant public relations officer. She soon was promoted to the rank of captain. Things did not turn out well for Kay in California. On February 12, 1947, she was the victim of an attempted rape. FBI files show that a twenty-two-year-old Marin City janitor broke into the WAC barracks at Hamilton Field and apparently picked out her room at random. She screamed, and in all the noise and commotion the attacker fled, but he was soon caught and arrested. He was eventually sentenced to fifteen years of imprisonment by a San Francisco federal court.

A few months later, in July 1947, Kay was engaged to be married, and, at her request, she was discharged from the service, effective May 28, 1947. But the engagement ended, and she moved to New York.[15] On December 2, 1947, Eisenhower wrote in his diary, "I heard today, through a mutual friend, that my wartime secretary (rather personal aide and receptionist) is in dire straits. A clear case of a fine person going to pieces over the death of a loved one, in this instance the man she was all set to marry [a reference to fiancé Colonel Richard Arnold, who died in North Africa in 1943]. . . . I trust she pulls herself together, but she is Irish and tragic."[16] Around the same time, Harry Butcher shared with Ike that he had received a letter from Summersby saying her engagement with the man in San Francisco was broken abruptly by a telegram telling her he could not go through with it.[17]

Margaret Chase, a fellow WAC who worked closely with Kay at SHAEF, wrote Eisenhower a lengthy personal letter that said in passing that Kay had broken her engagement to a fine young man whom she (Margaret) had known for years.[18] It appears we will never know who initiated the breakup or the reasons for it. What we do know is that Kay makes no mention in either of her books of the 1947 fiancé and very brief engagement. It was apparently a decision she wished to forget.

According to records at the Eisenhower Library, Ike saw Kay only once after the war when she visited his office in the Pentagon in December 1947. She probably did not have a formal appointment as the meeting does not show up in the appointment schedules for the army chief of staff. In her memoir, she indicates she brought along Telek, the headquarters' office pet dog during the war, and who she had brought with her to the US.

After that Pentagon visit, Eisenhower responded to a letter from Margaret Chase, former WAC at SHAEF headquarters and mentioned seeing Kay. Ike told Margaret that he thought Kay looked very well, despite the many difficult things she had encountered in the past two or three months. He was sure that Kay would soon get herself established and really settle into something she would like and be happy.

When Kay left California, she moved to New York City. Kay became a naturalized American citizen on January 19, 1951.[19] There is little record of her work there; however, in a 1951 letter to Ike, Captain Harry Butcher noted as an aside that he and his wife had a cocktail in the city one evening with Kay and she was doing fine. She was working at Bergdorf Goodman as a sales lady, and Butch reported Kay seemed in very good humor. Telek was also there. The dog remembered Butch and insisted on sitting on his knee, expecting to be scratched just as he was in London.[20]

Eisenhower and Summersby exchanged a few letters in the years immediately after the war, keeping each other updated on members of the "SHAEF family" they had seen or heard from. Kay wrote General Eisenhower a "Dear Ike" letter each Christmas from 1945 to 1950, wishing him well and in passing usually saying something like "I'm spending Christmas in Washington with my WAC friends. . . . I will not take up any more of your time, knowing how rushed you are." Eisenhower would reply in a short acknowledgement letter saying something such as "I think I have heard from almost everyone who was on my personal staff during the War and it has been nice to hear from them again. This note brings my good wishes for a happy holiday season and a prosperous New Year. Sincerely, DE."[21] There is no record of Kay ever having been to the White House to see President Eisenhower.

The last letter between the two was apparently in 1952 when Ike congratulated Kay on her marriage to Reginald T. H. Morgan, a New York stockbroker. Kay's bad luck in love continued, as the marriage ended in divorce six years later in 1958. Eisenhower's dozen original letters to Kay during the period of November 1945 through 1948 were sold at auction by Sotheby's in 1991. They were a part of Kay's estate after her death. The exact dollar figures Ike's letters to Kay brought are undetermined, but the asking prices in the catalog ranged from $3,000 to $15,000 each.

Eisenhower had strong views regarding the propriety of his former staff writing what we would today call "kiss and tell" books. His naval aide, Capt. Harry Butcher, wrote *My Three Years with Eisenhower* (1946). In a December 1945 letter, Eisenhower explained to Butch his feeling about the ethics involved, knowing of the impending publication:

> My feeling is that you were admitted into a circle where every individual had a right to believe that the matters discussed were to remain secret. Your admission into that circle was by reason of the fact that as my Aide I was responsible for bringing you into the secret. In the over-all story there is no objection that I can see to your telling about these things except in those instances where, because of the mention of personalities or other equally delicate subjects, I or any other participant in the discussion had every right to believe that the matter died at the instant it was born. There is no possibility of my giving you any line of demarcation but you know how repugnant it would be to me to appear in the position of having violated good faith.

In this same letter, Eisenhower admonished Butcher to avoid passages that could rightly irritate people with whom Eisenhower would have to work in the future or where international amenities were involved. He specifically reminded Butcher he had already agreed to rewrite the paragraph concerning Mr. Churchill to which he (Ike) took such earnest exception.[22] In a letter to Kay Summersby a couple of months later, Ike said, "Butch's diary is getting me into plenty of hot water with my British friends! Golly, I don't see why I have to have such 'added' troubles—I have enough I cannot dodge."[23]

In 1948 Kay published her first memoir, *Eisenhower Was My Boss* (302 pages for $2.75). It was well-received and certainly made no claims of a romance between the two. Kay informed Ike in advance that she was writing the book, and the general did not discourage her. In describing *Eisenhower Was My Boss*, one reviewer said, "Miss Summersby adds one more dithyramb to the chorus of praise. She has chosen to humanize the one general who perhaps needs it least."[24] (A dithyramb is a writing in an exalted or enthusiastic vein.)

Eisenhower did express his one objection and that was concerning the original title of the book as it was first proposed—*Eisenhower's Girl Friday*. Ike believed he had no "Girl Friday" in the office. He wrote to the publisher before the book came out and apparently his reservations about the title held sway: "Kay Summersby had an important position in my office and one which demanded complete reliability and loyalty on her part. However, there were a great number of individuals in that office, including a number of women. Therefore, I believe that to use the title you suggest is scarcely indicative of the situation."[25]

Kay sent Eisenhower a copy of *Eisenhower Was My Boss* in September 1948, but the record seems to indicate that Eisenhower never read Kay's book in full. He told Butcher he had managed to read the first and last chapters.[26] Interestingly, I checked this book out of the Abilene Public Library in doing research for this chapter and discovered it was an autographed copy that had been sent to the library by Kay, with the handwritten inscription, "To: The Abilene Public Library, 8 Nov. 1948, signed Kay Summersby." It appears nothing is sacred, however. Several decades later, a library staff member had innocently put the library's circulation bar code sticker over a portion of the inscription, not realizing the possible historical significance of the autograph.

Look magazine serialized the Summersby memoir and employed the rejected title *Eisenhower's Girl Friday*. The magazine also focused on the more suggestive elements of the book. Kay's editor felt he had been "taken for a ride" by *Look* when they sensationalized the series.[27]

Then there is the "Kay Summersby Diary." At General Eisenhower's request, Kay had taken on the duty of maintaining a handwritten, desk-calendar-type diary at SHAEF headquarters. From the beginning of 1944 and through November 10, 1945, she recorded the names of the VIPs meeting with the general each day. She would frequently write a few words regarding the purpose of the meetings and sometimes even note General Eisenhower's feelings about how the meetings went. After the war, Summersby still had these two seven-inch by ten-inch books in her possession. They eventually found their way to the Eisenhower Presidential Library seventy years later in a somewhat unusual manner. More on that saga shortly.

After the war: General Eisenhower, in his new role as army chief of staff in the Pentagon, spent his free hours preparing his wartime memoir *Crusade in Europe*, which would eventually be published in 1948. On September 17, 1946, Ike sent a personal wire regarding Kay Summersby to General Lucius D. Clay in Berlin, military governor of the US occupied zone in Germany, who, as noted previously, now had Kay on his staff: "Some time back Captain Summersby engaged to type out a diary kept by herself in my office during the European Campaign. It has become important that I learn timing of my movements during fall of 1944. Please ascertain if part of diary covering June 1944 through December 1944 has been typed."[28]

It did not take long for Kay to finish the assignment. She went beyond Eisenhower's requested time period and typed up her diary entries from not only from June 1, 1944, through December 31, 1944, but continued her transcription through April 30, 1945. In sending the lengthy document to Washington, Kay prepared a handwritten cover note to the WACs she had served with during the war who were now working in Ike's Pentagon office. "Dear Sue and Chick," she said. "I've typed the diary up very quickly. As you know I am no typist. Nevertheless, I hope you will be able to retype it for the Boss."[29] Sue Sarafian and Margaret Chick did not have to do that, and the rough manuscript served its purpose for Eisenhower's work on his book. Kay's typed transcript of the diaries has been part of the Pre-Presidential Papers in the holdings in Eisenhower Library archives since the 1970s. The library had always assumed the original two handwritten volumes were lost to history; however, that was not the case.

In June 2001, Mr. Richard Woodman of North Carolina contacted the Eisenhower Library. He told us he had some handwritten Eisenhower diaries from the war years. As deputy director and head of the archives at the library, I oversaw the twenty-six-million-page manuscript collection and was also charged with acquiring new historical materials. In my first telephone call with Mr. Woodman, he was very cryptic about why he had these volumes, which made us at the library doubtful about their authenticity. There was good reason for us to be skeptical. Just a few weeks prior to this, I had spoken on the phone with a woman who believed she was Eisenhower's illegitimate daughter. The woman claimed her mother was— who else?—Kay Summersby! Guess where the woman was calling from? Roswell, New Mexico. You see my point. (The woman maintains she was adopted by a family in Kentucky in the 1930s—that would be a decade before Eisenhower met Kay Summersby.)

After we received faxed copies of several pages, we realized these diaries were indeed the real thing. I called Mr. Woodman and told him our examination confirmed his discovery. He then became more forthcoming. He had just placed his sister in an assisted living home because of her dementia. Her name was Barbara Wyden, and she was a freelance writer. She had ghostwritten Kay Summersby's second memoir, *Past Forgetting: My Love Affair with Dwight D. Eisenhower.* Woodman had found these

diaries in his sister's closet when clearing out her apartment in Connecti-
cut. She apparently possessed them since the early 1970s to use in writing
Kay's book. He wanted to donate this material to the Eisenhower Library,
as that was where it belonged, he said. I told him he was making a great
contribution to history. Within three weeks, I had flown to North Carolina,
met Dick Woodman and his sister in person, and carried the diaries back
to the Eisenhower Library. Mr. Woodman and Barbara Wyden did a wonderful service in donating these volumes to the library for posterity.

A couple of things can be said about the two-volume diary: (1) It is a
very important firsthand account of the activities of the Supreme Allied
Commander during the last half of World War II and the early days of the
occupation of Germany, and (2) boy is Kay's handwriting hard to read!
The new handwritten original diary also covers a much longer period
than the earlier diary typescript that had been in library holdings since
the 1970s. Therefore, entries for the early months of 1944 and second half
of 1945 are new to history. In addition, the library found many small but
sometimes important differences between Summersby's typed transcript
and the handwritten original. Sometimes she apparently *added* details of
events from memory a year or two after the fact when typing up the diary
for Ike's work on his memoir. And equally important, she occasionally
"self-edited" by omitting information that was in the original handwritten
version. Both versions are important records, and researchers visiting the
Eisenhower Library can study and compare the minor changes and omis-
sions and be the judge in determining their significance.

Then there is what I like to call Truman's Revenge. The Truman-
Eisenhower relationship began in 1945 upon FDR's death and had not
been close, but it was perfunctory and cordial. That all changed in 1952
during the election to succeed President Truman. The presidential campaign of that year was a hard-fought battle between Eisenhower and the
Democratic nominee Governor Adlai E. Stevenson, and there were bitter
feelings in its aftermath. Eisenhower had pledged during the campaign
that, if elected, he would personally go to Korea to see firsthand how the
very unpopular war could be ended. This was a bold move; a five-star
general war hero going to Korea to see what could be done to bring resolution to the seemingly endless quagmire as the war entered its third year.
After the election, outgoing President Truman implied that Eisenhower's
campaign pledge, "I shall go to Korea," was purely an insincere political
ploy. Truman sent President-elect Eisenhower a telegram offering to put
a presidential plane at Ike's disposal for the trip and added, somewhat

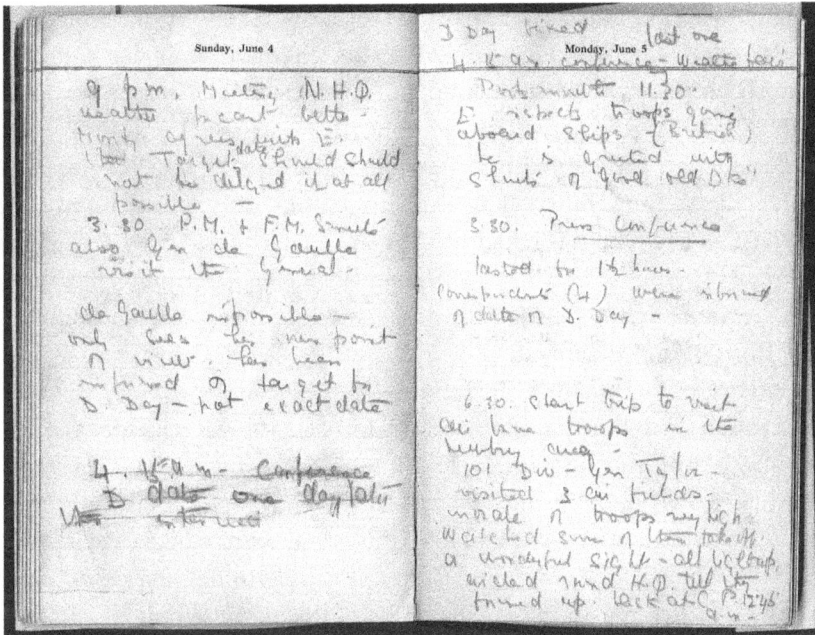

Kay Summersby's handwritten diary entries recording General Eisenhower's activities on June 4th and 5th, 1944, on the eve of D-Day. As an example of her account was this notation, "De Gaulle impossible—only sees his own point of view. Has been informed of target for D-Day—not exact date." (Courtesy Eisenhower Library)

caustically, "if you still desire to go to Korea." This insult caused severe damage to their relations. John Eisenhower described his father's reaction: "This dig hit dad as tantamount to calling him a liar. From that time on the two were on cool terms."[30]

The strain in the relationship had begun earlier in the presidential campaign when candidate Eisenhower declined an invitation to sit down with Truman and his cabinet in August 1952 to discuss issues facing the nation. Ike felt he needed to distance himself from the Democratic Party and President Truman. He told Truman, "It is my duty to remain free to analyze the policies and acts of the present Administration whenever it appears to me to be proper and in the country's interests." Eisenhower had not declared his Republican Party affiliation until the 1952 election and had in fact worked for Democrats Roosevelt and Truman in his highly visible military roles during World War II and later as NATO supreme commander. Truman felt this rejection of a meeting with his cabinet was political betrayal and told Ike this in an angry handwritten note on August 16. "I am extremely sorry that you have allowed a bunch of screwballs to come between us." He then made a veiled threat, "You have made a bad mistake." But Truman signed off on his letter to Eisenhower with the almost comically sad closing salutation, "from a man who has always been your friend and who always wanted to be."[31]

During the presidential race, Ike and the Republicans blamed the Democrats, among other things, for the loss of China to communism in 1949 and the failure to end the Korean War. They accused President Truman of being too soft on communism abroad and corruption at home. K_1C_2 became the Republican campaign strategy—"Korean, Communism, and Corruption." It worked, of course, and Ike was elected in a landslide over Democratic candidate Governor Adlai Stevenson.

Truman's longtime bitterness toward Eisenhower was no doubt behind the apocryphal story he allegedly told author Merle Miller, which appeared in Miller's 1973 book *Plain Speaking: An Oral Biography of Harry S. Truman.* Truman claimed that right after the war, Ike wrote his boss General George Marshall from occupied Germany asking to be relieved of duty, allowing him to return to the United States to divorce Mamie "so that he could marry this 'Englishwoman.'" Truman then said that General Marshall "wrote him back a letter the like of which I never did see." According to Truman:

> He (Marshall) said that if Eisenhower even came close to doing such a thing, he'd not only bust him out of the army, he'd see to it that never for the rest of his life would he be able to draw a peaceful breath. He said it wouldn't matter if he was in the army or wasn't. Or even what country he was in.[32]

In Miller's account, Truman said, "I don't like Eisenhower; you know that. I never have, but one of the last things I did as President, I got those letters from his file in the Pentagon, and I destroyed them." This incredible story has been discounted by all serious scholars, including respected historian Forrest Pogue, who spent most of his career writing and researching the life of General Marshall and found no record of such a letter from Ike.[33] The tale told to Miller was no doubt a bitter diatribe by Truman (1884–1972), who, conveniently for Merle Miller, died the year before *Plain Speaking* was published and could not be asked about the veracity of Miller's stories.

Historian David McCullough won a Pulitzer Prize in 1993 for his highly respected biography *Truman.* When asked in an interview why the alleged divorce letter from Eisenhower to Marshall was not included in the book, McCullough said it was so clearly a figment of Truman's imagination that it did not merit a reference. He said it was just as fictitious as Truman's notorious account of his Wake Island meeting with General Douglas MacArthur that the former president had also related to Merle Miller; a narrative that differed from those of others who had witnessed the meeting.[34]

In fairness to Harry Truman, it should be noted that two respected scholars have come to the former president's defense. Distinguished professor of political science Dr. Francis H. Heller at the University of Kansas and Dr. Robert H. Ferrell of Indiana University, both Truman experts, vehemently discounted many of the stories cited by Merle Miller in *Plain Speaking*. They said Miller lost all credibility when he interspersed frequent profane Truman quotes in the book and many references to the former president imbibing in alcohol excessively during breaks in the interviews. This was not the Truman that Professor Heller knew firsthand. There were many other factual errors in the Miller book according to Heller, who had spent considerable time with Truman when he took a leave of absence from the University of Kansas to assist the former president in writing his memoirs. He also served on the board of directors of the Harry S. Truman Library Institute for almost fifty years and was intimately knowledgeable about the content of Truman's personal papers at the presidential library. Dr. Ferrell wrote voluminously on Truman, devoting more than a dozen books to his life and presidency. Professors Ferrell and Heller state that the original Merle Miller interview tapes in the Truman Library, on which the book was based, contain almost nothing about Dwight D. Eisenhower. Furthermore, there is absolutely no mention of Kay Summersby on the tapes.[35] Interestingly, former President Truman once threatened Merle Miller with a lawsuit because of so many inaccuracies in a draft article Miller had written earlier for *The Saturday Evening Post*, forcing the author to withdraw the piece. Perhaps that is why Miller waited until Truman died to publish his book *Plain Speaking*.[36]

What has since become known is that General Eisenhower did indeed write George Marshall on June 4, 1945, but not about divorcing Mamie. Rather, Ike requested a policy be established whereby military personnel remaining in occupied Germany after the war could be joined by their wives. Ike asked Marshall if such a wholesale policy could not be approved by the War Department at that time, and whether public opinion would allow Eisenhower at least to bring his own wife over. Ike reasoned with General Marshall:

My real feeling is that most people would understand that after three years continued separation at my age, and with no opportunity to engage, except on extraordinary occasion, in normal social activities, they would be sympathetic about the matter. . . . While I am perfectly willing to carry on in this assignment as long as the War Department may decide I should do so, I really would like to make it a bit easier on myself from the personal viewpoint.[37]

General Marshall's answer was negative. He did not approve this favorable treatment Ike requested regarding bringing Mamie to postwar Germany. "The time has not yet come for such procedure and I am rather dubious about ever restricting it to a select group if authorized."[38]

In 1987, Merle Miller authored another book—this time an "oral history" of General Eisenhower entitled *Ike the Soldier: As They Knew Him*. Written fourteen years after his Truman book was published, Miller quietly offers a correction. In the Eisenhower volume Miller says that, upon further research, the record seems to show that the facts reported earlier in *Plain Speaking* regarding postwar correspondence between Ike and George Marshall "are completely at variance" with Truman's story. In other words, Eisenhower did not seek General Marshall's permission to divorce Mamie. So, just as corrections in newspaper stories are often buried well inside the front page, so Miller's "correction" to his salacious account of Ike seeking a divorce from Mamie appeared over a decade later, on page 642 of *Ike the Soldier*.[39] But the damage had been done. Truman did indeed get his revenge against Eisenhower. The question is, was it the former president's intention or was it simply Merle Miller's effort to sensationalize *Plain Speaking* and increase book sales?

In late 1973, a dying Kay Summersby decided to write a second memoir. She had developed liver cancer and doctors gave her only six months to live. She survived another year, dying in January 1975. Kay kept busy during her fight with cancer, working as a fashion consultant for the film production of *The Stepford Wives* (1975). Possibly inspired by the new attention she received from the media in the recent aftermath of Merle Miller's just published *Plain Speaking*, it was now that Kay decided to write her second memoir, entitled *Past Forgetting: My Love Affair with Dwight D. Eisenhower*. The book was not published until November 1976, almost two years after her death.

In the foreword to *Past Forgetting*, the publisher says Kay felt it was time to set the record straight. "I was always extremely discreet, but now the

General is dead," she said. "And I am dying. Once I am dead, then I would like this book to speak for me. I would like the world to know the truth of the Eisenhower affair."[40]

Readers of *Past Forgetting* can be forgiven if they are left disappointed by its dearth of steamy stories. The book describes no torrid love affair within its 251 pages. Kay does tell of only a single alleged attempt to make love with the Supreme Allied Commander. In her account she says that one evening during the North African campaign, they were alone in his quarters at the end of a long and tiring day. After dinner, Ike refilled their glasses several times. Kay says they soon found themselves in each other's arms "in an unrestrained embrace." But it was not what Kay had hoped for. They slowly calmed down. Eisenhower apologized, "Oh God, Kay. I'm sorry. I'm not going to be any good for you." She didn't know what to say other than, "You're good enough for me. What you need is some sleep."[41]

It may not have been her intention, but Summersby herself gave good reasons in *Past Forgetting* to discount the stories of her romantic relationship with Ike. First, Kay wrote that the conversations in her book "ring true to my ear and my heart, but it must be understood that they have been reconstructed from my memories."[42] As experience shows, sometimes thirty-year-old memories recalled from the heart differ from reality. And, in fact, some of the "memories" in the book may well have been created out of whole cloth by the ghostwriter.

Kay also asked her late 1970s readers to consider the time period that the alleged relationship occurred, as well as the year of her first, more innocent, book—published in 1948. She said it used to distress her enormously when people asked "did she . . . or didn't she" have a romantic relationship with Eisenhower. If one were able to fast-forward through time from World War II to when her second book was published—over three decades later—Kay maintained no one would even wonder. "Today people would simply assume that we did—and given modern mores, forget the whole thing."[43]

Kay may well have been right about the difference thirty years make in what a more cynical and jaded public would believe about her relationship with General Eisenhower. In 1998, during the height of the Clinton-Lewinski Scandal, historian Gil Troy wrote, "Only later—after the sexual revolution of the 1960s undermined many Americans' faith in the private probity of public figures—did the Eisenhower-Summersby 'affair' become a topic of widespread public conversation." He noted that, four decades later, the public's willingness to turn the uncertainties about Ike and Kay into fact says more about us than about Eisenhower.[44] That our expectations of our leaders have been lowered does not establish the veracity of Kay's claims made in *Past Forgetting*. Rather it is an indictment of the ongoing eroding of societal morals. It is worth noting that John S. D. Eisenhower told his daughter Susan that Ike "would have made a lousy philanderer because he was so damned Victorian and moral."[45]

Speaking of the gradual erosion of mores in modern society and what is now easily believed about our politicians, allow me to digress a moment and share a sad example. The following is the text of an email reference inquiry the Eisenhower Presidential Library received in 2002 from an unnamed middle school student. It is indeed a sad commentary coming from a fourteen year old:

> Hello. I am doing a report on Maime [*sic*] Eisenhower for my 8th grade social studies class. We are comparing a woman from the 1950s to a woman of today. I chose to compare her to Hillary Clinton. There are some rumors that Dwight Eisenhower was cheating on Maime [*sic*] and wanted to get a divorce. I was wondering if you could clear that up for me so I can compare that to the Monica Lewinsky deal. Thank you for your time.[46]

While I do not have a copy of the library's response to the young student's query, I am confident we replied that we could not confirm the veracity concerning rumors of such a romantic relationship and that historians had discounted it.

Kay made an interesting self-observation in *Past Forgetting* about the heady experience—at times "seductive," to use her word—she had working at Ike's headquarters and meeting world leaders and top generals during the war:

> I was more than a trifle star dazzled. Working with great men, men whose actions affected people's lives all over the world, has a very seductive glamour about it. The men themselves were very seductive. I don't mean that in a sexual sense, but they would not have had the power they possessed if they did not also possess this magnetism. And the great men I met while working for the General all possessed it.[47]

The publisher claims that *Past Forgetting* was written by Kay Summersby herself, but in literary circles it is understood two ghostwriters authored the book: initially Sigrid Hedin and finally Barbara Wyden. Reportedly, Wyden did most of the writing, having access to Kay's tapes. This would seem to be the case, as Barbara Wyden also had possession of the original World War II diaries from the time of Kay's death until they were donated to the Eisenhower Library, as noted above.

It is very revealing that Kay Summersby's own brother, Colonel J. C. F. MacCarthy-Morrogh (Seamus), corresponded with the law firm handling Kay's estate one month after her death, attempting to stop publication of *Past Forgetting*. MacCarthy-Morrogh was serving with the British army in the Transvaal (South Africa) at the time. He had visited his sister in the US during Christmas 1974 and knew of her fragile physical and emotional condition. On February 21, 1975, he wrote to Burlingham, Underwood & Lord in New York City:

> I would appreciate you informing me of my "rights" as sole next-of-kin to stop publication of a book on my sister's association with General Eisenhower in the war. My sister was under some pressure from the publisher to develop such a book. Now that she is not present to refute any statements attributed to her by the publisher, I would like as next-of-kin to have publication withheld.[48]

The law firm replied politely on March 4, informing MacCarthy-Morrogh that because he had not been named by his sister in her will as one of the beneficiaries in her estate, he had no "rights." Furthermore, even if the all the residuary beneficiaries named in the will (Mr. and Mrs. Saxe, the Saxes' two sons, and Summersby's goddaughter in England) were to agree that the publication of the book should not go forward, there would remain the question of the rights of the publisher and the ghostwriter under certain contracts executed by Kay. Those legal questions had not yet been resolved, so the law firm could not provide any definitive advice on the fate of the book. Eventually, publication of *Past Forgetting* went forward, despite the protestations from Kay's brother that she was no longer around to refute any of the statements attributed to her in the book.[49]

Upon Kay's passing in January 1975, journalist Bob Considine wrote a tribute entitled "To Kay Summersby from a close friend" in his syndicated column, which appeared in newspapers across the US. Considine had been a war correspondent in Europe and he and his wife Mildred became close friends of Kay after the war, living in New York City. Considine was a well-known and prolific ghostwriter and Kay had asked him to "spook" her first book *Eisenhower Was My Boss*, but he was busy with other projects and had to decline. As her friend, Considine was disappointed when the book did appear because, while it may have "made her a few bucks," it also plunged Kay deeper into the fantasy world of being "Ike's girl" even as Eisenhower was moving on to become NATO Supreme Allied Commander and then president of the United States.[50]

Considine goes on to share a conversation between his wife Mildred and Kay that took place late one night at the famous Stork Club in New York City. "Kay, did you ever sleep with General Eisenhower?" Kay, with tears in her eyes, looked at her good friend and said, "You know, you are the first person I have ever met who has had the courage enough to ask me that question." Kay continued, "I've seen that question in too many thousands of eyes during the years but you, God bless, are the first one to give me a chance to answer."[51] Kay then told Mildred, "The answer is no. Never. I loved him as everybody in uniform or out of uniform loved him around the world. If he had asked me, beckoned a finger to me, I would have done anything he asked me to do. But he never asked me."[52]

As previously noted, Barbara Wyden (1922–2020) was a well-published author and ghostwriter who worked with Summersby on *Past Forgetting* during the final weeks of Kay's life. Bob Considine observed that the ghostwriter eventually gave the manuscript a "racy flavor" that corresponded to what by then had become accepted belief that Kay and Ike were lovers. It is interesting to note that Ms. Wyden's past literary history included ghostwriting such books as *The Brothers System for Liberated Love and Marriage* by Joyce Brothers, *The Doctor's Case Against the Pill* by Barbara Seaman, and *Jane Fonda's Workout Book* by Jane Fonda.

In 1972, Mamie Eisenhower pointed to a box in the corner of her bedroom at the Eisenhower Farm in Gettysburg and told her son that it contained all the wartime letters Ike had written to Mamie between June 1942 and November 1945. The box held 319 original letters, almost all handwritten, that General Eisenhower wrote from North Africa and Europe during this three-and-a-half-year period. This was an average of two letters to his wife each week throughout the war years. John Eisenhower admitted, "Like a dutiful son, I removed the box, took it home to Valley Forge, and promptly forgot about it."[53]

It was about a year before John got around to taking a serious look at the letters and he quickly realized they needed to be published. The personal letters showed a different side of Ike, one that up to this time was unknown to the public. "What these letters lack in historical material they make up with a transcript of inner thoughts, worries, and philosophical ponderings, rare in the Eisenhower literature." John put off work on the letters project, as he was busy completing his own memoir, *Strictly*

Kay Summersby's 1960 US passport photograph. She was fifty-one at the time. This was her third US passport, as she became a US citizen in 1951 and had passports dated 1952 and 1956. (Courtesy Eisenhower Library)

Personal (published in 1974), but by 1976 he began compiling and editing the letters for publication as *Letters to Mamie by Dwight D. Eisenhower.*[54]

Merle Miller's *Plain Speaking* (1972) told the unsubstantiated Harry Truman tale of Eisenhower seeking a divorce from Mamie at war's end. Kay Summersby's deathbed book *Past Forgetting* appeared in late 1975 and built upon that story. The grief and embarrassment these two books caused his mother provided John Eisenhower with even greater determination that now was the time to publish Ike's wartime letters. John wrote in the foreword to *Letters to Mamie* that the opinions regarding Kay Summersby's book ranged from "certain sentimentalists considering it a beautiful love story to others charactering it as rubbish." John refused to evaluate her writing effort but noted that he himself was an eyewitness to many of the events Kay described in *Past Forgetting*, and that "her imagination played a stupendous role" in the book. When it came to President Truman's allegation in Merle Miller's *Plain Speaking* that Eisenhower had written Marshall—in a "lost" letter—for permission to divorce Mamie, John said *Letters to Mamie* exposes the story to be "the spiteful falsehood that it was. Ike's letters home to Mamie reflected his sincere devotion to his wife."[55]

As Ike's granddaughter Susan Eisenhower has noted, her father John Eisenhower "has always likened Kay Summersby's relationship to Ike as roughly that of Mary Richards (Mary Tyler Moore) to Lou Grant (Edward Asner)."[56] Younger readers will need to search for television reruns of *The Mary Tyler Moore Show* (1970–1977) to understand the analogy; a fond relationship between an older male mentor and younger female staffer. It should also be noted that John Eisenhower did not downplay the seriousness of the relationship, telling biographer Jim Newton that even if Eisenhower and Kay were not intimate, "a rapport is much more serious than a roll in the hay."[57]

Ike's 319 letters to his wife reflected not only his love for Mamie, but also gave revealing insight into the worries and stress he endured as wartime commander of Allied forces in the European Theater. Ike frequently complained about the lonely existence he had and asked Mamie to send him news from home. He longed for the private life he enjoyed with his wife. "I live in a fishbowl," he wrote.[58] There was no "home" to go to, where there would be incentive to forget the work part of his existence, even if only momentarily. He told Mamie she could not imagine how much she had added to his efficiency in the hard months in 1942 in Washington before he took on the commander in chief role in Europe. He confessed he did not fully realize that fact at the time but did now, and he was so grateful to her.[59]

Eisenhower also missed his son John, who was attending West Point and busy preparing to become an army officer in his own right. Ike complained to Mamie that in the last two months he had only received one short note from John containing just three lines. He lamented that John was unaware of how a letter would help his father fight the loneliness. "Sometimes I worry a bit about the possibility that he may be just a bit spoiled," Ike said. He wrote Mamie that he would like to hear from Johnny as to his desires and possible army assignment when he graduated from West Point but had heard nothing. "He can keep silent in many languages," Ike observed sadly. In another letter to Mamie, he noted that John is "the champion non-letter writer."[60]

By July 1943, General Eisenhower had become a world-renowned figure after leading the defeat of the German forces in North Africa. Mamie
had written to her husband about her sadness that, because he was now
on the world stage, he no longer belonged to her. Ike wrote back immediately, reassuring her that she was wrong. "In spite of all the publicity you
are quite mistaken in saying that I no longer belong to you and Johnny."
With conducting a winning war there was naturally acclaim and that was
part of his official life now. But for Ike, it was still all about family. "So
far as I, as a person, am concerned—I'm just 1/3 of the family (your and
John's and mine). So don't fret your head about that phase of the thing."
He went on to add an interesting comment about things to come: "At
least no crack-brain has yet started running me for political office. That's
something!"[61] In less than ten years, Eisenhower would be in the White
House.

There was self-deprecating humor in his letters to Mamie. When
talking about having to meet in total secrecy to plan Operation Torch, the
invasion of North Africa, Ike wrote, "Think I'll wear a false mustache and
dark glasses." The almost bald Eisenhower then added that in his case,
rather than the mustache and glasses, "Possibly a wig would be more
effective!" And perhaps most importantly, Ike wrote to Mamie about how
he longed to be alone with her in their Washington, DC, apartment. "If
I could only take forty-eight hours and have it all at the Wardman Park
Hotel, I think I could face the next few months with much greater enthusiasm." Eisenhower shared with Mamie that the daily stress of his position
meant having to fight to not become cynical and morose. He found he
wanted to sneak off alone and stop arguing the same things each day with
the other generals, staff, and politicians. He then added, "It would be lots
more fun to sneak off to see you." Five days later, in another letter, he said,
"I swear I think I miss you more and love you more than I ever did."[62]
John Eisenhower notes in the afterword of his book that when Dwight
D. Eisenhower wrote his first wartime letter home in June 1942, he and
Mamie had been married for slightly less than twenty-six years. After the
last letter on October 31, 1945, they still had nearly twenty-four more years
ahead of them.[63]

In a 1977 oral history, John Eisenhower said of Summersby, "Dad and
everybody else was fond of her. I liked her too." John had met Kay in June
1944 after he graduated from West Point and visited his father in the war
zone. He was also her escort stateside when she was part of a group of
SHAEF staff who visited Washington in the summer of 1944. John also

confided that if he were ever to find written evidence that there had been an affair, he would not make the document public. "If I found a real smoking gun letter, I'd probably destroy it. I haven't found any."[64]

Granddaughter Susan Eisenhower found it significant that Mamie did not confide any concerns about Kay Summersby to her friends or to her parents. In times past, she had confided her deepest feelings to them. To Susan, this suggests Mamie was not terribly worried about the veracity of these rumors, but she did resent the gossip. Years later Mamie would refute any notion that her husband had had a romantic relationship with his wartime driver, saying simply, "I know Ike."[65]

It is enlightening to read the considered opinions by Eisenhower scholars regarding the true nature of the Eisenhower-Summersby relationship. These historians have delved deeply into the archives and oral histories of the period and have interviewed Ike's wartime associates. There appears to be a commonality in the resulting conclusions most have drawn. Peter Lyon authored *Eisenhower: Portrait of the Hero* (1974). He writes that, in his view, the fact of the Eisenhower-Summersby matter is that the whispers were not true. Further, if those whispers ever had a purpose beyond idle malice, they have long since outlived it. But, sadly, these stories have been "sanctified" by appearance in newsprint. Lyon says they will therefore be labored over the next few generations by candidates for a PhD in history and live on until God's final judgment on Earth.[66]

In *Eisenhower Declassified* (1979), historian Virgil Pinkley interviewed many members of Ike's wartime headquarters who were eyewitnesses to Ike's and Kay's relationship, and he came away with the strong impression that Kay Summersby loved to be associated with glamour and had sensationalized an affectionate but platonic relationship with one of the most prominent men in recent history. Pinkley wrote that his long investigation of the Summersby claim led him to a triple-headed conclusion: (1) Eisenhower is innocent; (2) Kay Summersby and her ghostwriters were most imaginative; and (3) sexual content helps the sale of books.[67]

In his 1983 volume, *Eisenhower: Soldier, General of the Army, President-Elect 1890–1952*, Eisenhower biographer Dr. Stephen Ambrose observed that in Ike's high-powered world of generals, admirals, prime ministers, and French politicians, he needed a soft touch, a light laugh, an escape from the constant pressure of war and death, and Kay met those needs. Ambrose says *Past Forgetting* might simply be the fantasy of an older woman looking back thirty years and that no one will ever know for certain about the true extent of the relationship. What is important to note, he points out, is that not even Kay ever claimed that they had a "genuine love affair."[68]

In 1997, historian Garry Wills wrote a scathing commentary in the *New York Post* about the role Ike's predecessor in the White House played in promoting the Eisenhower-Summersby scandal. Wills said that the recent debates over fraternization in the military reminded him "what a lying little twerp Harry Truman was." Wills asks rhetorically, "How did everybody get the impression that Eisenhower had this affair? No one claimed that while Eisenhower was alive. It took a cowardly liar to spread the smear after his death. That coward's name was Truman."[69]

Geoffrey Perret in *Eisenhower* (1999) wrote that not even one of the half dozen people who were part of Ike's wartime "family" believed then or later that there was any kind of romance between Ike and Kay. Captain Butcher, Sgt. McKeogh, and the WACs on the staff, with whom Kay shared rooms and forged friendships that lasted until her death in 1975, all poured scorn on her claim. Perret concludes tellingly that Summersby could not produce a single piece of material evidence to confirm it."[70]

In 2015, Eisenhower biographer Carlo D'Este authored a series of articles entitled *The Myth of Ike and Kay Summersby* for *Armchair General* magazine. He stated that once myths are unleashed, they are difficult if not impossible to shatter, and that the alleged affair between Ike and Kay Summersby had evolved from juicy gossip into folklore. In the articles, D'Este outlines why he is very doubtful the affair ever took place. He also speculates that it is hard to verify how much of *Past Forgetting* was based on Kay's dictation to the ghostwriter from her deathbed and how much might have been made up to protect Simon & Schuster's substantial investment in view of the large six-figure advance reportedly given by the publisher. He concludes with some praise for Kay Summersby. Whether driving an ambulance in London during the Blitz or chauffeuring General Eisenhower across England, North Africa, and Europe, Kay was as much a soldier as her boss, says D'Este. "She deserved a better fate."[71]

Then there is the testimony of Ike's wartime staff. "I was with the Boss almost everywhere during World War II," said Captain Harry Butcher, Eisenhower's naval aide. "He was commanding the most-critical war in the nation's history. He worked incessantly, was always protected, always watched. There was no time or opportunity for an affair."[72] Butcher recalled to Carlo D'Este in 1980 that there was no sign of a romance. "We were a close family. . . . If a romance had been brewing between Ike and Kay, I could hardly have missed it . . . hell, even his son John was fond of her!"[73]

General Eisenhower's wartime chief of intelligence, British Major General Kenneth Strong, also did not believe there was an affair. Lieutenant Colonel Kenneth Keith (later knighted as Lord Keith of Castleacre) was military assistant to General Strong during the war and remained close friends with Strong until the end of his life. Colonel Keith felt compelled to write a letter to the editor of the *Washington Post* in 1997 saying he wanted "to place firmly on the record General Strong's firmly held view and also my own" that there was no such affair. Since his boss oversaw all intelligence operations and the security services in the European Theater, they would have known if there was any truth to such rumors that circulated from time to time about General Eisenhower and Kay Summersby. "I am certain we would have known," he said, and both he and General Strong remained convinced that there was no truth in the suggestion the Eisenhower had an affair.[74]

Sergeant Mickey McKeogh served as Eisenhower's personal orderly. In an interview with Virgil Pinkley, McKeogh said, "That stuff about an affair with Kay is sheer nonsense. I put the Boss to bed every night, and there was no one else in the bed. In the mornings when I would wake him up, there was no one else in the bed, except one time when I found Telek, his black Scotty, on his pillow." McKeogh went on to say that General Eisenhower worked incessantly and was always protected, always watched. He explained there was no time or opportunity for an affair. There were at least a dozen staffers who made up the Eisenhower wartime household, who became known as "the family." If there had been any unusually warm exchanges—looks, remarks, or touching or caresses—between Ike and Kay, someone would have seen or learned about it. McKeogh added somewhat cynically, "Someone would have told or written that story for money. You can usually count on one Judas among twelve, but no one ever told such a story."[75]

Ike's grandson David Eisenhower, in *Eisenhower at War, 1943–1945,* shares a further assessment of Kay Summersby provided by Sgt. Mickey McKeogh. Ike's orderly admitted that General Eisenhower needed "unmilitary types" like Kay to relieve the austere and disciplined routine he otherwise led. But her unmilitary approach at times intruded on Mickey's keen sense of his place within the headquarters setup. He said, "She was nice, unmilitary, and very emotional." Kay had a habit of crossing jurisdictional lines, ordering him and the other lower staff members around. Mickey once appealed to General Eisenhower for relief, but Ike's reported response to his orderly was, "Bear with her, she's not a very well person."[76]

Anthea Saxe served as a fellow driver in British Motor Transport Corps during the war. She was Kay's good friend and, like Kay, also emigrated from England to the US shortly after the war. She and her husband served as trustees for Summersby's estate after her death in 1975. Mrs. Saxe told me in a 2002 telephone call, "Ike trusted Kay completely. They lived in a fishbowl." Mrs. Saxe said that *Past Forgetting* is a total fabrication. "Kay didn't write a word of it. The first book was the true picture. Kay did play up the relationship to open some doors for herself."[77]

Sue Sarafian Jehl was a key member of Eisenhower's clerical staff during the war. She said of Summersby, "The first time I met her, I thought she was one of the most beautiful women I had ever seen, and very gracious. . . . Every person who came to visit the General would always stop in and see Kay first. They all loved her, she was a very likable person." Jehl added, however, "Whatever was in that book was not true." However, Sue Jehl went on to tell an interesting story about the personal impact of the Kay Summersby rumors. Sue said that Mamie resented all the women in uniform because of all the rumors about Kay during the war. This resentment was especially applied to those like Sue, who were connected with Kay because of wartime service. Sue could not blame Mamie and understood, but it cost her a trip to her hometown of Detroit in 1946 or 1947. Jehl, now a lieutenant, was still working for Eisenhower in the Pentagon, where he served as army chief of staff. She was transcribing Ike's dictation for his forthcoming World War II memoir *Crusade in Europe*. The general accepted an invitation from the chamber of commerce to speak in Detroit. He took Sgt. Leonard Dry with him but not Lieutenant Jehl. Eisenhower apologized to Sue after the trip and explained that since Mamie was not making the trip, he could not take Sue along. Sue and her family in Detroit were very disappointed.[78]

Ann Whitman may provide an interesting parallel to Ike's relationship with Kay Summersby. She was the same age as Kay, both born in the year 1908. Ann served Eisenhower as personal assistant for the entire eight years of his presidency, sitting at her desk right outside the Oval Office. She had worked initially in the 1952 presidential campaign and was then brought onto the staff after the election. Ann was married and living in New York City when she came to the White House in 1953. She was ahead of her time with her commuting marriage, but the relationship with her husband suffered during her long absences from New York. Sadly, she divorced shortly after the end of the Eisenhower administration.

The hangover from the Summersby controversy was reflected in Mamie Eisenhower's concern about Ann Whitman. Mamie feared the close working relationship developing between her husband and his bright secretary, eighteen years his junior, might get out of hand or appear to. Appearances were very important to Mamie Eisenhower. A senior official on Ike's presidential election campaign confided to Ann that Mrs. Eisenhower had told him she wanted Ann removed as her husband's secretary. Ann wrote her husband in New York saying: "I don't know what will be the outcome of the problem . . . the Gen [General Eisenhower] knows nothing of it—but knowing Mrs. E's power, I'm pretty sure I'm out." Ann thought this was absurd. She told her husband, "Imagine! At my age!"[79]

But of course, she was not "out" and indeed served at her desk just outside the Oval Office the full eight years of the Eisenhower administration. I conducted an oral history interview with Ann Whitman in 1991 and she shared she had indeed paid a high personal price by working for Eisenhower. Being in Washington, DC, while her husband lived and worked in New York City had ended her marriage. Ann admired and adored Eisenhower and I asked in the interview, "If you could do something over again in those years in the White House, what would you do?" Her answer: "I wouldn't go!" Then there was a very long pause. Ann said, "I don't know whether I mean it or not. It was a great, great, great experience, but I loved my husband very much."[80]

It is only logical that "historical fiction" books about Ike's alleged affair would eventually emerge. In this genre, fiction writer Susan Wittig Albert authored *The General's Women* (2017) and James MacManus wrote *Ike and Kay* (2018). One critic of a different book by Ms. Albert noted that, whether or not you agreed with her basic premise, the swift-moving novel was "engrossing and very satisfying."[81] I guess that means the author fulfilled the readers' prurient hopes. We can all agree that "engrossing and satisfying" may indeed be more enjoyable than the truth.

In Albert's historical fiction work on Eisenhower and Kay Summersby, entitled *The General's Women* (one of the general's women was Kay and the other his wife, Mamie), there are disclaimers that appear on the reverse of the title page and later in a section entitled "Author's Notes." Albert reasons that her fictional true lovers are deserving of some fictional satisfaction, even if that did not occur in reality.

This is a work of fiction. Names, characters, places, and incidents are the product of the author's imagination or, in the case of historical persons, are used fictitiously. . . . I feel that both Ike and Kay deserve to wrest a least a little passionate pleasure out of those dark days, so I have given them that, at times and places where I think it might have been possible. In offering this fictional satisfaction to my fictional lovers, I have trusted to my own romantic imagination and the testimony of Sigrid Hedin, the first ghostwriter on *Past Forgetting*.[82]

And it was not merely historical fiction books that appeared after *Plain Speaking* was published. In 1979 an ABC made-for-television, four-hour miniseries, *IKE: The War Years*, was shown on TV screens across America. Actor Robert Duvall was great as Eisenhower, and Lee Remick was impressive as Kay Summersby. But critics complained that the dramatization gave Kay too much alone time with Ike and portrayed the general as constantly using Miss Summersby as a sounding board. The only thing missing would have been General Eisenhower asking, "Gee Kay, do you think we should go ahead with the plans for the Normandy Invasion?" Susan Eisenhower noted, "What a pity that the network mini-series, based on a book the author didn't even see, made 'fact' of the 'affair.'"[83]

In *Past Forgetting*, Kay recounts the long evening she drove General Eisenhower to the airfields to watch as the airborne troops departed England for the Normandy landing drop zones. In her version of events, when they returned to the headquarters that evening, Ike wanted her to share his solitude as he waited for messages about the early success of Operation Overlord (codename for the Normandy invasion). She wrote that Ike asked her that night, "What are your thoughts, Kay?"[84] Summersby's nephew, Michael MacCarthy-Morrogh would find this difficult to believe. In 2020, he published an article entitled "Kay Summersby – Helping Ike Win the War," in an Irish local historical society journal. The article is very detailed about his "Auntie Kay's" life, affectionate and most informative. MacCarthy-Morrogh admitted that Kay was undeniably an important part of the wartime "family"— that close-knit team of half a dozen who lived cheek by jowl with him for three years—but continued as follows:

Whatever Kay's relationship with Eisenhower was, she had absolutely no historical influence on the conduct of the war. Just to imagine it is absurd. The General strode into the room, smoking furiously. "God Dammit how are we going to pressure the Germans from behind once the invasion lands?" Kay stood up, "I have an idea, Sir. "Let's hear it, Irish." "Why not have a second invasion of France from the Mediterranean?" Ike stared at her. "Why, that's brilliant, Kay."[85]

John Eisenhower wrote a letter to Virgil Pinkley noting, "Ironically, ABC, with their television mentality, believe they are making Dad look good—a sort of Humphrey Bogart type—in the distasteful screenplay they have produced." John's irritation was less with the role that Harry Truman or Merle Miller's *Plain Speaking* might have played in leading to this television miniseries, but rather with the American public for accepting the story with almost universal belief in its truth.[86]

In the fall of 2002, I surveyed my archives staff at the Eisenhower Presidential Library regarding their personal assessment of whether Dwight D. Eisenhower had an affair with Kay Summersby. The results were interesting. Please note that the library is totally non-partisan, and these staff professionals keep their personal opinions to themselves when dealing with researchers or the public visitors. Over the years, we have provided equally professional reference service to Holocaust deniers, UFO true believers, Ike-haters, and all who do research. However, around the staff coffee break table an opinion is allowed.

Please be advised also that these nine staff members had collectively over 200 years of experience reviewing, arranging, declassifying, and responding to reference queries on the twenty-six million pages of original archival materials in the Eisenhower Presidential Library. Also, in case you're wondering, a majority of the staff were not registered Republicans. My instructions to them in an email were as follows:

> Based on working here at the Library for many years and having delved into the papers, oral histories, etc. . . . and "knowing" Eisenhower the way you do . . . Do you think the rumors of an affair were true or false? Pick an answer. Please email with "reply to sender only"—I don't want you "influencing" the "votes" of others. I'll share results with everyone later.

The results of the survey were as follows:

Using the survey's scoring system—True = 4, Probably True = 3, Could be Either = 2, Probably False = 1, and False = 0—the composite score is 1.15. This is very slightly above the "Probably False" assessment. You can see that one wishy-washy staff member split their vote and that is taken into consideration in the scoring. The bottom line is that these career

Table 2. The "Ike—Kay Survey." November 2002

	True	Probably True	Could be Either	Probably False	False
Staff 1					X
Staff 2				X	
Staff 3				X	
Staff 4			X	X	
Staff 5				X	
Staff 6			X		
Staff 7				X	
Staff 8				X	
Staff 9			X		

archivists and archives technicians who each lived and worked for a couple of decades with the original historical records of the Eisenhower era tend to discount the affair. This proves nothing but is certainly worth noting.

In 1986, grandson David Eisenhower wrote a massive and well-researched history of General Eisenhower's wartime service. In *Eisenhower at War 1943–1945*, David touched briefly on the relationship with Miss Summersby. From his interviews with headquarters staffers who were on the scene, David gleaned that Summersby no doubt exaggerated the tale of romance in her second book, but there was no exaggeration of her importance on the headquarters staff. David Eisenhower concluded, "However far it went, the two were attached. Eisenhower was under tremendous pressures and in need of company." Let's concede that Kay Summersby played a necessary role in Ike's wartime headquarters.[87]

What are we to conclude? Members of General Eisenhower's immediate wartime staff (aka "the family") were very fond of Kay, but they all went on record in oral histories and interviews saying the rumored affair between the two did not happen. It is difficult to overemphasize the importance of these statements. We realize that times have changed; perhaps personal and professional loyalty meant more back in the 1940s and 1950s. Nevertheless, the fact there was not a single "kiss and tell" book about Eisenhower and Kay speaks volumes. (Except the brief vignette in Kay's second book of course.) The *National Inquirer* has been publishing since 1926, yet not one of Ike's confidants sold out to the press.

Historians and Eisenhower biographers who have studied the man and his role on the world stage have by and large also concluded that the affair probably did not happen. These are scholars who have not shied away from disagreeing with Ike's decisions and policies during the war or as president. But there was near unanimity in their positive view of his personal life. In my informal survey of archivists at the Eisenhower Presidential Library, these knowledgeable staffers were largely of the opinion that the rumors were probably false.

I spent almost four decades of professional work studying and preserving the history of the Eisenhower era. My belief is that Eisenhower was extremely fond of his young chauffeur. He enjoyed and probably even needed her presence at his wartime headquarters to give him respite and relief from the relentless burden of the awesome responsibilities of his military command. But, in the final analysis, Ike loved Mamie and was guided in life by a strong set of morals.

Mildred Considine asked Kay directly about the alleged affair and Summersby's response was that it did not happen. At this point, it is very fitting to cite Kay's own words about Eisenhower's integrity, which she wrote in the conclusion of her first book: "No single characteristic lifts a man from the crowd. Yet General Eisenhower does have one outstanding distinction: his unconquerable honesty. . . . I find it unique that a man of his prominence has never once, as far as I know, been accused of dishonesty or lack of integrity."[88]

In my informed opinion, it is very unlikely that Dwight D. Eisenhower had an affair with his wartime driver, Kay Summersby.

CHAPTER TWELVE

THE PROFANE IKE

"Oh, goddammit, we forgot the silent prayer."
—*President Dwight D. Eisenhower at a Cabinet meeting*[1]

During the cold, wet winter of 1945, as the Allies were slowly driving toward Germany, Supreme Allied Commander Eisenhower received a letter from a shocked lady who deplored his selection of adjective when he was quoted in a newspaper referring to the "damnable weather" hindering the war-fighting effort. Ike wrote home to Mamie that the lady not only disliked his swearing but also reminded him that "since the Lord sent the weather, I had no right to curse it. She really put me over the jumps."[2] Little did this lady realize this was just the tip of the iceberg when it came to Eisenhower and profanity.

Sergeant Mickey McKeogh, General Eisenhower's wartime orderly, had a front-row seat to colorful language used by "the boss." "I suppose everybody knows he uses a good deal of profanity," McKeogh wrote in his 1946 autobiography. However, he went on to point out that the general's swearing was "pretty clean" and not the kind of talk a good many men used in the army. Eisenhower himself was annoyed by any complaints about his language, and Mickey quoted the general as saying, "I don't curse. I just use some words as adjectives."[3]

Sue Sarafian Jehl was a member of the Women's Army Corps (WAC) and served during the war as one of General Eisenhower's personal secretaries at his headquarters. In a 1991 oral history interview for the Eisenhower Library, I asked her if she experienced Eisenhower's temper firsthand; she replied, "Oh yes, a lot." She added, "And he swore, he loved to swear . . . very much." Jehl went on to explain, "But that was the army. And we got used to it, we never paid any attention to it."[4] This language in no way lessened her strong admiration and respect for Ike.

General Eisenhower's Irish born wartime driver Kay Summersby had been assigned to the US Army in London long enough to understand that swearing was as natural as punctuation in the spoken word of many US military personnel. She tried to explain to her British friends that "Yanks used curses in such a natural way that no one could take offense." Kay also shared with General Patton her memory of the time she had yelled "god-damn!" while sitting at a desk outside Ike's office at the Grosvenor Square London headquarters. General Eisenhower buzzed her in right away and asked where she had acquired such shocking language. Ike then smiled meekly when Kay confessed she had learned that word from none other than Dwight D. Eisenhower.[5]

In Kay Summersby's ghostwritten, posthumously published second memoir, *Past Forgetting*, the author felt compelled to quote Eisenhower's profanity as the very last words in the final paragraph of the book. Kay said that she was close to the end of her life and had a sense of being close to Ike again. As she neared death, she was fondly remembering the good times she shared with the general. If Ike were with her again, she remi-nisced, he might say, "Oh, that was a great day. Didn't we have a good time that day!" Kay said it was almost as if Ike were looking over her shoulder as she imagined his last words to her. Her closing sentence in *Past Forgetting*: "Right now, he's saying, 'Goddammit, don't cry.'"[6]

In 1991, I conducted a revealing oral history interview with Ann Whit-man, who served eight years as Eisenhower's personal secretary in the White House. I asked Ann about the president's use of profanity in the Oval Office. She explained that Ike was a retired soldier after all, and hab-its do die hard. Ann was not bothered by the swearing and noted it was never directed at her personally. She explained that Eisenhower would say, "Goddamn it to hell and that sort of thing, yes, sure, but none of the four-letter words or anything like that." Four-letter words? I always thought that included "hells" and "damns." But her point was that Ike's profane vo-cabulary did not wander much beyond these constrained bounds.[7]

Doug Price, another White House staffer, confirms Ann's assessment. He recalled that Ike cursed privately, "but only in light blue, not dark four-letter words." Anyone who made the mistake of using scatological or vulgar language in Eisenhower's presence regretted it. Also unacceptable were off-color stories. Price said that Eisenhower had too much respect for the presidency to allow such behavior.[8]

Ike's secret recordings of conversations in his offices at Columbia Uni-versity and in the White House confirm the limits of his profane vocab-ulary. It was indeed mostly hells and damns. For example, in May 1950 while at Columbia, Eisenhower met with John Henshaw Crider, editor of *Boston Herald* newspaper. Crider appeared to be urging the retired general to run for president and an irritated Ike replied: "If ever I become ready or willing or feel I have any goddamn duty to touch politics, even to announce to which party I want to adhere, it will be done publicly. You don't need to fear about any goddamn inner circle."[9]

Eisenhower's frustration with issues at the Civil Aeronautics Board was evident in a recorded Oval Office conversation with the Chairman of the Republican National Committee and Secretary of Commerce in January 1955. "I'm so sick of that goddamned body. It must have been doing a horrible job or there wouldn't be so damned much fighting." The tenure of CAB board member Oswald Ryan was brought up and an angry Ike interrupted, warning his White House visitors, "Every other person who comes in wants to talk about Ryan. I'm so sick of the name that I could practically choke, but go ahead."[10]

Ike could even be creative in his profanity. He had strong feelings toward the renowned, and often critical, Washington political columnist Drew Pearson and in 1958 wrote to his boyhood friend Swede Hazlett about Pearson. "I have not read a word of his in fifteen years. Personally, I think he is a 'spherical' SOB which makes him one, no matter from what angle you may view him."[11]

In another secret White House recording, Ike showed he could become very frustrated by paperwork and minutia in general. Sitting at his desk in the Oval Office, he was handed a finished letter to General Omar Bradley for his signature. "I have to sign so much goddamned paper I haven't had a chance to read these days!" He was assured by the staff member who said, "I know. I'm very careful with these things." The situation did not get any better just a few minutes later when the White House social secretary was outside the Oval Office, seeking permission to enter to ask the president to review the names on the invitation list for an upcoming formal dinner. Eisenhower barked, "Oh, for Christ's sake, I don't give a damn about this . . . have her come in." Ike's irritation grew even greater when he learned he was being asked to pare down the number of attendees. An exasperated Eisenhower finally said, "Certainly some of them will be sick or dead or something," and then the recording shows he abruptly left the office.[12]

Speaking of presidential frustrations, we can safely assume Ike's frequent hook shot into the famous Eisenhower Tree on the seventeenth hole at Augusta National Golf Course was also the occasion for a blue tirade by the commander in chief. Early on, when John Eisenhower as a boy accompanied his father on the golf course, he noted that if a shot went awry, "the air would be punctuated with certain expletives that I had thought were unknown to adults—only to kids."[13] Ike was apparently in good presidential company when it came to the frustrations caused by the game. As early as 1908, William Howard Taft once said about golf, "I don't know of any game that after a while makes you so ashamed of your profanity."[14]

Blame the army. In perhaps an unintended moment of self-analysis, Eisenhower wrote his good friend, and fellow general officer, Arthur Nevins in 1954 venting about the criticism he was receiving from the media for taking too many vacations as president. Like all presidents, the frustrated Eisenhower felt time away from the White House is never truly a vacation, since the stress and responsibility as world leader are sure to follow wherever you go. Ike wrote Nevins, saying when he hears these criticisms, "I feel like turning loose a little bit of barrack room language!"[15] Eisenhower's own words, "barrack room language," do indeed explain the genesis of his profanity habit; one that extended well after his almost forty years in uniform. One writer remarked, "One of the many reasons for Eisenhower's popularity with the troops was that he was a general who could swear like a sergeant."[16]

I grew up a military brat. My career military father was known to swear occasionally, when angry or frustrated. The example clearest in my memory is what was said as I held a wrench or the flashlight for him when his work under the hood of our 1956 Chevy station wagon was not going well. But, as with Ike, it was hells and damns—nothing more off-color than that. When Dad was older and retired from the military, he used very little profanity, if any. It was no doubt in deference to us kids. He was more likely to exclaim "dadgummit" or "what the Sam Hill!"

A decade later, I found myself in a virtually all-male, military environment while serving at the US Seventh Air Force headquarters in Saigon, Vietnam. Profanity flew around quite steadily during that year-long tour of duty, and I participated. In retrospect I believe the root cause was being away from the moderating influence a man experiences when going home at night to his family.

So why profanity? One cause, in my estimation, is the fact Dwight D. Eisenhower grew up in and worked in a male environment for the first three-quarters of his life. Granted, swearing was no doubt taboo in the Eisenhower boyhood home, with his strict River Brethren parents. But there were only sons and no daughters. One wonders what was said by the Eisenhower boys playing on the baseball field across the street from the house when mother and father were out of earshot? Also, young Ike was a great outdoorsman and enjoyed camping with his pals along the banks of the Smoky River south of town. From an early age, Eisenhower demonstrated that he was a man's man, enjoying and being most comfortable among the male species. I'm guessing there might have been a few damns and hells sprinkled among the bravado of Eisenhower's "old Woodbine Gang" as the teenagers sat talking around the campfire along the riverbank.

Then there was Ike's boyhood hero Bob Davis to consider. Davis, in his fifties, was a crusty old bachelor living in Abilene and, surprisingly enough, Ida Eisenhower allowed her son to spend weekends with him camping along the river, fishing, trapping, and shooting. Although Davis was illiterate, he was smart. He taught young Ike the rudiments of poker, drilling percentages into the lad's head, so he soon had an inkling which cards were likely to be drawn.[17] This was to come in handy later when Cadet Eisenhower was playing poker in the barracks at West Point, not to mention giving him a good head start on acquiring the skills to play bridge, the card game he really came to love later in life. It is not hard to imagine that Bob Davis might well have included an expletive or two in his teachable moments when poker fledgling Ike played his cards wrong. And who knows? The youngster may have responded in kind.

Unlike in today's US military, Ike's forty years of service in uniform occurred during a virtually male-only environment. The hells and damns of those years were an accepted form of routine speech in the army, and rather innocuous. And Eisenhower's habit of using them continued after he was out of uniform. The more serious expletives in the English language have certainly been around for generations (centuries in fact!) and would not have been alien to Eisenhower's ear. According to the first-hand testimony of his military and White House associates, Ike's swearing could quite correctly be described as very restricted in its vocabulary, even if not so limited in the frequency of its use. The secret recordings of office conversations that exist from his time at Columbia and in the White House make the strongest case for that conclusion. Compare the rather tame damns and hells on the Eisenhower tapes with the "expletives deleted" on the later Nixon Watergate tapes.

Dwight D. Eisenhower was indeed very restrained in his swearing when compared to modern society's public use of much coarser language. "Our society's comfort level with offensive language and content has drastically shifted over the past few decades," according to a Canadian scholar.[18] Eisenhower was somewhat of a Victorian and would no doubt be shocked and outraged at today's public use of profanity in our society. Mamie Eisenhower obviously would have been aware of Ike's proclivity toward the use of profanity. Nevertheless, when writing home to Mamie from Europe during the war, a more sensitive Eisenhower would use d—, instead of spelling out the word "damn" in his letters. That is restraint.

Eisenhower was indeed a career soldier and possessed a temper. One cannot deny the man could be profane when it suited his mood. But it appears Ann Whitman was correct when she defended her boss in the White House, explaining he might say "goddamn it to hell and that sort of thing, yes, sure, but none of the four-letter words or anything like that."

No disqualifier from being placed on Mount Rushmore, in my humble opinion.

CHAPTER THIRTEEN

"DWIGHT VAN GOGH"

> "I refuse to refer to my productions as paintings. They are daubs, born of my love of color and in my pleasure in experimenting, nothing else."
> —*Dwight D. Eisenhower,* At Ease

Ask most people what colors they would associate with Dwight D. Eisenhower, and they would say olive drab or khaki. Not too many know that he was just as comfortable with the cadmium red, cobalt blue, or yellow ochre of his artist's palette.

One art historian speculates that the artistic spark within Ike may have first been lit during wartime in England, as General Eisenhower observed Winston Churchill absorbed in painting for relaxation, "lost in his love of pigments."[1] Eisenhower attempted his first oil painting just a few years later, while he was president of Columbia University. That first venture was the basis of one of the stories he told to friends in *At Ease.* Thomas E. Stephen, a New York artist, was visiting the university president's official residence to paint a portrait of Mamie. Ike was a very interested spectator. While Stephens and Mamie toured the house to locate the best place to hang the finished portrait, Eisenhower decided to use the remaining paint on the artist's easel for a little experimentation of his own. Having no blank canvas at hand, he and his aide stretched a clean dust cloth over the bottom of a box. The first subject that came to mind was Mamie, so he began his own version of the portrait Stephens was doing.

When the others returned, Ike displayed his painting, which was, in his words, "weird and wonderful to behold." Mamie pointed out laughingly that the small pink bow she was wearing in her hair had grown to relatively monstrous proportions on Ike's make-do canvas.[2] Stephens encouraged him to keep trying, but Ike had decided that painting was not his talent. The artist asked to have the painting as a keepsake and Ike was happy to oblige. (I hope the Thomas Stephens heirs still have this very first piece

NOTE: This chapter is based in part on an article that appeared in *Overview* (Winter 1982), a publication of the Eisenhower Foundation, Abilene, KS.

of Eisenhower artwork. Can you imagine its value?) A few days later, Ike received a package from Stephens. Ike described what he found inside as "everything I could possibly need—except ability—to start painting." Considering the gift a thoughtful gesture but a "sheer waste of money," Ike set it aside. But soon his curiosity got the best of him, and he embarked upon a new hobby, one in which, unlike golf, he could indulge on rainy days. He said the most urgent need as he started was "a generous-sized tarpaulin to cover the floor around the easel." In the beginning, Ike said he covered his hands, clothes, brush handles, and the floor with more paint than ever reached the canvas. While he grew to enjoy this new hobby very much, if the weather was fine enough to sit and paint outdoors, it was also good enough for golf. No contest![3]

Writing to Churchill in 1950 about his new hobby Eisenhower said:

> I have a lot of fun since I took it up, in my somewhat miserable way, your hobby of painting. I have had no instruction, have no talent, and certainly no justification for covering nice, white canvas with the kind of daubs that seem constantly to spring from my brushes. Nevertheless, I like it tremendously and, in fact, have produced two or three things that I like enough to keep.[4]

Ike found painting to be relaxing and a great diversion from the cares of the day. He continued painting periodically for the rest of his life. In the White House, he maintained a small room ("hardly more than a closet") on the second floor, just off the elevator, where he would occasionally escape for ten minutes when going to the residence for lunch. Granddaughter Susan explained that Eisenhower was like other decision-makers trying to "find coherence in a million parts" and that he could sometimes be found by himself in silent retreat. Press Secretary James Hagerty observed the same. "From time to time he would find the President in his studio surrounded by scattered paint tubes and unfinished daubs, just sitting, lost in thought, in front of a blank canvas."[5]

He tried still lifes and landscapes, usually pastoral scenes, but "with magnificent audacity" he tried more portraits than anything. "I've also burned more portraits than anything else," he wrote. "I destroy two out of every three I start."[6]

Even as his skills improved, Ike seldom took any pride in the finished product; he just enjoyed the process. He seemed genuinely amazed to the very end that his friends were pleased to receive his "daubs" as gifts. A

Eisenhower the artist is shown painting at Camp David, Maryland, August 1, 1954. Ike finished some 300 works during his lifetime and found great solace from the burdens of the presidency when sitting alone before his easel. (Courtesy Eisenhower Library)

newspaper columnist attempted to flatter former President Eisenhower by asking about the symbolism of one of his paintings that was on display for a charity fundraiser. Ike told him, "Let's get something straight. . . . They would have burned this [expletive] a long time ago if I weren't the president of the United States."[7]

It is somewhat surprising that Eisenhower went along with the suggestion that he make prints of some of his paintings as large-scale Christmas greetings, but prints were indeed given out six of the eight years he was in the White House. His cover letters reveal that he was always apologetic when presenting them. He wrote to Joyce Hall, a friend and president of the Hallmark Company, which printed the Christmas cards: "As you know, I always hesitate to inflict my 'art' on my friends and members of my staff, but Hallmark makes such a beautiful package job that I am and I hope others are distracted into the belief that the whole thing is a superior product."

His own modest opinion of his talent notwithstanding, publicity about his painting generated so much public interest during his presidency that the White House was deluged with requests from charities for an original Eisenhower painting to exhibit or to auction off. There were also letters from other amateur artists offering or requesting criticism, and requests from people who wanted Ike to paint a special portrait or scene just for them. Nearly all requests were turned down because Ike considered his painting a very private domain. He never sold his paintings and rarely kept them. As soon as they were dry, he generally gave them away, often to the subject of a portrait or to whoever was around and expressed an interest. The White House staff compiled a list of the disposition of most of Ike's paintings. Anyone wanting to know today who was truly close to Eisenhower could be advised to start with that list.

After retiring to Gettysburg, the former president was a little more open about his hobby and allowed exhibition of his works. A major showing was held at the Gallery of Modern Art in New York City in 1967. The *New York Times* noted, "The works of an American amateur painter better known for his prowess in war and in politics will get their first public exposure in New York this spring."[8] All rights to commercially reproduce the paintings in that exhibit were assigned, subject to permission for present owners, to Eisenhower College, Seneca Falls, New York, thus providing a sizable endowment to that newly founded school. The paintings subsequently appeared on calendars and in print portfolios and in a large coffee table book in 1972, entitled *The Eisenhower College Collection: The Paintings of Dwight D. Eisenhower*, for which historian Kenneth Davis (one of the early Eisenhower biographers) prepared a very lengthy accompanying text.

Professor Davis wrote that Ike quickly found his new painting hobby to be increasingly absorbing and delightful. It provided needed relaxation from the tensions of his official duties in the Pentagon, at Columbia University, or in the Oval Office. While golf continued to be his favorite recreation, the relaxation of painting was a welcome respite and utterly free of the anger or disgust of a missed putt or a hooked drive. In his painting, Eisenhower also discovered a passion for color and a sense of line he had not known he possessed. "Sometimes I'll take two hours to get just the shade I want." And when the president looked at other people's paintings, it was now with an appraising eye, an eagerness to discern how the work had been done, how the colors had been mixed and the brush applied.[9]

The Dwight D. Eisenhower Museum in Abilene has twenty-three

original Eisenhower paintings in its holdings, some from the family and several that were donated to the museum by other individuals who had received them from Ike. During his twenty years as an artist, Ike produced some three hundred finished paintings.

Conservative in most things, Ike was in art as well. He had no time at all for the avant-garde. He felt modern art could even be categorized as "morally wrong." Speaking at the dedication of his presidential library in 1962, he said: "Our very art forms (are) so changed that we seem to have forgotten the works of Michelangelo and Leonardo da Vinci . . . a piece of canvas that looks like a broken-down Tin Lizzie, loaded with paint, has been driven over it . . . what has happened to our concept of beauty and decency and morality?"[10]

Newspapers and magazine articles reveal that writers and art critics could not agree on the quality of Ike's painting. Some said that, had he started earlier, Ike could have made art his life's work. Others compared him to Churchill as a Sunday painter and rated Churchill superior. Some implied that the paintings' value was purely therapeutic. Whatever their place in the world of art, Eisenhower's canvases show a side of the general and former president that should be remembered. When Ike was not busy saving the free world, he appreciated color, harmony, beauty, and tranquility.

One art historian provided very interesting insight into Eisenhower's painting hobby. Frieda Kay Fall (1913–2002) was on the staff of the Los Angeles County Museum of Art and was well-published in the world of art history. She penned a lengthy essay entitled "The Painter Dwight D. Eisenhower: A Critical Look," which was included in the *Eisenhower College Collection* book of Ike's painting, published in 1972.[11] Ms. Fall said, "Eisenhower was not a visionary who fancied himself a great painter. He never laid claim to the title of artist and thought of his painting as a pastime. . . . Relaxation and pleasure were his sole reason for painting."

Some of Ms. Fall's other observations include:

- Ike did not seek acclaim for his artwork. He had no need to bask in any favorable commentaries from friends, relatives, or associates. The end results achieved in his paintings were relatively unimportant to him.
- As a military man and president, Eisenhower had dwelt upon the rising and falling tide of civilizations in mortal conflict. He used

This political cartoon by Joseph Parrish entitled "Art Talk," appeared in the *Chicago Tribune* newspaper in 1956. Fortunately for America, Ike continued to "dabble in politics," but he also continued oil painting and it remained one of his favorite hobbies. (Permission 1956 Joseph Parrish/Chicago Tribune/TCA)

the medium of art to express what was pleasing or inspiring to him. There was a basic tranquility in his art. Violence and ferocity were not a part of his paintings. Ike with his paint brush was not striving for the moral improvement of his fellow man, nor the world in general.

- Ike was not a practitioner of any tried or true method, or currently popular formula in his art. Thus, his paintings are charmingly lacking in any kind of academic formalism. In satisfying his creative inclinations, his approach to his individualistic interpretations was instinctive and unstudied.

Eisenhower was more concerned with color considerations than with a literal rendering of the subject. The beauty of trees, rivers, and lakes fascinated him. He got interested in painting because he liked color. For him nature seemed not to be a setting or a background for his paintings but a partner and a source. Ike created highly original genre canvases, many of them reminiscent of peaceful, rural areas. Susan Eisenhower said her grandfather knew exactly what painting did for him. It helped him see the world in another way, through color and light.[12]

Frieda Kay Fall concludes her commentary by noting that Eisenhower's paintings are not profound works, but they are not without positive appeal and charm. He did not paint them for posterity, nor was he concerned with attaining economic security or public acclaim for his daubs. Sometimes the ability of a painter is overlooked in the preeminence of the man. She believed that Dwight D. Eisenhower could not possibly have spent a lifetime of abandon in painting intimate and charming genre scenes. He developed a style to correspond with his interests and needs. It served his purposes admirably.

Although he may have possessed more talent than most amateur artists, it was good that "Ike van Gogh" viewed painting as merely a relaxing hobby and focused his primary efforts on being a world leader and providing his nation with eight years of peace and prosperity.

That said, I do believe most of us would be very pleased to have an original DDE-signed oil painting hanging on our wall.

CHAPTER FOURTEEN

IKE AND THE ATOMIC BOMB
A STEADY HAND

"Science seems ready to confer on us, as its final gift, the power to erase human life from the planet."[1]
—*Dwight D. Eisenhower, Inaugural Address 1953*

Upon examination, Dwight D. Eisenhower appeared to be quite inconsistent in his view of nuclear weapons. Consider the following chronological saga. Near the end of World War II in July 1945, General Eisenhower first learned of the existence of the top secret atomic bomb that had been developed by the Truman administration. His initial reaction was shock that the US could contemplate using such a weapon of mass destruction against Japan near the war's end. Yet, a few years later, as he entered the White House as president, Ike had concluded he must declare nuclear weapons as just another arrow in the quiver of the US arsenal.

In his first weeks in office in 1953, the new commander in chief used the not-so-subtle threat of employing atomic weapons to successfully bring a quick armistice to the Korean War, which had been dragging on for over three years. But in April 1953, six weeks after Joseph Stalin died, Eisenhower sent an olive branch to the new leaders of the Soviet Union in the form of a public speech despairing of the arms race as "humanity hanging from a cross of iron."

Two months later he declined to grant clemency to Julius and Ethel Rosenberg and the two spies were executed for passing atomic secrets to the USSR. Surprisingly, Ike's personal abhorrence of the nuclear bomb did not prevent him from implementing the Eisenhower administration's "New Look" defense policy, which moved away from large ground forces and relied instead on massive retaliation with nuclear weapons to deter America's enemies. During his eight years in the White House, he grew the US nuclear arsenal to record size. Yet Eisenhower's biggest disappointment upon leaving the White House was his failure to achieve a disarmament treaty with the Soviet Union. What gives with this apparent paradox regarding Ike and nuclear weapons?

In his World War II memoir, *Crusade in Europe*, Eisenhower describes a conversation with Secretary of War Henry Stimson during the Potsdam Conference in July 1945. It was here, in postwar Germany where cities lay in ruins, that Ike first learned of the existence of his country's new, top secret weapon of mass destruction. The test of the first atomic bomb occurred on July 16, the day before the conference began. General Eisenhower was surprised and even startled to learn about the weapon.

> I expressed hope that we would never have to use such a thing against any enemy because I disliked seeing the United States take the lead in introducing into war something as horrible and destructive as this new weapon was described to be. . . . In an instant many of the old concepts of war were swept away. Henceforth, it would seem, the purpose of an aggressor nation would be to stock atom bombs in quantity and to employee them by surprise against the industrial fabric and population centers of its intended victim. . . . Even the bombed ruins of Germany suddenly seemed to provide but faint warning of what future war could mean to the people of the earth.[2]

Fifteen years later in his presidential memoir, *Mandate for Change*, a now post-presidency Eisenhower doubled down on his statement of misgivings about use of the atomic bomb. He gave more detail of his memory of the Potsdam Conference conversation with Secretary of War Stimson, writing that he had advised against use of the weapon since Japan was on the verge of surrendering as soon as they could do so with a minimum of losing face. Ike said he felt use of the atomic bomb was no longer mandatory as a measure to save American lives. Eisenhower went as far as to say Stimson was "deeply perturbed by my attitude, almost angrily refuting the reasons I gave for my quick conclusions."[3]

In 1965, former President Eisenhower corresponded with John J. McCloy, who had served as undersecretary of war during World War II. Ike once again expressed his rationale for doubting the necessity of dropping the atomic bomb on Japan. He reiterated his previous argument that "Japan was already licked" and went further in saying that Secretary of War Stimson was under the influence of military sources who figured the US would lose one million men in an invasion of the Japanese islands. Eisenhower told McCloy, "I, of course, thought this a tremendous error in calculation." Ike went on to add that Stimson "got very impatient and I was glad to change the subject."[4]

There was a very interesting ten-page article published in 1987 by

Barton J. Bernstein, a professor of history at Stanford University, entitled "Ike and Hiroshima: Did He Oppose It?" Bernstein is a scholar of the Cold War and the history of nuclear weapons. His conclusion was that a close examination of the evidence (which included research in Ike's own papers at the Eisenhower Presidential Library) raised doubts in Bernstein's mind about whether General Eisenhower challenged the intention to use the bomb, as has now been accepted as fact in historical accounts. The professor cites circumstantial evidence from Stimson's diary and assessments from contemporaries that Ike's version of the conversation never occurred.[5]

As part of his research, Bernstein also quotes a letter he received from the president's son John Eisenhower, sharing his memory of a July 1945 conversation with his father about the atomic bomb. John was with his father in Germany during this time and said Ike was depressed primarily by the mere fact that the bomb had been invented. Ike told his son, "War is horrible enough with the weapons we've got, why the hell make it worse?" What seemed to strike the general most was the fact a single atomic bomb in the hands of the enemy could have destroyed the entire Normandy beachhead.[6]

Bernstein sought a rationale for Eisenhower the war hero going on the record in his two memoirs about his strong reservations concerning the dropping of the atomic bomb on Japan. After all, as chairman of the joint chiefs, and later as president, Ike oversaw the tremendous growth of America's nuclear arsenal during the early Cold War. His role looms large in bringing America into the nuclear age. Speculating about Eisenhower's motives, Professor Bernstein wrote, "In this context, his claims about pre-Hiroshima moral objections might salve his own conscience."[7] In fairness to Ike, he was the first to state that morality played a major role in his decisions regarding national security during the Cold War.

Ike's had a revealing one-on-one conversation in February 1950 in his office at Columbia University that sheds more light on his views. Eisenhower was the newly appointed president of Columbia University and had just completed service as chairman of the joint chiefs of staff, overseeing the growing role of nuclear weapons in the US armed forces. Eisenhower's visitor was Clarence William (C. W.) Boyer (1899–1988), who was on the General Sunday School Board of the Brethren in Christ Church. Boyer was a pacifist exploring the challenging issue of war in the new era of atomic weapons. He had visited Albert Einstein a couple of years earlier and was obviously continuing his examination of the views held by important people on war in general and atomic weapons in particular. Fortunately for history, the Eisenhower-Boyer conversation at Columbia was recorded by Ike's office taping system.[8]

In the seven-minute conversation, Eisenhower states he does not believe atomic power is the greatest element in the current unsolvable dilemma facing mankind. While, in Ike's words, atomic power is "a new and terrifying way of destroying gobs of people," he pointed out to Boyer that there has always been the power to destroy people. Eisenhower made the point that whoever invented the automobile created a way to kill 40,000 Americans every year. But Ike did acknowledge that the atomic bomb had captured our imagination as a weapon that can kill many people at one time. In the recording, Ike told Boyer that the weapon was not the critical point in our equation. Rather, there needed to be some understanding of the human soul that had to be incorporated into your "X." Putting it bluntly, Ike said we need "some realization that a divine power has got to give us a little more brains than we are exercising today or we are in a hell of a fix." The conversation continued about war in general. "You have no assurance in a war that the right side wins the war. Therefore, it's stupid to keep going." Then Ike admonished his visitor, "But don't for one minute believe that my philosophy will incorporate a completely pacifistic approach. I just can't see that."

Eisenhower then began quoting from the Bible to Mr. Boyer. He made the point of telling his Brethren in Christ guest, "By the way, I'm one of the few people who has read the Bible from cover to cover." Ike noted that while Christ did indeed admonish Peter for cutting off the ear of the soldier with his sword, he also told his disciples, "When a strong man armed keepeth his palace, his goods are in peace" (Luke 11:21). Eisenhower added for good measure, "Now personally, I believe that. I don't think it needs any explaining that the Lord knew exactly what he was saying." The general then ended the conversation by saying:

Now imagine that I am an inspired person who can do something in promoting respectful devotion to a deterrent. And then a perfectly senseless, stupid person comes along with a poison spear and is about to strike me. Well, should I shoot him or shouldn't I? I say I should. I don't believe in my mind that you can make much progress disassociating the instinctive reactions from a moral code, which is not in this case called Christianity. Now what you've got to do is show that they do go together. And if they don't, then there's something wrong. Well, this is interesting, but I must get back to work.

Three years after this conversation, the president of Columbia University found himself taking the oath of office as president of the United States. On January 20, 1953, in his inaugural address he asked the crowd gathered below the Capitol steps, "How far have we come in man's long pilgrimage from darkness toward the light?" He worried that the shadows of another night were closing in upon the world. This was no doubt a reference to the threat of communism, but also the growing nuclear dilemma he would face as commander in chief. In addition to all the good that modern technology had brought civilization, Ike feared that science seemed ready to confer upon the world, as its final gift, the power to erase human life from the planet. Mankind's power to achieve good or to inflict evil seemed to Ike to surpass the brightest hopes or sharpest fears of all previous ages. Eisenhower's solution for the nation (in addition to putting him at the helm) was a moral one. Americans must have "a conscious renewal of faith in our country and in the watchfulness of a Divine Providence."[9]

Sitting in the Oval Office on his first day as president, Eisenhower immediately faced a big moral decision involving the atomic bomb. His predecessor in the White House was noted for the sign on his desk that touted "The Buck Stops Here," but in one famous case, President Harry Truman definitely passed the responsibility to Ike. Julius and Ethel Rosenberg had been convicted in March 1951 of espionage and were sentenced to death. The Truman Administration received their petition for executive clemency on January 10, 1953, ten days before leaving the White House, but declined to make the decision. Thus, the question of whether the spy couple should serve life in prison rather than be executed was on Ike's desk when he arrived in the office on the morning of January 21.

The Rosenbergs had secretly passed classified drawings and information about the US atomic bomb development program to the Soviets during the mid-1940s. Americans were shocked and dismayed when the USSR successfully tested its first atomic bomb in 1949. Suddenly, the US nuclear monopoly was over, and the tensions of the cold war were dramatically elevated. Two years later, Julius and Ethel Rosenberg became the first Americans sentenced to death for espionage in peacetime.

Ike faced considerable public pressure on this commutation issue. The communist press screamed that the US had convicted the Rosenbergs because they were Jewish. Some argued the death sentence was too severe, considering others in the spy case who had been found guilty were only sentenced to prison terms. Many also sincerely believed that life imprisonment might be a better judgment because the Rosenbergs were the parents of two young boys and because one of the condemned was a woman.[10]

On February 11, just three weeks after assuming office, President Eisenhower made his decision. He said that after careful examination, there was neither any new evidence nor mitigating circumstances that should alter the original sentencing decision of the court. Clemency would be denied. The White House released a statement:

> The nature of the crime for which they have been found guilty and sentenced far exceeds that of the taking of the life of another citizen; it involves the deliberate betrayal of the entire nation and could very well result in the death of many, many thousands of innocent citizens. By their act these two individuals have in fact betrayed the cause of freedom for which free men are fighting and dying at this very hour.[11]

On June 19, the Supreme Court vacated a stay of execution. That night, there were communist and anti-communist demonstrations up and down Pennsylvania Avenue in front of the White House while the sentence of the court was duly executed. Ike wrote son John in Korea about his Rosenberg decision, saying it "went against the grain to avoid interfering in the case where a woman is to receive capital punishment." But the president argued there was another aspect of the case that was important to consider. First, it was Ethel Rosenberg who was the stronger and recalcitrant one of the two and who had obviously been the leader of everything the couple did in the spy ring. Secondly, Ike maintained that if there had been any commuting of the woman's sentence, without the man's also being commuted, "then from here on the Soviets would simply recruit their spies from among women." In addition, he argued, the Rosenbergs by their actions had exposed to greater danger of death literally millions of Americans. A just government must serve the interests of all its citizens.[12] The action of these spies led directly to an end of the US monopoly on atomic weapons and made the world a more dangerous place.

At a White House press conference on February 25, 1953, just two weeks after Eisenhower's decision on the Rosenberg's commutation, the president was asked if he was willing to meet with the Soviet premier.

Joseph Stalin had been quoted a few weeks earlier saying he would look favorably on a face-to-face meeting with the American president. Ike's response was, "I would meet anybody, anywhere, where I thought there was the slightest chance of doing any good, as long as it was in keeping with what the American people expect of their chief Executive." The question soon became academic as Stalin died ten days later.[13]

Eisenhower understood that the new leadership in the Soviet Union, no matter how strong its link with the Stalin era, was not automatically bound to follow the policy dictates of the dead leader who had been in power for thirty years. There was some hope for a slow move toward mutual trust between the two adversary nations, especially in reducing the burden of armaments on both countries and the entire world during these early years of the Cold War. There was indeed a "Chance for Peace," which became the title of his address delivered before the American Society of Newspaper Editors on April 16, 1953, just five weeks after the death of Stalin. In "Chance for Peace," Ike extended an offer and a promise to the new Soviet hierarchy. The alternative was a continuation of the threat of atomic war and an ongoing arms race that was draining the wealth of all peoples.[14]

In "Chance for Peace," Eisenhower gave the world eloquent examples of the true wastefulness for mankind of the arms race. The cost of one heavy bomber was not having a new schoolhouse in thirty cities or two fully equipped hospitals. We traded new homes for more than 8,000 people for a new destroyer. We were paying half a million bushels of wheat for a single fighter jet. In the most famous lines from the speech, Ike said, "This is not a way of life at all, in any true sense. Under the cloud of threatening war, it is humanity hanging from a cross of iron." He asked the rhetorical question, "Is there no other way the world may live?" Eisenhower was convinced that the hunger for peace lay in all men's hearts.[15] Unfortunately, the answer from the USSR was deafening silence.

During this same time, the Korean War armistice negotiations were dragging on without an end in sight. There was still heavy fighting involving US troops, including the famous Battle of Pork Chop Hill. In President Eisenhower's mind, the stalemate demanded definitive action "to put an end to these intolerable conditions." One action was to let communist leaders know that the US intended to move decisively to end the war without inhibition in the use of weapons, including atomic weapons.[16] The joint chiefs of staff produced a war plan calling for a massive bombing campaign, including hundreds of atomic bombs, against China as well as

North Korea. Ike had reached the point of being convinced that the atomic bomb had to be considered simply another weapon in the US arsenal. One of his articles of faith was that war was ever-changing and surprising when it came to weaponry, and that a country that relied on old technology and tactics did so at their own peril.[17] In his diary, he recorded the advice he had given his "friends" in the Pentagon: "An appeal to force, cannot by its nature, be a partial one. The appeal having been made, for God's sake, get ready! . . . We must study every angle to be prepared for whatever may happen, even if it finally came to the use of an A-Bomb (which God forbid!)."[18]

The essence of effective deterrence is to never let on that you are not willing to use your ultimate weapon. Dean Acheson had told President Kennedy this during the 1961 Berlin Wall crisis. Ike already embodied this precept. During World War II, General Eisenhower had repeatedly demonstrated his willingness to use the maximum force available to help guarantee success in every battle. His adversaries in North Korea and China were aware of this history. Fortunately, the communists accepted the US/UN peace terms in Korea just a few days after the National Security Council (NSC) had approved the war plan. We may never know whether Eisenhower was being totally forthright in his professed willingness to use atomic weapons. But when his White House Chief of Staff Sherman Adams later asked how he had achieved the armistice, the president responded instantly, "Danger of an atomic war."[19]

In early April 1953, after it was apparent the olive branch extended in the "Chance for Peace" speech was ignored by the Soviets, President Eisenhower decided to have his national security team design a program to provide a "reality check" to the American people about the atomic dilemma facing the nation. He once observed succinctly that in case of nuclear war with the Soviet Union, "You might as well go out and shoot everyone you see and then shoot yourself."[20] Ike believed the public did not fully grasp the fact they were living in an age of great peril. Thus was born Project Candor.

The initial plan was a series of fifteen-minute nationwide radio and TV talks by the president or other administration officials on several issues, such as the communist threat and the military capabilities of the USSR.[21] C. D. Jackson, Eisenhower's advisor on psychological warfare issues, had overseen the preparation of several drafts of speeches and draft plans for Project Candor, but Jackson and the president eventually agreed that the public relations campaign would leave the listener with only a new terror, not a new hope. A different approach was necessary.[22] Another important reason; on August 12, the Soviets exploded their first hydrogen bomb and, with that, joined the US in this exclusive nuclear club. The stakes had changed.

After abandoning Project Candor, Ike's next approach found itself in the form of a dramatic proposal Eisenhower made in a speech given at the United Nations on December 8, 1953. It became known as the "Atoms for Peace" address. The proposal was that the two nuclear powers would agree to share a portion of their respective nuclear stockpile with the UN to be used for peaceful purposes around the world.

Eisenhower knew that America led the world in nuclear technology but that it would not last. Soon, so many of the nuclear secrets the US jealously protected would be known throughout the world. Its monopoly on atomic power was a "wasting asset."[23] He was dedicated to participating in disarmament talks with the Soviets. But in his "Atoms for Peace" speech before the General Assembly of the United Nations in December 1953, Ike said more action was vital. "It is not enough to take this weapon out of the hands of the soldiers. It must be put into the hands of those who will know how to strip its military casing and adapt it to the arts of peace."[24]

Ike noted in his diary fourfold reasons for his message to the Soviets and the entire world in "Atoms for Peace." First, and the principal reason, was a clear effort to get the Soviet Union to work with the US in some manner that had peace and the good of mankind as a goal. The president felt that even the tiniest of starts might expand into something broader. He hoped that Soviet self-interest would eventually win them over to participating in some kind of joint humanitarian effort.

Secondly, Ike was hoping to make the "smaller nations" aware that they were, in essence, supplying the two atomic powers with the raw materials necessary to make the bomb. Perhaps these countries would be convinced to see the wisdom of new and promising opportunities to use these materials and skills to the benefit, rather than to the destruction of mankind.

Third, even if the USSR decided to cooperate minimally with the "Atoms for Peace" proposal for only "propaganda purposes," the United States could afford to reduce its atomic stockpile two or three times more than the Soviets might contribute to the United Nations. The always calculating Ike knew that the American advantage in numbers of atomic weapons meant that any modest reduction by the USSR would still improve the US position in the Cold War and even in the event of an outbreak of a hot war. America could not lose.

Finally, the speech provided the opportunity to inform American citizens and the world about the very considerable size and strength advantage of US nuclear capabilities vis-à-vis the USSR, while doing it in a manner that argued for peaceful negotiations rather than as a threat to the Soviets. In the dark shadow of the atomic bomb, the United States did not wish merely to present strength by promoting its overwhelming numerical advantage over the Soviets, Ike wrote in his diary, but also demonstrate a sincere desire and hope for peace.[25]

Eisenhower was sensitive to maintaining this drive for peace throughout his presidency. In 1956, three years after the "Atoms for Peace" speech, he shared with senior Pentagon officials that he personally would like to watch a test firing of the new Nike missile but felt unable to do so because of the need to give "psychological support" to peaceful rather than military things.[26]

Eisenhower wrote in his diary that "underlying all of this, of course, is the clear conviction that as of now the world is racing toward catastrophe—that something must be done to slow down this movement." He was the first US president confronted with the reality of a world where two enemies faced off with weapons that could destroy civilization. One historian said Ike was the first man in history to make real the mythical power of a god. And because of his upbringing, he made most decisions, thank goodness, by weighing the moral dimension from all sides.[27]

Ike was also a realist, knowing that the words in his "Atoms for Peace" speech—no matter how eloquent or sincere they may have been—would not apply brakes on this race toward the destruction of mankind. However, he believed that if people in America, the Soviet Union, and around the world heard the warning and began thinking along these lines, there was at least hope of devising ways and means by which the possible nuclear disaster of the future could be avoided.[28] It was predictable that the USSR would balk at Eisenhower's proposal of donating nuclear material to the United Nations. Nevertheless, a tangible result of "Atoms for Peace" was the eventual establishment in 1957 of the International Atomic Energy Agency (IAEA). The IAEA operates to this day within the United Nations system, promoting peaceful use of nuclear energy around the globe.

Ike's proposal concerning the peaceful use of atomic energy received favorable comment in the press initially, but after a short time it was out of the news. In a creative move to revive the world's interest in this search for non-military uses of atomic energy, Eisenhower's team devised a plan for a series of international scientific conferences to be held in Geneva, where technical information could be discussed and exchanged in an open atmosphere. Dr. Isidor I. Rabi was Ike's leader in organizing this effort. Professor Rabi was a renown physicist at Columbia University and served on the advisory committee of the Atomic Energy Commission. The initial reaction to the proposal was lukewarm among scientists in the US and Europe. As Rabi later explained: "There was a hopeless feeling that the conference could not succeed, that it would be regarded as a propaganda stunt, that the Soviets would not join, that the papers presented at the conference would be of inferior quality because of atomic secrecy, and that, in general, more harm than good would come of it."[29]

Because of the persistence and persuasion of the conference organizers, most of those world nations initially indifferent about participating in the "Atoms for Peace" gathering were won over by the attractive list of subjects to be covered. There were a variety of topics but they centered around one principal problem: how to use the vast source of energy latent in the nucleus of the atom more productively to the benefit of mankind.[30]

After the first conference in 1955, scientists were very impressed with the contributions of the Soviet delegates. Dr. Rabi noted that while the US demonstrated to the world the strength and rigor of American scientific study, at the same time the scientific world learned something about the Soviet scientists and became impressed with their education and the extent of their abilities. The two conferences demonstrated that science and technology in the USSR had achieved maturity and independence. Also critically important was the major effort by the US to reduce a great deal of the security classification surrounding information about nuclear power. There was a sincere effort by the Eisenhower administration to declassify technical data and promote awareness of the peaceful benefits of nuclear energy with the world.[31]

One "Atoms for Peace" program with truly lasting implications was the American program to share data with the world concerning the production of power from controlled thermonuclear or fusion reactors. In 1958 the US began to sign agreements to assist individual countries with their development of nuclear power plants, and within five years, thirty-seven of these "peaceful bilaterals" had been arranged.[32] The World Nuclear Association (located in England and Wales) reported that of as of the year 2024 there were 440 nuclear power reactors operating in thirty-two countries, with more in the planning stage. These plants were estimated to provide 10 percent of the world's electricity.[33]

Eisenhower's peace initiative to confront the great atomic dilemma

The "Atoms for Peace" postage stamp was issued in 1955 as part of the Eisenhower administration's all-of-government effort to promote awareness of Ike's historic offer to share the peaceful use of atomic energy with the entire world. (Courtesy Eisenhower Library)

paid dividends according to Dr. Rabi. In a 1960 speech he said, "I feel that we have made a dent in the cold war, a dent which has been exploited in favor of the reduction of tensions to a more bearable level."[34] And Ike's focus on promoting the non-military uses of nuclear power had a lasting impact beyond his presidential administration. By 1967, the chairman of the Atomic Energy Commission under President Lyndon Johnson asserted proudly that over half of his agency's $2 billion budget was allocated to the peaceful atom. "Atoms for Peace" was alive and well.[35]

Since the end of World War II there had emerged a "nuclear taboo" of sorts regarding nuclear weapons. There seemed to be a growing moral consensus prohibiting their use in the aftermath of Hiroshima and Nagasaki, largely because of the inevitable massive civilian casualties. This development is outlined very well in Dr. Nina Tannenwald's book *The Nuclear Taboo: The United States and the Non-Use of Nuclear Weapons Since 1945*, published in 2007. Tannenwald notes, however, that the special status that encouraged political leaders to view them as weapons of last resort did not automatically carry over from the Truman to the Eisenhower administration in 1953. Already during his time in the Pentagon, prior to entering the White House, Eisenhower's thinking on nuclear weapons had evolved to the point that he personally viewed smaller, tactical nuclear bombs as a part of the general arsenal that could quite properly be used in time of war against troop concentrations or hardened targets.[36] The nuclear taboo, while an unwelcome constraint, did not prevent the Eisenhower administration from implementing a defense strategy that relied heavily on nuclear deterrence.[37] This was Ike's New Look strategy, and it in fact employed the concept of "massive retaliation" whereby any first strike on US soil by an enemy would result in an overwhelming nuclear counterstrike, making the foe realize their county would lie in ruins as a result. While Eisenhower's New Look continued the Truman administration policy of "containment" of the Soviet Union, Ike carried it out with a large nuclear arsenal rather than a massive buildup of more costly conventional forces. The frugal Ike believed that the potential bankruptcy of America with an oversized Pentagon personnel budget presented as much a threat to national security as the Soviet Union.[38]

To Ike, his budgetary reasoning behind the New Look policy was paramount. He gave a nationwide radio address in May 1953, just four months after entering office, on the issue of national security and its costs. The president told his fellow countrymen there was no such thing as "maximum military security" unless a nation was willing to mobilize all its national resources. To achieve such an unrealistic goal, America would have to put every able-bodied man in uniform and regiment all civilian workers, farmers, and businessmen. Price controls would need to be reinstated, as they were in wartime. In essence the whole nation would become a garrison state. Eisenhower said such grim measures "would compel us to imitate the methods of the dictator."

In his radio address, Ike informed the citizenry that he and his associates had studied and analyzed national security needs, and he assured his listeners that his administration had arrived at a sound and prudent program to protect the nation without bankrupting it. It was not a magical formula, but he promised it was the best that competent men could devise. US nuclear deterrence was going to be strong enough to deter aggression. Beyond that, the military would maintain sufficient conventional forces to protect the nation in the event of any attack, while the nation moved quickly to full mobilization. The New Look military strategy, with its reliance on nuclear deterrence, would not require the funding of a massive army and navy.[39] An aptly coined phrase by Defense Secretary Charles E. Wilson described the Eisenhower administration strategy as "a Bigger Bang for the Buck."[40]

Toward the end of his time in the White House, Eisenhower viewed US national security policy as having stern resolve and a forceful argument regarding the use of nuclear weapons. It was in essence all or nothing—either effective deterrence or death. As he told his NSC in January 1959, if the Russians start a war, "we will finish it." A major war between the Soviet Union and United States would devastate both nations. The hope was the threat of this reality would keep the enemy at bay. Eisenhower's son John told one biographer, "It was a terrible gamble, but Ike was a terrific poker player."[41]

During his years in the White House, Eisenhower rebuffed the call for ever-increasing military spending from each branch of service. He told his chiefs of staff that American strength was a combination of economic, moral, and military force. The armed services were established to defend a way of life, and they needed to find the balance between the minimum requirements in the costly implements of war and the health of the US economy. In 1956, Ike wrote his boyhood friend Swede Hazlett a letter expressing his worry about the future:

> But some day there is going to be a man sitting in my present chair who has not been raised in the military services and who will have little understanding of where slashes in their estimates can be made with little or no damage. If that should happen while we still have the state of tension that now exists in the world, I shudder to think of what could happen to this country.[42]

According to one historian, Eisenhower's keenest insight was that the arms race with the USSR was less about weapons and more a contest between two very different economic and political systems. Dr. Alex Roland, professor emeritus of history at Duke University, said the old general did not believe the Cold War would become a shooting war. The real conflict was not one of weaponry. "We would win the war against a garrison state if we did not become a garrison state ourselves."[43]

It seems Eisenhower agreed with Dr. Roland, at least in part. In May 1953, Ike himself had written his long-time military colleague General Al Guenther, "Our organized resistance must be maintained over a long period of years and that this is only possible with a healthy American economy."[44] In his presidential memoir *Mandate for Change*, Eisenhower pointed out that national security could not be measured in terms of military strength alone. To him, the relationship between military and economic strength was "intimate and indivisible."[45]

In the era of "nuclear taboo" against the use of such weapons, a strategy of massive nuclear retaliation was a deterrence perhaps only the five-star general and war hero Eisenhower could make credible. In war, General Ike had consistently demonstrated his willingness to use overwhelming force to meet any enemy. In a 1955 press conference, President Eisenhower said, "Nobody in war or anywhere else, made a good decision if he was frightened to death. You have to look facts in the face, but you have to have the stamina to do it without just going hysterical. That's what you are really trying to do in this business."[46] For Ike, "this business" was defending his nation against foreign adversaries and making the difficult decisions without hesitation.

In the Oval Office, President Eisenhower told General Maxwell Taylor and Admiral Radford that his emphasis on atomic weapons gave the US its greatest safety and security. The memorandum documenting the meeting went on the say that Ike "did not claim to be all wise in such matters, but he was very sure that as long as he is President, he would meet an attack in the way indicated."[47] There was little doubt that, if the US underwent a surprise attack, Eisenhower would retaliate with an annihilating nuclear counterstrike. And that was enough to keep the Soviet Union at bay.

Susan Eisenhower, Ike's granddaughter, once asked her father about President Eisenhower's most important assumption regarding the nuclear policy of the Soviet Union. John S. D. Eisenhower had served in his father's administration as an aide on top-level security matters. John told Susan that Ike's view was that the leaders of the USSR had one objective: to survive and retain their power. "The Soviet elite are not early Christian martyrs." They knew the total destructive nature of nuclear weapons and were not likely to engage the US in a first strike and risk their annihilation and loss of their own power. For Eisenhower, a related important consideration was avoiding small regional wars that might draw the Soviets in. If a war were underway and the USSR was losing, all bets were off on their use of nuclear weapons.[48]

Critics of the Eisenhower's New Look policy believed America was in danger of falling behind the Soviets in development of conventional weapons such as aircraft, tanks, missiles, and other sophisticated military technologies. Fortunately, Ike's experience as Supreme Allied Commander in war and chairman of the joint chiefs of staff in postwar times gave the old general an insight into the insatiable appetite of the military-industrial complex, about which he would later warn the nation in his presidential farewell address.

In addition to this healthy skepticism about the actual needs of the military, Eisenhower had another secret weapon he relied upon during the Cold War: the Central Intelligence Agency (CIA). One CIA historian has stated that no president before or since has so heavily relied on the National Intelligence Estimates and overhead reconnaissance provided by the U-2 spy plane. Intelligence resources gave Ike reasonable confidence he could predict the threat of a Soviet attack in time to craft a non-military response, or—worst-case scenario—fashion a US response that would not escalate into nuclear conflict.[49] He also was not reluctant to use CIA covert operations against overseas adversaries.

In John S. D. Eisenhower's eulogy for his father in 1969, he very fittingly reminded America of how fortunate the nation was to have had President Eisenhower in the White House during these dangerous Cold War years. We had a leader who would indeed have used atomic weapons as a last resort to defend the nation. Of that there can be little doubt. But the blessing was that because of Ike's unmatched credibility on the world stage, this decision never proved necessary. As John said of his father, "He was the vaunted warrior who hated war. He was nearly indispensable. The people of the United States were lucky during the 1950s to have Good Soldier Ike in control of our nuclear arsenal."

As a closing footnote, buried in Ike's post-presidential files among the twenty-six million pages of documentation at the Eisenhower Presidential Library is a handwritten document, dated May 18, 1965, with several of the retired president's personal predictions for future years 2000 and 2020. It includes an echo of the hope brought about by the "Atoms for Peace" initiative. One salient prediction captured the retired president's optimism regarding the long-term legacy of the splitting of the atom. As commander in chief, Eisenhower had indeed carried the heavy burden of guarding America against the threat of nuclear war, but his projection was that in the distant future of the twenty-first century, energy would become plentiful in America because of the "success in the economical use of atomic fuel."[50]

In recent years, nuclear plants have provided around 20 percent of US energy needs. This is a considerable amount, but one wonders whether President Eisenhower would be disappointed that the number was not higher. We can well imagine he would have worked hard, if still in office, to overcome the reservations about nuclear energy held by much of America's citizenry in the aftermath of the accidents at Three Mile Island (1978), Chernobyl (1986), and Fukushima (2011). But alas, to use Ike's own words, perhaps 20 percent is, after all, a "plentiful" amount provided by the peaceful atom.

What we can say about the legacy of Dwight D. Eisenhower is that he was the vaunted warrior who kept the US, and in fact the entire world, safe from nuclear war. Ike also initiated the national conversation regarding the role of nuclear science and technology in American society. He was indeed a founding father of the "Great Nuclear Debate," and his "Atoms for Peace" speech was its Declaration of Independence.[51]

CHAPTER FIFTEEN

MOVE OVER RICHARD NIXON!

"Eisenhower was far more complex and devious than most Americans realized."
—*Richard M. Nixon*, Six Crises, *1962*

Somewhere, former President Richard Milhouse Nixon had to be feeling relieved and be smiling upon the discovery there were secret Eisenhower Oval Office recordings among the historic holdings in Ike's presidential library. Nixon's name has been long synonymous with the practice of surreptitiously recording conversations in the Oval Office. What are we to make of Dwight D. Eisenhower now that he is guilty of the same sin?

Truth be told, the archivists at the Eisenhower Library over the years had seen very detailed Oval Office meeting notes prepared by Ike's personal secretary, which sometimes included lengthy verbatim quotes from those in attendance. Ann Whitman was a fantastic executive secretary, but it seemed highly unlikely her skill at taking dictation was that good. Ann admits in her biography that shorthand note-taking was not her forte.[1] Ergo, a recording system of some type was always somehow indicated, even if no existing tapes could be found. In fact, Ann Whitman occasionally referred to a recording system in the written summaries of meetings she prepared at the time. It was usually to complain about the quality of the recordings and the extremely cumbersome job of verbatim transcription. There was also the difficulty of understanding muffled conversations. Some examples from her notes:

October 21, 1953—Cong. John Taber (NY)
Note: Large portions of the tape were completely garbled. The noise of the machine itself is so great that the words, while loud enough, cannot be understood

Saturday, November 7, 1953—9:00 a.m. appointment with Secretary of Commerce
First time any adequate use of "gadget" for recording conversations made. It is now fine and a complete verbatim report of the conversation could be made—but the work! Anyhow here are the highlights of this

conversation (apparently the President did not turn his switch until conversation was underway).

May 29, 1954—Haile Selassie, Emperor of Ethiopia

It was impossible to understand the conversation and words of any of the Ethiopians.

While the Eisenhower Library staff had seen indication of some sort of taping system over the years, it could not be confirmed. In the fall of 1979, news of an Eisenhower White House recording system was made public by historian Francis Loewenheim of Rice University. While doing research at the Eisenhower Presidential Library, Professor Loewenheim had come across these same verbatim transcripts of Oval Office conversations that pointed to the existence of such a system. He published a series of articles in the *Houston Chronicle* newspaper during November 1979 that included excerpts of the transcribed texts. Loewenheim speculated that Ike selectively recorded meetings with no apparent pattern, but probably ones the president regarded as covering politically or potentially sensitive issues. The archivists at the Eisenhower Library had previously identified twenty-five documents in the Ann C. Whitman Diary Series that were clearly transcripts of recorded conversation and approximately fifty other "memcons" (memoranda of conversations) that included verbatim quotes and could possibly be partial transcripts from recorded conversations. But still no tapes were to be found.[2] Even after the Loewenheim article series appeared in the Houston newspaper, there was no groundswell of interest in this issue by the public, the media, or historians.

Almost two decades later, in the summer of 1996, another researcher finally followed up on this story. William Doyle visited the Eisenhower Library in research for his book *Inside the Oval Office: The White House Tapes from FDR to Clinton*, which was published in 1999. Doyle pursued a new theory. Rather than tapes, he surmised the recordings might have been done on a Dictaphone machine. Doyle's suspicion in this regard stemmed from an article in *Time* magazine's international edition in 1982, in which renowned journalist Hugh Sidey reported that, before he was president, General Eisenhower had used Dictaphone equipment to record conversations while serving as Supreme Allied Commander at NATO and as president of Columbia University. Sidey received this tip from a retired Dictaphone technician who had done the equipment installation work in both New York City and at NATO headquarters in Paris.[3]

In response to Doyle's request, Eisenhower Library archivists conducted an exhaustive search of the archives, not for tapes or discs, but this time for Dictabelts relating to the conversations in question. Ten Dictabelts suspected of being tied to Oval Office conversations were eventually found in the library's massive audiovisual archives holdings, where they had sat in the downstairs stack area, unnoticed for two decades. Why did it take the Eisenhower Presidential Library such a long time to discover the existence of tapes? Well, first, because there were no tapes.

Unbeknownst to the staff, the recording medium for Ike's Oval Office recordings indeed turned out to be Dictabelts. Belts of this type were normally used for letter dictation and over three hundred other Dictabelts had been found previously in the archives, filed among the twenty-six million pages of manuscript documents in the Eisenhower Library. It was logical to assume these latest ten were also from dictation that resulted in a typed finished letter or report, for which the flattened Dictabelt was then filed in the same folder with the resulting paper copy. This was common practice. To cite another example, there are in the post-presidential papers at the library many Dictabelts containing Eisenhower's own dictation for his book *At Ease*, written during his retirement years in Gettysburg.

When the Ann Whitman Files were originally reviewed by the archives staff and opened for research in 1977, ten flattened belts were found stuffed in envelopes among the files. Archivists logically assumed the belts must contain letter or memo dictation by Eisenhower and they were routinely transferred to custody of the audiovisual section of the library, as were any Dictabelts, photographs, and other non-paper media. Because they were found in the Ann Whitman papers (the president's most important files), the Dictabelts were kept in the library's security vault as a precaution, since they could possibly cover a topic that included sensitive national security information. (Members of the archives staff had top secret security clearances.) The staff believed the flattened and creased belts were damaged and unplayable and, in any event, the library did not have the antiquated equipment necessary to listen to the belts.

Dictaphone is a brand name for the state-of-the-art dictating equipment that dates from 1910. The original Dictaphone equipment used a wax cylinder to record, but starting in 1947 a vinyl belt was introduced. These upgraded Dictabelts were one-time use, disposable, thin 5-mil vinyl belts that are three and one-half inches wide and twelve inches around. The Eisenhower era, 1950s Dictaphone machine is now a true museum relic and, unfortunately, the Eisenhower Library does not have one in its equipment inventory.

In March 1953, the White House chief of staff office asked the US Army's White House Signal Detachment (WHSD) about the possibility of installing a recording device for President Eisenhower in the Oval Office.[4] The signal detachment had been created by FDR in 1942 to provide both routine and secret communications in support of the president. This included everything from mobile radio, teletype, telegraph, telephone, and encoded messages.

In an oral history interview done with Eisenhower's personal secretary in 1991, Ann Whitman said, "They put this monster in my office, and of course, it did not work at all." She added that if the president wanted to tape a meeting, he was supposed to push a button and the red light on Ann's desk would come on. "If he'd forgotten, I'd forgot."[5] According to the signal detachment technician who installed the equipment, the president had the "on button" out of sight, in the knee well of his desk, and he was the person who actually started the recording. When the president began a recording, Ann's red light would warn her that a recording was in progress and alert her to be prepared to change the belts, which only lasted from fifteen to thirty minutes, depending on the recording speed and quality desired. The signal detachment technician also said the microphone was in the receiver of "a dummy telephone" on the president's desk.[6] Since the recording system was secret, Ann said she alone did any transcribing of the recorded conversations. "We didn't want other people to know about it."[7]

Whatever the planned White House procedure may have been, we later learned by listening to one existing recording that the belt had continued to run after the Oval Office meeting adjourned and Ann Whitman can be heard entering the office and trying to demonstrate to the president the proper operation of the Dictabelt machine. Obviously, Ike was a slower learner when it came to the mechanics of secret taping systems.[8]

In any event, in 1996 researcher William Doyle made a formal request to listen to the Dictabelts, the first such request. The library decided it was time to attempt to determine what was on the ten suspect belts. We learned that Dictaphone Corporation had a working version of one of the old machines in their Melbourne, Florida, facility. Shortly thereafter, I had the responsibility to fly to Florida with the precious belts locked in a briefcase sitting on my lap all the way. On February 4–5, 1997, I spent two days at the facility in Melbourne in a closed room, observing the process as their product support engineer, Mr. Peter Meyers, converted the belts to tape for us. The cost of this endeavor was $5,700, which in retrospect was certainly a relatively small price to help preserve unique history.

I was always present as Mr. Meyers made the transfers. This was a precaution as there may have been security classified information discussed on the belts, which were playing out loud for us both to hear during the format conversion. I had a top secret clearance, but my new engineer friend was not cleared. I was to stop the tape and "debrief" Peter if a security violation occurred. That was better than shooting him. Fortunately, that proved not to be necessary. When the conversion process was completed, I made the return trip to Abilene with both the old and new format versions of the recordings in my tightly held briefcase.

Why does the Eisenhower Library have only the ten surviving Dictabelts for five White House conversations, dating from the period January to March 1955? And why were these and all other recorded conversations not transcribed verbatim? I would say first that the transcription process was too much work for a very busy Ann Whitman, and the sound quality was so poor it made the task at times almost impossible. During the eight years of the Eisenhower administration, it appears Ann listened to the recordings and transcribed only twenty-five conversations in whole or in part, and for approximately fifty others she typed up a few direct quotes she felt were important. The Dictabelts were then discarded. Why were the ten surviving Dictabelts not transcribed and tossed as the others were? Perhaps because this was a hectic time at the White House. The State of the Union Address was being prepared, the Formosa Straits Crisis was happening, and the new Interstate Highway program was being introduced to Congress. This was a logical time to discontinue these time-consuming efforts to record and transcribe endless meeting discussions. Hereafter, simple note-taking it would be.

The quality of these recordings was certainly bad, and you could have great pity on Ann Whitman for having the burden of transcribing belts added to her myriad assignments. Anyone with firsthand experience in transcribing and/or editing an oral history interview can relate to the challenge. Count me among them.

When opening the newly discovered material for research, the Eisenhower Library initially planned to provide the now-available cassette tapes of the conversations, along with a complete transcription for each of the ten Dictabelts. I oversaw the project, and we soon realized there was an inherent danger in the "complete transcription" approach. Two listeners may hear different words. We had that experience among our own staff involved in the project. The recording quality was so poor it was necessary to include frequent parenthetical notes in the transcript or summary that said "[unintelligible portion]." Note that this also occurs in normal oral history interviews. In any event, the library did not want to be the final arbiter of interpreting what was said on these unique tapes. After the experience of transcribing the first Dictabelt and releasing the tape and text to the public, we quickly realized that for all subsequent Dictabelts a general summary of the conversations would have to suffice. The poor sound quality of the belts, as well as the tremendous labor time involved, made it too difficult, and we stopped any attempt at full transcriptions. Summaries it would have to be.

Case in point that our decision was correct: shortly after the public release of the first tape in early 1997, I had a telephone call from nationally known television newsman Bob Clark, White House correspondent for ABC News. He was doing a story on the new revelation of Eisenhower's Oval Office taping systems and had recently purchased a copy of the Roy Howard (American newspaperman) conversation tape from our parent agency the National Archives in Washington, DC. Over the phone, Mr. Clark politely, but firmly, wanted to inform me that he disagreed with the Eisenhower Library's version of the transcribed text of the Roy Howard conversation we had released. In our version, we had President Eisenhower saying this about the prime minister of India: "I am not very hopeful about Nehru. I think he is a bastard [unintelligible portion]." Bob Clark said on ABC's better equipment the second sentence was in fact: "I think he [Nehru] is a bastard to talk to." I understandably went back and listened to the tape myself and we were both wrong. My hearing is good, and after replaying it several times, repeatedly, with my headset on, I am very confident I heard Ike say, "I think he [Nehru] is a son of a bitch." Seriously. Take your pick: Bastard or SOB? But the case is closed on why we got out of the transcribing business for these hot potatoes.

But wait, there is more. The Dictabelt recordings saga was not yet over at the Eisenhower Presidential Library. About a year after the ten Oval Office recordings were discovered, there were additional "smoking guns" found. They were lying in the bowels of the archives in the large collection of unprocessed personal papers of Robert Schulz, still waiting for the page-by-page archives staff review before being opened for research. Brigadier General Robert Schulz served as military aide to Eisenhower from

1947 to 1969. A staff archivist beginning the processing review of the 100,000 pages of Schulz papers discovered thirty-eight Dictabelts in one of the collection's 125 boxes. These were recordings of nineteen conversations recorded in 1949 and 1950 in Eisenhower's office while he served as president of Columbia University in New York City. Soon, we were on the phone with our old friend Peter Meyers at Dictaphone Corporation in Melbourne, Florida. This time Peter flew out to Abilene with his equipment and did the conversion from Dictabelt to reel-to-reel tape on-site at the library.

So the question is why did Eisenhower feel compelled to record conversations? He was a self-described farm boy from Kansas and a simple soldier. But, of course, truth be told he had been tested in the political fires of Washington while coming up in the military in the 1920s and 1930s. He spent much of his career working in the War Department for high-profile bosses, such as General Douglas MacArthur. He gained invaluable bureaucratic "combat" experience. Just like President Roosevelt before him, and Nixon and others after him, Ike was acutely aware of the need to sometimes document what was said and by whom in meetings.

There is an oft-quoted statement allegedly made by Ike at a White House cabinet meeting in July 1954. "You know boys, it's a good thing when you're talking to someone you don't trust to get a record made of it. There are some guys I just don't trust in Washington, and I want to have myself protected so that they can't later report that I said something else."[9] While the sentiment expressed by Eisenhower in the quote might have been true, there is no factual documentation in existence in the Eisenhower Library archives to show he said this. Nevertheless, one respected historian included the apocryphal quote in his biography of Eisenhower and other historians have simply repeated it. Thus, it has now entered the Ike lore.

In Eisenhower's case, the practice of recording meetings did not begin during his years in the White House. As we have seen, he recorded office conversations earlier while at Columbia University and at NATO military headquarters (no Dictabelts exist for these Paris conversations). In fact, the practice goes back even further. In *Crusade in Europe*, Ike described a recording system he set up in his War Plans Division office in the Munitions Building in Washington, DC, during 1942:

> Most of the conferences were held in my own office. Out of them were
> developed decisions, many minor but some of great significance. . . . To

insure that none would be forgotten and that records for subordinates would always be available, we had resorted to an automatic recording system that proved most effective. . . . The method was complete wiring of my war room with Dictaphones so placed as to pick up every word uttered in the room. . . . I made it a habit to inform visitors of the system that we used so that each would understand its purpose was merely to facilitate the execution of business.[10]

Historian Evan Thomas interviewed the president's son for his 2012 book, *Ike's Bluff: President Eisenhower's Secret Battle to Save the World.* John S. D. Eisenhower was a former US ambassador, retired brigadier general in the Army Reserve, and well-respected professional historian and author himself. In recalling his famous father, the younger Eisenhower said he had a loving but complicated relationship with his dad. John said there were two sides to Ike, seemingly evenly balanced between open warmth and cold-bloodedness. "He thought for a moment and said, with a slight smile, 'Make that 75 percent cold-blooded.'"[11] In his 1962 memoir, Richard Nixon provided an additional insight. He served eight years as Ike's vice president and noted that Ike was not shackled to a one-track mind. Eisenhower preferred the indirect approach when it would serve him better to solve problems. Nixon went on to say that Eisenhower "was far more complex and devious than most Americans realized"—Ike's former VP then added, "in the best sense of these words."[12]

It seems that Dwight D. Eisenhower may hold the prize for the president who recorded office conversations in the most venues and in the most positions held. As described above, the historic record shows he recorded conversations in the War Department during World War II, at Columbia University while serving as its president, in Paris as Supreme Allied Commander of NATO, and finally at the White House.

What does this mean for history? Some perspective is in order. According to rough calculations, these recordings and the transcripts (or summaries) constitute approximately .000001 percent of the entire twenty-six million pages in the archives of the Dwight D. Eisenhower Presidential Library. That, in a word, is minuscule in terms of volume. Furthermore, in my judgment the actual historical importance of information contained in the small number of tapes/transcripts is negligible. However, I would say these recordings are important for providing an insight into how Ike spoke in these largely one-on-one conversations. What I do know from speaking with many dozens of researchers over my thirty-four years with

the Eisenhower Library and Eisenhower Foundation is that the rich archival holdings in Abilene are often praised by historians and political
scientists for having the best written record of any presidential library for
its historical period. It turns out that Ike's penchant for documenting his
work was truly a historian's dream.

Ironically, evidence of recording systems is one more factor among
many that helps debunk the myth of Eisenhower as an uncomplicated
man who just happened to be elevated to the highest office in the nation
by sheer luck and timing. It is no surprise that Ike served his nation very
well for two decades in war and peace. Scholars of the Eisenhower era
have learned that it is not wise to underestimate Ike.

CHAPTER SIXTEEN

IKE THE CULTURAL WARRIOR
THE ~~EISENHOWER~~ KENNEDY CENTER FOR THE PERFORMING ARTS IN WASHINGTON, DC

"Military drill was a problem . . . For days I was assigned to the Awkward Squad until I could co-ordinate my feet with the beat."
—*Dwight Eisenhower*, At Ease

It is easy to imagine that the magnificent Kennedy Center for the Performing Arts in Washington, DC, might well have been named for Ike. "To neglect the role that Eisenhower played in the (National Cultural) Center's chancy beginnings not only omits a significant item of cultural history but also serves to perpetuate an image of the man that does disservice to his memory." So said Ralph Becker in his masterful history entitled *Miracle on the Potomac: The Kennedy Center from the Beginning*.[1] Becker was appointed by Eisenhower to serve as a founding trustee and general counsel of the National Cultural Center in 1959.

As early as January 1955, Eisenhower discussed the need for a government commission on the arts in his State of the Union message to Congress:

In the advancement of the various activities which will make our civilization endure and flourish, the Federal Government should do more to give official recognition to the importance of the arts and other cultural activities. I shall recommend the establishment of a Federal Advisory Commission on the Arts within the Department of Health, Education and Welfare, to advise the Federal Government on ways to encourage artistic endeavor and appreciation. I shall also propose that awards of merit be established whereby we can honor our fellow citizens who make great contributions to the advancement of our civilization.[2]

Ike also envisaged for Washington a dedicated public building whose architecture would symbolize the nation's desire for international understanding and whose concert halls would provide foreign tourists with a steady display of America's aesthetic sensibilities, a side of the US that

The Kennedy Center for the Performing Arts, located on the Potomac River in Washington, DC, near Georgetown. (Courtesy Rob Crandall/Alamy Stock Photo)

overseas visitors rarely had a chance to see.[3] Washington, DC, had venues for theater and music when President Eisenhower took office in 1953, but no facility in DC compared with the best in other capitals of the world. Especially lacking were theaters designed for ballet and grand opera. There was growing concern that Washington's inadequate cultural life did not promote the proper image for the great power that the United States had become. This issue was especially concerning for the country at this point in the Cold War, when a positive image of the US abroad was paramount.[4] The negative perception of the US described so vividly in *The Ugly American* (a 1958 political novel by Eugene Burdick and William Lederer) was bad enough. There was no need to compound that image problem with the persistent view of the "uncultured American."

Eisenhower had personally experienced the patronizing comments from foreigners about his country's lack of culture. As a former president, he shared his reflections in remarks he gave during a television program entitled American Pageant of the Arts, broadcast on November 29, 1962. President Kennedy in Washington, DC, recognized Ike, who was participating by remote television hookup from Augusta, Georgia. Kennedy said, "We are particularly pleased to have as our guest tonight . . . the man under whose administration this project [the National Cultural Center] was started and who has given it wholehearted support—ladies and gentlemen, General Eisenhower." Ike said to the television audience:

> Many years ago when we were in Europe, it was not too rare at all to hear our country spoken of as another colony. When a European spoke of coming to America, he would say, "we are going out there next year to see you people," and it was in sort of a condescending tone . . . in the later years when I was acting as the chief executive, the idea was born that in Washington there should be a center of culture—an American center of culture . . . then people would come to see in sort of a nutshell what America was capable of showing, not only in her factories, in her productivity, in her great strength, her wealth, and in her prosperity, her great roads and highways, but . . . in the arts and in those things that appeal to all that is spiritually aesthetic to the senses of man . . . in making this Center a true mecca for artists—one that will give everybody who visits Washington, whether from our own country or from the four corners of the world, a true appreciation, a better appreciation of America.[5]

Here is a bit of irony. Harry Truman, Eisenhower's predecessor in the White House, was a very accomplished piano player—a gifted amateur in fact—while Ike was a piano lesson dropout. His mother Ida had given all the Eisenhower boys lessons on the piano in the small family room of their boyhood home on the very piano she had bought with the modest inheritance she received on her twenty-first birthday. Ike's oldest brother, Arthur, and the youngest, Milton, continued to play in their adult lives, but Ike and his other brothers quit as quickly as they could.

According to his wartime military orderly, Sgt. Mickey McKeogh, when General Eisenhower had access to a piano, he would frequently sit down and play "Chopsticks" with two fingers. However, on one bleak occasion in Tunisia when German troops were breaking through the Kasserine Pass, the general looked worried and tired when he returned late at night after visiting troops at the front lines. McKeogh noted that General Ike sat down and slowly picked out notes on the piano, then played "Taps." "He then got up, without saying anything, and went off to bed. I don't think I ever saw him lower than he was that night."[6]

This is not to say that Eisenhower had no musical talent. In the January 31, 1953, issue of *Collier's* magazine, there was a brief vignette by roving reporter Walter Davenport telling readers not to fret about any lack of

Ten days after President Eisenhower was inaugurated, a *Collier's* magazine cartoon in the January 30, 1953, issue depicted Ike playing the harmonica while President Truman departed the White House pushing his baby grand piano ahead of him. The cartoon caption said not to worry, "there will still be music at 1600 Pennsylvania Avenue, Washington, D.C." (Permission Irwin Caplan Cartoon Collection)

music when President Truman, an excellent pianist, left the White House. Davenport had it on good authority that Ike "was no fumblemouth with the harmonica" and that the new president planned to have at least one on every mantel in the mansion at 1600 Pennsylvania Avenue. The article featured an accompanying cartoon by Irwin Caplan depicting newly installed President Eisenhower playing the harmonica in the foreground while President Truman departed the White House pushing his baby grand piano ahead of him.[7] As a result of the article, Ike received at least five harmonicas as gifts from the general public in 1953.

Also, in response to an inquiry from a freelance writer in 1954 about presidential musical abilities, the White House assistant press secretary wrote back saying, "The President, sometime ago, was a harmonica player and always has enjoyed group singing."[8] No further information is available about this little-known talent of Ike's. The Eisenhower Museum surprisingly has no harmonicas among the gift collections—my guess, probably all were given to the grandkids.

Kay Summersby, General Eisenhower's Irish driver during the war, recounts an evening in January 1945 when Ike invited some of his staff and General Carl "Tooey" Spaatz (commander of US Strategic Air Forces) over to his quarters to celebrate after the hard-fought Allied victory in the Battle of the Bulge. Ike insisted that Tooey bring his guitar, and the two of them let off the previous month's steam by booming out a medley of slightly off-key but boisterous West Point songs (General Spaatz graduated from West Point a year ahead of Eisenhower). Kay noted that the festivities that evening seemed to signify the worst part of the war was over.[9] Sergeant McKeough also said that during the North Africa Campaign, the supreme commander would have other generals over to his quarters in the evening and, if someone were good at the piano, they would commence to sing a variety of songs—not just West Point songs, but also western songs. Additionally, one of Ike's favorites was the 1942 hit "One Dozen Roses," made popular by Harry James and His Orchestra with Jimmy Saunders as vocalist. Sergeant Mickey said the boss sang that one for weeks. He could hear the general singing, usually when he was shaving or in the bath, crooning, "Give me one dozen roses and put my heart in beside them."[10]

As president, Eisenhower used the White House as a showcase for promoting the arts and the idea that America did indeed have culture. According to Ralph Becker, while Harry Truman had a lifelong affection for the classics, formal musical programs were held at the White House during only one of the eight years of his presidency. It remained for Eisenhower, whose own tastes ran to the popular and sentimental (he liked Lawrence Welk) to make musical programs— twenty-four of them in all—a regular feature of head of state dinners. Ike offered a wide cross section of music in his White House events, with some restrictions. The East Room was off limits to bop, rock and roll, and electronic jazz.[11] Dear reader, you may also be pleased to learn that Muzak (elevator music) was never pumped through speakers in the White House, at least according to a detailed search of records in the archives of the Eisenhower Presidential Library in response to a reference inquiry.

Surprisingly enough, Ike also released a long-playing record album in 1956. It was entitled *The President's Favorite Music* and included the Boston Symphony performing Beethoven's "Coriolan Overture" and the Boston Pops Orchestra playing Gershwin's "Porgy and Bess." Eisenhower penned this powerful message on the album's back cover:

I wish to salute musicians and the important part they play in the life of our people. American music has brought us pleasurable distinction at home and abroad. Millions of Americans are engaged in the creation, performance and active appreciation of music. Indeed it is a rare day when any one of us does not hear some form of music. It is hard to imagine our lives without it.

The enjoyment of music—speaking for myself, at least—has a moral and spiritual value which is unique and powerful. It reaches easily across lingual, racial and national boundaries. The development of American music, like the native development of any art, is therefore the development of a national treasure.[12]

Eisenhower believed the arts were important to the life of America and did his best to promote that idea while in the White House. However, he felt that the arts were not an elitist activity and that the president's mansion should not be their only government-endorsed showcase in Washington. The nation's capital needed another venue. In July 1955, he signed Public Law 128, creating the "D.C. Auditorium Commission," which included planning for the design, location, financing, and construction in the District of Columbia of a civic auditorium that would include an Inaugural Hall of Presidents and a music, fine arts, and mass communications center. This was the origin of the concept of a future national center for the performing arts.[13]

In 1956, President Eisenhower initiated a ten-year project to revitalize US national parks, designated "Mission 66" (as 1966 was the target end date). Ike's project also called for the preservation and renovation of the historic Ford's Theatre in Washington, DC, which was under the auspices of the National Park Service. The theater had been closed since the assassination of President Lincoln, but because of Ike's Mission 66 program, it reopened in January 1968. By that date, those enjoying the performances at Ford's Theatre had long forgotten—or more likely had never known—the decisive role that Eisenhower had played in their cultural evening at the historic theater.[14]

Concerned that too many foreign people saw the US as materialistic and militaristic, President Eisenhower felt strongly that our artists, at home and abroad, could make an implicit statement to the contrary. In his 1954 message to Congress, Ike requested $5 million for cultural exchange programs. As a result, the New York Philharmonic performed in Latin America, the New York City Ballet and Boston and Philadelphia symphony orchestras toured the capitals of Europe, and the Gershwin opera *Porgy and Bess* was performed in Moscow. Eisenhower understood well that the arts and culture transcended language and could promote "world friendship."[15]

The importance to President Eisenhower of American culture and values extended to official US foreign policy during his administration, as demonstrated in a top secret document entitled "Basic National Security Policy" prepared by his National Security Council in 1956. The now declassified NSC policy paper stated:

> The spiritual, moral, and material posture of the United States of America rests upon established principles which have been asserted and defended throughout the history of the Republic. . . . These concepts and our institutions which nourish and maintain them with justice are the bulwark of our free society and are the basis of the respect and leadership which have been accorded our nation by the peoples of the world . . . In interpreting abroad U.S. policies and actions, the United States should seek to delineate those important aspects of U.S. life, culture and institutions which facilitate understanding of the policies and objectives of the United States.[16]

Official US foreign policy was not Eisenhower's only focus when it came to promoting American culture to enhance the US image abroad. Ike established the non-government program People to People International (PTPI) in 1956. He knew the average American citizen could be an effective cultural "weapon" for their country. In September 1956, the president told attendees at the first PTPI planning conference of the important role that this fledgling cultural exchange organization would play in creating understanding between peoples during the height of the Cold War:

> In short, what we must do is to widen every possible chink in the Iron Curtain and bring the family of Russia, or of any other country behind that Iron Curtain, that is laboring to better the lot of their children—as humans do the world over—closer into our circle, to show how we do it, and then to sit down between us to say, "Now, how do we improve the lot of both of us?"[17]

On September 2, 1958, while on summer vacation in Newport, Rhode Island, President Eisenhower signed the National Cultural Center Act— Public Law 85–874. His dream was now definitely on its way to becoming reality. Ike's message to the nation was clear: "The cultural center belongs to the entire country. The challenge of its development offers to each of us a noble opportunity to add to the aesthetic and spiritual fabric of America."[18] Ralph Becker, in his role as a director of the Greater Washington Board of Trade, had testified before Congress in support of the proposed national cultural center legislation in August 1958, before its passage. Becker was more direct than Ike had been earlier on the importance of culture in the ongoing fight against communism in the Cold War: "We cannot afford the Soviets to outdo us in the cultural field any more than we can in ballistic missiles. In my humble opinion the inadequacy of cultural facilities in Washington is the one major area of emphasis on the arts that has been neglected in our efforts to match the Communists."[19]

There were challenges to the center's development, as Ike had said there would be. Other than funding, the major problem was the initial site proposed for the cultural center on the National Mall near L'Enfant Plaza. That prime location in Washington had been under study for twenty years as the site designated for a future "national air museum" to be operated by the Smithsonian Institution. Indeed, the National Air and Space Museum did eventually open on that mall location in 1976. In 1971, the planned National Cultural Center found a new proposed building home site along the Potomac River in the Foggy Bottom part of Washington, DC, closer to Georgetown.[20]

Within days of JFK's assassination on November 22, 1963, actions began around the world to honor the martyred president. Idlewild International Airport in New York City was changed to John F. Kennedy International Airport by the governor. Canada designated one of its tallest peaks (at the time still unnamed) as Mount Kennedy. This 13,944-foot peak is in the Yukon Territory along the Canadian border with Alaska. Every country on every continent around the world had cities with a boulevard or bridge renamed for the fallen president. Even in Ike's own Abilene hometown, a new elementary school—destined originally to be named for Eisenhower—was instead named Kennedy Elementary by the local school board. In Washington, DC, there was discussion about renaming Pennsylvania Avenue, which connected the White House to the US Capitol, as Kennedy Avenue. Finally, it was decided instead to designate the future National Cultural Center as the Kennedy Center for the Performing Arts as a fitting tribute. On January 23, 1964, only two months after Kennedy's death, President Lyndon B. Johnson signed Public Law 88–620, naming the center after JFK.[21]

The Kennedy Center formally opened on September 8, 1971, with a dedication of the Opera House. The inaugural performance was Leonard Bernstein's *Mass*, commissioned by Jacqueline Kennedy Onassis as a tribute to the assassinated president. The next evening, the concert hall opened with violinist Isaac Stern performing. President Nixon and his wife attended, along with Mamie Eisenhower and other dignitaries. One month later, in October, the Eisenhower Theater in the Kennedy Center was dedicated. The inaugural performance in the theater was *A Doll's House*, staring British actress Claire Bloom. To honor Eisenhower, who had passed away two years earlier, President and Mrs. Nixon were in attendance, as were Mr. and Mrs. John S. D. Eisenhower, Ike's son and daughter-in-law. Mamie Eisenhower was unable to attend the opening, as she was in Abilene, Kansas, for the dedication of the Eisenhower Presidential Museum.[22]

Though not widely recognized today, it was a combination of Ike's signature on the 1958 act to create a national cultural center and then his vigorous endorsement of the idea that made culture and arts a legitimate concern of public policy in this country. Eisenhower's efforts were perhaps our government's strongest commitment ever to that most intangible of the inalienable rights advanced in the Declaration of Independence—"the Pursuit of Happiness."[23] This dream was not Ike's alone. Before he became our nation's second president, John Adams prophesied that someday in the future America's capital would become a center of the arts as well as the seat of government. In a 1780 letter from Paris written to his wife, Abigail, when he served as minister in France, Adams explained that the early generations must do the difficult work of building and securing a nation, so that future generations can enjoy the "pursuit of happiness" promised in the declaration:

> I must study Politicks and War that my sons may have liberty to study Mathematicks and Philosophy. My sons ought to study Mathematicks and Philosophy, Geography, natural History, Naval Architecture, navigation, Commerce and Agriculture, in order to give their Children a right to study Painting, Poetry, Musick, Architecture, Statuary, Tapestry and Porcelaine. Adieu.[24]

In February 1960, during his last year in office, Eisenhower called for a "President's Commission on National Goals." This non-official body's purpose was to develop a broad outline of national objectives and programs for the next decade and even longer. The commission operated under the auspices of the American Assembly, which was a non-partisan educational organization established in 1950 by Ike while he served as president of Columbia University. The American Assembly studied a wide range of issues, including Equality, The Democratic Process, Education, Art and Sciences, Economic Growth, Technological Change, and Health and Welfare. The commission's final report was issued in late November 1960, just a few weeks before President Eisenhower left office. The thirty-two-page document could rightly be viewed as a philosophic think piece meant to accompany his now famous, televised "Farewell Address" to the nation given on January 17, 1961, which included Ike's well-known warning of the dangers of a military-industrial complex. The national goals report provided an equally strong statement about the critical importance of "the arts" as a priority for the country. John Adams would have been very pleased with Eisenhower's words. "The arts are a vital part of human experience. In the eyes of posterity, the success of the United States as a civilized society will be largely judged by the creative activities of its citizens in art, architecture, literature, music, and the sciences."[25]

On March 24, 1969, Dwight D. Eisenhower was in Walter Reed Hospital dying of congestive heart failure. Against his doctors' wishes, he dictated and signed one last letter. It was to composer Irving Berlin, whom Ike had admired for decades. Berlin had written patriotic songs during both World War I and World War II and many other popular tunes such as "White Christmas," "There's No Business Like Show Business," and "God Bless America." He had even composed the "I Like Ike" election campaign song in 1952. Ike's admiration and affection for Berlin was long standing.

Dear Irving:

I have cajoled my doctors and nurses into letting me dictate this letter—it is a brief but very sincere note of thanks to you for the wonderful melodies you have created over the years.

A good part of my days here at Walter Reed are occupied with expert treatment by attentive doctors and nurses and some reading, but always with background music. I have wanted you to know what pleasure you have brought to me not only during my recovery but for so many years.

No music has meant so much to me as yours. I hope all is well with you and yours—please do not bother to respond.

With warm regard to you and Mrs. Berlin in which Mrs. Eisenhower joins.

Cordially,

DDE

D D E

Walter Reed Hospital
March 24, 1969

Dear Irving:

I have cajoled my doctors and nurses into letting
me dictate this letter---it is a brief but very
sincere note of thanks to you for the wonderful
melodies you have created over the years.

A good part of my days here at Walter Reed are
occupied with expert treatment by attentive doctors
and nurses and some reading, but always with background music. I have wanted you to know what
pleasure you have brought to me not only during
my recovery but for so many years. No music
has meant so much to me as yours.

I hope all is well with you and yours---please do
not bother to respond.

With warm regard to you and Mrs. Berlin in which
Mrs. Eisenhower joins.

        Cordially,

        NDE.

Mr. Irving Berlin
17 Beekman Place
New York, New York   10022

The last letter written by Dwight D. Eisenhower was to composer Irving Berlin.
As Ike lay in Walter Reed Hospital he expressed his final gratitude to Berlin. Four
days before he passed Eisenhower wrote, "no music has meant so much to me as
yours." (Courtesy Eisenhower Library)

The letter to Irving Berlin was the last written by Ike. He passed away four days later on March 28, 1969. I had the privilege of traveling to New York City in 1996 on behalf of the Eisenhower Library to meet with Berlin's daughter. Elizabeth Irving Peters presented me with this very poignant letter to her father, as a donation to the library, where it is now so rightly preserved for history.

The National Cultural Center in Washington, DC, was begun by Eisenhower and then pursued by Presidents Kennedy, Johnson, and Nixon before it became a reality in 1971. We owe a debt of gratitude to all four presidents. But if not for the fateful events in Dallas in November 1963, audiences might well be enjoying opera, concerts, and theater in the grand "Eisenhower Center for the Performing Arts."

A soldier, politician, writer, painter, and music lover. Ike was a true Renaissance man.

"I'm going to ask Congress for more money to build up Border
Patrol. If we have to build fence down there, the Mexicans will be
mad. That's too bad."[1]
—*Dwight D. Eisenhower, March 1, 1954*

I wager you may not have heard of a deportation program entitled Operation Wetback, conducted by the US government in 1954 and 1955. It may surprise you that things have not changed much over of the past several decades when it comes to the controversial issue of the flow of workers from Mexico crossing the border, legally or illegally, to work in the United States. This issue confronted the Eisenhower administration some seventy years ago in the 1950s, just as it does today. The response was a massive program to return illegal aliens to Mexico.

Dr. Frank Tannenbaum (1893–1969) was a professor of Latin American history at Columbia University. He once said, "Mexico is a beautiful place in which to live, but a hard place to make a living."[2] This reality is at the heart of the Mexican-US immigration issue.

First some discussion over the very term "wetback," which would certainly and quite correctly be viewed today as very derogatory. Webster's dictionary defines wetback as "a Mexican who enters the US illegally (as by wading the Rio Grande)." The term initially referred specifically to those Mexicans who crossed illegally into the state of Texas, by crossing the Rio Grande River, which forms Mexico's border with Texas. By swimming or wading across the river, the illegal alien was often wet when apprehended by the border patrol; ergo the graphic term "wetback."[3] The term would certainly never be used in official documents by any organization today. Many younger readers may have never heard the word "wetback" (and that is good). It will be used in this chapter only as it appears in excerpts from the original records from the time period when it was used as an official term to describe the illegal immigrants all along the southwest border of the United States. It is important to note that neither Dwight D. Eisenhower nor US Attorney General Herbert Brownell used this pejorative term in their written accounts of the White House years.

In 1942, the Bracero Program was initiated by the US government as concern grew over the labor shortage caused by the mobilization of millions of young American men for service in World War II. Bracero in Spanish meant "manual labor," derived from the word for "arm." The Mexican Farm Labor Agreement was signed by the US in August 1942 and guaranteed decent living conditions and a minimum wage for legal Mexican workers who were to come by the many thousands to work in factories and on farms on a temporary or seasonal basis. This Bracero Program lasted twenty-two years (1942–1964) and, after an initial slow start, it took off—and from 1951 until it ended in 1964 averaged some 315,000 legal workers per year.[4]

Many scholars of the history of immigration to the US have concluded that the Bracero program, while very beneficial, also had the unintended effect of serving as a magnet for illegal immigration. Thousands upon thousands of eager Mexican workers came to the Bracero recruitment centers hoping to win one of the approved slots for a work visa to the United States. They had heard exciting tales of the money that could be earned in El Norte. Those who had already been Braceros quite naturally reapplied for the opportunity the following year, as did increasing numbers of their fellow citizens. The result was that the number of applicants far exceeded the labor needs established by the US Labor Department.[5]

The issue was complicated from Mexico's perspective as well. Mexican growers did not want to open Bracero recruiting stations near the border because they would lose many workers to the US and be required to pay higher wages themselves to compete in Mexico. The Mexican government also wanted to limit the number of Braceros who entered each year to operate the program more efficiently and keep the demand high for this controlled number of legal immigrants in the US.[6] One estimate by the Migratory Workers Affairs department in the Mexican foreign office was that during the period of 1947–1960, only one out of every ten Bracero applicants received a contract for a legal work visa. That did not stop the unauthorized entry of many of the remaining 90 percent with their hopes and dreams of working for a better life for their families. Thus, the Bracero program proved to be a catalyst for illegal entry across the US border.[7]

In 1954, in response to the growing crisis on the southern border, the Eisenhower administration initiated Operation Wetback, which aimed at deporting illegal immigrants. President Eisenhower's attorney general, Herbert Brownell, prepared a cabinet background paper entitled "The Wetback and Bracero Programs," which was presented to Ike and members of his cabinet on January 26, 1955, for advanced reading in preparation of a meeting scheduled two days later. The attorney general's six-page statement described measures being taken to curb the entry of illegal aliens and assist in the employment of legally admitted Mexican farm laborers.[8] Arrests for illegal migration along the border had grown exponentially from only 10,492 in 1940 to 885,587 in 1953; an over 800 percent increase.[9] There was a growing immigration crisis.

Attorney General Brownell began his presentation by informing President Eisenhower and the cabinet that in recent years, a mass invasion of Mexican "wetbacks," with the accompanying social and economic ills, had taken place along the southern US border. To correct this alarming situation, the Immigration Service since June 1954 had been engaged in removing "illegals" from this country and preventing their return. This action was named Operation Wetback.[10]

The border patrol had created mobile task forces using planes, jeeps, and ground teams. When illegal aliens were caught, planes, trucks, and buses were used to convoy these individuals to staging areas. To discourage reentry, those apprehended were removed from the staging areas to the interior of Mexico by train and ship. Brownell reported to the cabinet meeting that 250,356 illegals had been apprehended and removed in the first six months of the program, and that since the inception of Operation Wetback, only 1.8 percent of those returned to Mexico by ship had been caught reentering the US. As conditions along the southern border improved, the effort moved to industrial areas inland, such as Los Angeles, San Francisco, Chicago, and other cities. No doubt very surprising to today's reader, the American Civil Liberties Union publicly commended the methods used in the removal program.[11]

A direct result of Operation Wetback was increased use by US employers of the Bracero program for legal immigration of workers, viewed as a very positive improvement. Brownell reported that 309,000 contract workers were brought into the country in 1954, a 54 percent increase over the 201,000 admitted in 1953, which had been the highest year previously. The roundup of illegals was having a positive impact on utilization of the legal framework. He noted that employers previously addicted to the hiring of illegals were now cooperating in the use of Braceros in their workforce.[12] The attorney general also cited the positive social and economic consequences of Operation Wetback. According to the California Department of Employment, claims for unemployment insurance benefits in

the state dropped 10 percent the very first month of the removal operation, saving taxpayers $325,000 per week. There was a similar report
from Texas where the Employment Commission estimated that some
30,000 Americans residing in south Texas, who customarily were forced
to migrate northward for seasonal work, were able to remain at home
because of higher wages and better working conditions brought about by
the absence of Mexican workers. In other words, in both states more US
workers were hired for this seasonal work. There were also numerous reports received from police and welfare agencies testifying to the fact that
crime and disease rates in their localities had declined sharply.[13] This is
one more indicator of the sad conditions illegal workers often endured in
the underground economy.

Brownell made a visit to the Mexican border area and at night watched
the illegals steal across the Rio Grande River. On this tour of the southwest
and California, he saw firsthand the inadequate nature of existing reception centers and how understaffed the border patrol was. Much as the
situation today, the attorney general was also briefed by law enforcement
and social welfare agencies concerning the problem confronting illegals
who, by definition, lived outside the law and were preyed upon by exploit-
ers. During the trip, Brownell also had a planned meeting with General
Joseph Swing, commanding general of the US Sixth Army at the Presidio
in San Francisco. General Swing provided sound advice on the illegal immigration problem and, shortly thereafter, retired from the army and was
appointed as commissioner of the Immigration and Naturalization Service (INS) in the Department of Justice. Brownell wrote, "He [Swing] developed a brilliant plan, in cooperation with Mexican local officials along
the border, to stem the influx. Within a couple of years, he was able to
report to Congress that the problem had been brought under control."[14]

There is an interesting follow-up anecdote on this immigration issue.
One day Attorney General Brownell was tipped off by a newspaper reporter
that the Senate majority leader, Lyndon Baines Johnson, was planning to
entrap him in testimony before Congress by showing that Brownell, the
very person charged with responsibility of the nation's immigration law,
was employing an illegal Mexican domestic worker in his home. Soon
enough, the attorney general was called before the Senate committee in
the largest hearing room available. After testifying to the Senate on the
Eisenhower administration's law enforcement program along the border,
sure enough, as if prearranged, the cameras flashed on and LBJ asked

Table 3. Number of Undocumented Persons
Apprehended 1951–1964

Year	Number
1951	500,628
1952	543,538
1953	875,318
1954	1,075,168
1955	242,608
1956	72,442
1957	44,451
1958	37,242
1959	30,196
1960	29,652
1961	29,877

Source: US Immigration and Naturalization Service

Brownell, "I understand you have a Mexican immigrant in your domestic service at home—I don't suppose by any chance she entered the country illegally, did she?" Brownell had his answer ready: "No, Senator, I have her entry visa here in my pocket," and he displayed it for the committee and the cameras and an embarrassed Lyndon Johnson. The camera lights quickly went off. Thereafter, Herbert Brownell's relationship with Senator Johnson was somewhat strained, and from that point on LBJ went directly to President Eisenhower when working on civil rights issues, even though the attorney general was the point man for the administration.[15]

Government and public officials, as well as private citizens and organizations, deemed Operation Wetback a success. The program was effective in expelling illegal immigrants; that was obvious. But most also believed it thereby protected American wage levels, reduced crime, shrunk welfare rolls, and cut down on public health problems.[16] But in President Eisenhower's mind, there was an even more important reason for Operation Wetback, and it involved national security. The program addressed the threat of communist infiltration through the southern border, which was indeed a valid concern at this high point in the Cold War. Ike wrote his friend Swede Hazlett in 1954:

Already in that country there is a strong communist leaning among certain groups . . . including one of the most popular men in Mexico, ex President [Lazaro] Cardenas. . . . If that country should turn communist, and without considering all the other evil consequences that would follow in the wake of such an event, just think of the job that we would have in closing that border tightly. The financial outlay alone would be colossal.[17]

In his 1955 annual report, the new commissioner of Immigration and Naturalization, General Joseph Swing, stated "The so-called 'wetback' problem no longer exists. . . . The border has been secured." In congressional testimony in March 1955, Swing declared that the invasion of undocumented workers had been stemmed for the first time since before World War II. The number apprehended had been cut from 3,000 to 300 per day. Herbert Brownell and Joseph Swing used the newly earned respect for the INS and the success of Operation Wetback to gain an increase in congressional funding for the agency.[18]

With the decrease in illegal immigration and increased use of the Bracero Program, the situation along the southern border seemed to stabilize during the remainder of the Eisenhower administration. The Bracero Program was discontinued by Congress during the Johnson administration in 1964. The US now has the H-2A temporary visa program for migrant agriculture workers.

Today, US immigration policy continues to be a controversial issue, and it may surprise readers to learn the extent to which Dwight D. Eisenhower felt it necessary to confront this situation in a very strong manner many decades ago. He believed the border needed to be secured. For Ike it was even a national security issue.

CHAPTER EIGHTEEN

IKE AND THE EMMY
THE FATHER OF THE MODERN
PRESIDENTIAL PRESS CONFERENCE

"Why don't you just get an actor?[1]
—*Dwight D. Eisenhower*

"And the Ike award goes to Dwight D. Eisenhower for his distinguished use and encouragement of the Television medium." The "Ike" is what Eisenhower's 1955 Emmy would have been called if the original name proposed for the statuette had been selected. Ike wins an Ike? It would have been confusing.

The Oscar for films naturally predated the Emmy television award. The first Oscar was given out on May 28, 1929, by the Academy of Motion Picture Arts and Science, and was for best actor Emil Jannings (1884–1950) for his lead role in two silent films, *The Last Command* and *The Way of All Flesh*. Actually, Rin Tin Tin, the German Shepherd dog film star, received more votes in the 1929 balloting, but the academy thought better about setting an unusual precedent by allowing an animal to win.[2]

Movies did indeed predate the advent of television by over two decades, but in 1948 the Academy of Television Arts and Sciences (ATAS) began awarding their own prize. During the planning phase two years earlier, Syd Cassyd, the founder of ATAS, originally suggested the name for their new award be the "Ike." This was the nickname for the iconoscope tube, used in television cameras in the 1930s and 1940s. However, because General Eisenhower was already a war hero by this time and known around the world as Ike, the academy board instead sought a name not associated with a famous person. ATAS president Harry Lubke suggested the "Immy," which was the industry nickname for the image orthicon camera. The name stuck and was later modified to "Emmy," which board members thought was more appropriate for a statuette depicting a female with wings, holding an atom above her head. The Television Academy's website explains that the wings represent the muse of art, and the atom represents the science and technology that goes into making television.[3]

So, in 1955, Eisenhower did indeed receive an Emmy and the inscription on the statuette read:

To

DWIGHT D. EISENHOWER
PRESIDENT OF THE UNITED STATES
FOR THE DISTINGUISHED USE AND ENCOURAGEMENT
OF THE TELEVISION MEDIUM
PRESENTED BY THE
ACADEMY OF TELEVISION ARTS AND SCIENCES
1955

The academy contacted the White House in August 1954 to arrange a formal presentation of the award; however, it seems Ike was not interested in participating in such an event. As an alternative, the director of the academy was going to be in New York City and offered to travel down to Washington, DC, to make a presentation at the White House, but the president was "unavailable." Another possibility was a presentation in Denver when Eisenhower was scheduled to be there, and this was declined as well. Bernard Shanley, secretary to the president, explained the situation in a letter to George Murphy with MGM Studios, who was representing the academy in their efforts to make the presentation of the Emmy. Shanley wrote:

As you know, these are extremely busy days for the President and his schedule continues to be constantly filled with many urgent, official matters. . . . The President has asked that we not add further to his personal appointments unless they are of an urgent nature.[4]

Finally, a year later, the Emmy was brought to the Eisenhower Farm in Gettysburg by two men from the WCAU television station in Philadelphia. White House Press Secretary Jim Hagerty formally accepted the award on Ike's behalf. One of the secretaries at the Gettysburg Farm prepared a brief description of the presentation ceremony and sent it to Ann Whitman in Washington to share with the President. It read, "There was a great presentation with cameras, etc. Jim said he knew the President would deeply appreciate it, etc. and that he would see that it got to the President."[5]

On November 29, 1955, Eisenhower acknowledged receipt of this prestigious award in a letter to the president of the Academy of Television Arts and Sciences. Ike wrote that he was "highly complimented" by the award and that it was especially gratifying to be called a "professional" by members of the distinguished Academy. Eisenhower added, "I am proud to display the 'Emmy' that you have sent me" and asked the academy president to convey to his board of governors his deep appreciation of the honor he was paid by receiving an Emmy. Ike's Emmy now resides in the Eisenhower Presidential Museum in Abilene.

As noted on the Emmy inscription, the award was not simply for a particular performance; rather it was for Ike's groundbreaking employment of the new medium of television. In his 1952 presidential campaign, Eisenhower used a series of first-ever thirty-second TV campaign spots. Ike originally resisted this suggestion by showmen from Hollywood and Madison Avenue, but eventually he reluctantly agreed. During these taxing filming sessions, an exhausted Ike once exclaimed, "Why don't you just get an actor?" But the result was a series of very successful "Eisenhower Answers America" spots, which demonstrated the potential of advertising, entertainment, and political campaigning in presidential politics. Eisenhower won the 1952 election in a landslide and his media team's innovation had created a new celebrity political culture that helped usher in the modern candidate-centered presidential campaigns.[6]

On January 19, 1955, President Eisenhower held the first-ever "on-the-record" filmed White House press conference. This was indeed a major change. For the first forty years of presidential press conferences—from Woodrow Wilson to Harry Truman—the sessions were off-the-record. Press conferences favored the president. Without White House permission, the media could not directly quote anything the president said in responding to questions. And furthermore, the White House could edit the official transcript or alter a quote if they deemed the president had misspoken or perhaps been too honest.[7] Heretofore, it had been customary to state the president's replies in indirect discourse only. Now, direct quotation was being authorized. Eisenhower's change in policy was truly groundbreaking. As the press conference began, Ike said to the press: "Please be seated. Well, I see we are trying a new experiment this morning. I hope it doesn't prove to be a disturbing influence. I have no announcements. We will go directly to questions."[8]

For this January 19 press conference, television, newsreel, and newspaper camera equipment was present for the first time. Candid photos of the president and portions of the film and soundtrack were released for broadcast that night over television and radio. This practice of releasing only portions for broadcast continued for four months, but after a trial run, and beginning with President Eisenhower's press conference of May

Eisenhower's 1955 Emmy Award received for his distinguished
use and encouragement of the television medium. The Emmy
is in the museum collection at the Eisenhower Presidential
Library in Abilene. (Courtesy Eisenhower Library)

18, 1955, footage of the entire White House presser was released from
here on out.

Emmy Award–winning Ike was very aware of his limitations when
speaking off-the-cuff. There was no concern about a lack of knowledge of
the intricate details of most issues. Not at all. He was a very well-informed
and astute president. Rather, as White House speechwriter Robert Kieve
noted in an oral history interview, Eisenhower realized he tended to use
run-on sentences, as most of us do. He quoted Ike as once saying:

> Look, this speech we're about to give, for god's sake, don't let me give it
> extemporaneously, because I have a capacity for starting a sentence on
> something that's happened in my backyard and before I put a period on
> the sentence, I'm talking about the Normandy Landing.[9]

Interestingly, Eisenhower used this tendency to his advantage on at least one occasion. At a scheduled press conference on March 23, 1955, the White House was forewarned by the State Department about the likelihood of touchy questions regarding US policy on the use of nuclear weapons to defend Taiwan in the crisis that was currently brewing in the Formosa Straight. State advised the White House it would be best if the president said as little as possible. When told this, a grin spread across Ike's face as he was leaving the West Wing for the Old Executive Office Building to meet the press. He told press secretary James Hagerty, "Don't worry, Jim, if that question comes up, I'll just confuse them."[10] Sure enough, the question about the use of nuclear weapons was asked by a White House reporter. Eisenhower's non-specific answer rambled on in memorable fashion and resulted in a follow-up question by the same reporter. Ike then provided an answer that has been called "a classic of obfuscation" on the unpredictable nature of war and the need for wisdom in national leaders. It might be summarized as Ike saying, "I know war. Trust me."[11]

In his morning newspaper column, Pulitzer Prize–winning White House reporter James "Scotty" Reston (1909–1996) once made light of Eisenhower's twisted syntax as the president had attempted to explain a tough national security issue during the previous day's press conference. Press Secretary Jim Hagerty explained in an oral history interview that, in spontaneously crafting his response to the question, Ike spoke slowly and deliberately, discerning as he spoke exactly what information he could share with the public that was not classified. Hagerty noted that while reading a verbatim transcript of the president's answer, it might appear to be twisted syntax, when listening on radio or watching the response on television, Eisenhower spoke like most Americans spoke, and it was warm and personal. Hagerty called Reston that same afternoon and the reporter once again professed "shock" at the president's confusing syntax. Hagerty asked Reston, "Scotty, can I read you the question that you asked yesterday morning?" He read Reston the exact wording of his own question to the president and then asked, "Will you please parse this for me?" Recognizing his own confusing wording, Scotty gulped and replied, "You know, you've got something." And that was the end of the conversation. Hagerty said he thought that was the last time Reston wrote a column on Ike's syntax.[12]

Eisenhower was aware of his own limits as an orator, but he quite adroitly put the importance of this skill, or lack thereof, in proper perspective in

President Eisenhower poses for the cameras prior to beginning a White House press conference on February 3, 1954. Later, on January 19, 1955, Ike brought the presidential press conference into the modern era by allowing the first-ever "on-the-record" filmed session. Prior to this historic change, the press conferences were off-the-record. (Courtesy Eisenhower Library)

a conversation with one of his administration officials. Arthur Larson recalls the occasion during the last weeks of the 1956 presidential election campaign when he was treated to a long dissertation by Eisenhower about the true qualities of leadership. Ike had become very irritated with Stevenson's repeated cracks about Eisenhower's weak leadership as president. Stevenson, a Princeton graduate, was known for his great speaking ability. Ike told Larson he recognized Stevenson's facility with words but added that if being a wordsmith were a qualification for the presidency, "we ought to elect Ernest Hemingway."[13]

Hagerty had reason to be pleased about Ike's performance at the groundbreaking press conference on January 19, 1955. He wrote in his diary the next day that there was resignation to the inevitable among the print media that the new media age had arrived. And it had political implications as well. Practically all the White House correspondents admitted that the televised press conference was a very potent way of getting the president's personality and viewpoints across to the people of the country. The press reports noted that the Democratic National Committee was also concerned about this fact as well but "can do nothing about it at all." Hagerty went on to say Ike being on television was almost the same thing as the advent of Roosevelt's famous fireside chats on the radio and, by implication, just as revolutionary.[14]

For sixty-seven years, Eisenhower was the first and only US president to have received an Emmy, until President Barack Obama was awarded one in 2022 as "best narrator" for his excellent work on Netflix's five-part documentary series *Our Great National Parks*. Which Emmy was more significant? Obama's was for an outstanding oratory performance and certainly well-deserved. But Ike's was groundbreaking in a truly historic sense. As the inscription on his Emmy reads, President Dwight D. Eisenhower was recognized for his distinguished use and encouragement of the television medium.

Ike brought the White House press conference into the modern era.

CHAPTER NINETEEN

A NATURAL CURIOSITY
HOW IKE INVENTED THE INTERNET AND OTHER NEAT SCIENTIFIC STUFF

"Scientific research is a great adventure of the human mind."
—*Dwight D. Eisenhower, October 24, 1957*

One can easily imagine that Dwight D. Eisenhower began his fascination with technology while he was just a young lad lying in bed at night upstairs in his boyhood home, listening to the train whistles. Ike grew up not just on the wrong side of the tracks in Abilene but between two sets of train tracks. The Eisenhower home was nestled between the Santa Fe tracks, a stone's throw to the north, while the Kansas-Texas railroad tracks were just on the south side of the property. Not surprisingly, at the turn of the twentieth century young, Ike's dream in life was to become a train engineer and drive a powerful locomotive to distant places. Little could he have imagined he would travel the entire world and be recognized a hundred years later in America as the "Transportation Person of the Twentieth Century." The American Road & Transportation Builders Association awarded Eisenhower this title in 2002 in recognition of the president's extraordinary vision and leadership in developing the Interstate Highway System and the Federal Highway Trust Fund. With his wistful dreams of becoming a train engineer as a youth, it is also poetic that it was the railroad that brought his body back to Abilene in 1969 for burial in the chapel on the Eisenhower Library grounds.

There are other hints of Eisenhower's connection with technology during his youth in Abilene. Later in life Ike always wanted to claim he was just a simple "farm boy" from Kansas. In actuality, the three acres of land surrounding his boyhood hardly qualified as a farm. That said, he grew up very much in a farming community and no doubt spent long summer days and evenings working on area farms. If you labor on a farm, you are by default exposed to the latest in agriculture technology and even self-taught in how to repair that same equipment. As rudimentary as the farm implements were during Ike's youth, this exposure nevertheless gave him a lasting appreciation of the importance of technology. Fast-forward to 1960, his last year in the White House: President Eisenhower addressed representatives from fifty-nine countries around the world at the Fifth International Congress on Nutrition held in Washington, DC. The group was focused on solving the nagging issue of hunger in third world nations across the globe through improvements in the science of nutrition. In his remarks, Ike shared with the gathering of nutritionists the importance of scientific developments in agriculture:

> Each of you is selflessly and wholeheartedly dedicated to the advancement of a science that underlies human health . . . science has given us a set of tools designed for human betterment. Farm people, in the United States and elsewhere, have translated these tools into a capability for constructive action.[1]

After graduating from high school, before he eventually departed for West Point, young Eisenhower worked for two years in Abilene, first for a local company making steel grain storage bins. He quickly became a self-described "straw boss" overseeing the cold riveting of these large bins. Ike then moved on to a higher-paying job at the Belle Springs Creamery, just three blocks from the family home. Initially, his main task was moving three-hundred-pound blocks of ice around the creamery using a hand crank windlass. Quick promotions followed. From "iceman" he was elevated to "fireman" and then eventually became a "second engineer" working the twelve-hour night shift in the creamery's ice plant.[2] Ike, the "engineer" at the creamery, would earn an actual engineering degree four years later at West Point in 1915.

In June 1915, newly commissioned Second Lieutenant Dwight D. Eisenhower did indeed graduate with a Bachelor of Science degree in engineering from the United States Military Academy (USMA). While Eisenhower's education was different from today's college of engineering degree, it nevertheless included a lot of challenging and technical coursework. An examination of the curriculum during Ike's time at West Point shows the following subjects were included among the courses taken by Cadet Eisenhower:

Astronomy	Sound and Light
Analytical Geometry	Differential and Integral Calculus
Chemistry	Geology
Elements of Electricity	Building Construction Drawing
Machine Drawing	Isometric Projection
Topographical Sketching	Plane Surveying

The Slide Rule	Ordnance and Gunnery
International Law	Constitutional Law

The army wanted their officers to be well-rounded men and Eisenhower's studies at West Point also included liberal arts classes such as history, literature, English, Spanish, and even a course on the "Theory and Practice of Military Hygiene." Ike got his highest marks in English composition, a talent later reflected in his great skill as a writer throughout both his military and political careers. He was also a world-class doodler, as evidenced by the drawings in the margins on his copies of the White House cabinet meeting agendas. USMA had trained him for this artistic practice with engineering courses in "Topographical Sketching and Drawing" and "Freehand Mechanical, Perspective, and Memory Drawing."[3] These skills also became very helpful when Ike began his oil painting hobby some three decades later while serving as president of Columbia University.

After West Point, Lieutenant Eisenhower's first army assignment was Fort Sam Houston in San Antonio, Texas. Two fateful events occurred very early during this tour of duty. First, he met nineteen-year-old Mamie Geneva Doud and was quickly smitten. The couple wed just a few months later in July 1916 and celebrated fifty-two years of marriage before Ike's passing in March 1969. The second life-changing event also involved Mamie, but in this case, it was Eisenhower's future father-in-law, Mr. John Sheldon Doud (1870–1951). Before he met Mamie, Lt. Eisenhower had applied for the Aviation Section of the US Army and was waiting to learn whether he had been accepted in the fledgling branch. Just twelve years after the Wright brothers' flight, here was another example of Ike's desire to become involved in the latest technology. He was eager for the excitement of a new adventure as a pilot but also confessed to being motivated by the promise of a 50 percent hazard pay increase in his modest monthly military salary of $141.67 per month. When an excited Ike came to the Doud residence to share with Mamie and her parents the good news of his acceptance into the Aviation Section, there was a sudden chilliness in the atmosphere. Mr. Doud spoke up and said they had been ready to take him into the family, but if Eisenhower were "so irresponsible" as to want to go into the flying business just when he was thinking of being married, that he and Mrs. Doud would have to withdraw their consent. They did not want their daughter to become a young widow. After a couple of days of consideration, Ike gave up (temporarily at least) his plans to fly.[4] As fate would have it, this was a history-changing decision in a most positive way.

Dwight D. Eisenhower with his natural leadership skills would no doubt have risen to general officer rank in the Army Air Corps during World War II. However, he would not have become the five-star Supreme Allied Commander in Europe, a national hero, and thirty-fourth president of the United States. But Ike's dream of flying was merely postponed.

During World War I, Eisenhower was tasked with establishing a US Army Tank Corps training center at Camp Colt, Pennsylvania. While disappointed at not serving overseas to fight in the war, Ike as commander of the brand-new unit was responsible for overseeing the training of troops in the army's latest technological weapon. After the war in 1919, Lieutenant Colonel Eisenhower found himself stationed at Fort Meade, Maryland, working with legendary tank officer Colonel George S. Patton, who had served with tank units in France. Using their joint experiences with this new weapon, the two officers developed revolutionary concepts for the operational use of the tank with infantry soldiers. In Ike's words,

> We were pioneering with a weapon that could change completely the strategy and tactics of land warfare. . . . These were the beginnings of a comprehensive tank doctrine that in George Patton's case would make him a legend. Naturally, as enthusiasts, we tried to win converts. This wasn't easy but George and I had the enthusiasm of zealots.[5]

In 1920, Eisenhower authored an article for *Infantry* magazine (his branch of the army), while Patton wrote one for *Cavalry Journal*. Both visionary officers advocated the rethinking of the US Army's combat tactics for use of this new armor weapon. The current army doctrine saw no reason for the tank to have a speed greater than three miles per hour, as that was the walking pace of the infantryman on the ground. The tank's only role as defined at the time was one of support, i.e., simply proceed a short distance in front of the troops who were on foot and eliminate enemy machine gun nests that might be encountered. In Ike's article, "A Tank Discussion," he advocated developing tanks with greater speed and reliability. The machine gun battalion in infantry divisions should be replaced with a tank battalion. "The clumsy, awkward, and snaillike progress of the old tanks must be forgotten, and in their place we must picture this speedy, reliable and efficient engine of destruction."[6]

Eisenhower soon found himself called before the US Army's Chief of Infantry for this heresy. In his dressing down, Ike was told that his ideas were not only wrong, but dangerous and that henceforth he must keep them to himself. He was never again to publish anything "incompatible" with solid infantry doctrine. If he did, he would be hauled before a court-martial. George Patton was given a similar message in his cavalry chain of command, and Eisenhower said "this was a blow" to both officers. One effect was to bring them even closer together. Ike noted, "With George's temper and my own capacity for something more than mild irritation, there was surely more steam around the Officers Quarters than at the post laundry."[7] Despite the admonishment, Eisenhower did not waver in his belief in the importance of new thinking when it came to military tactics and the utilization of technology. This was on full display during World War II.

One important personal introduction to modern technology may have been postponed for Ike, but it was not denied forever. With his father-in-law, Mr. Doud, located conveniently some 7,500 miles away in Denver, Lieutenant Colonel Eisenhower quietly took up flying while stationed in the Philippines in the late 1930s. One of his fellow American officers gave Ike flying lessons during off-duty hours, and his deferred dream of becoming a pilot became a reality when he earned his license in 1939. As a private pilot, Ike accumulated an impressive 180 hours of flight time during his tour in Manila.[8] This makes Eisenhower one of three US presidents—and the first—who achieved pilot status. George H. W. Bush flew with the US Navy in the Pacific Theater during World War II and had 1,228 flight hours and 126 carrier landings.[9] George W. Bush earned his wings while serving with the Texas Air National Guard. From 1969–1972, the younger Bush logged 576 flying hours, including 333 hours in jets, primarily in the F-102 Delta Dagger fighter interceptor.[10]

Eisenhower had already proposed a "heretical" new doctrine for the US army involving that technological wonder known as the tank. Ike was soon to do the same with the airplane. With the threat of World War II looming on the horizon, Ike's personal interest in flying brought home to him the potential importance of airpower. Just a few years later as Supreme Allied Commander in Europe during World War II, General Eisenhower demanded Allied air superiority as an integral part of every military campaign. He once said, "I believe that the airplane, from the day it was invented, has grown in importance to warfare." In 1947, as US Army chief of staff, General Eisenhower successfully pushed for the establishment of the US Air Force as its own separate branch of service. It would no longer be the Army Air Corps and could now develop its own doctrine. This was no easy decision on his part and was counter to the wishes of most senior army officers with whom Ike served. Later, Eisenhower considered his support for an independent air force as one of his greatest contributions to the nation's security.[11] Technology won the day.

President Eisenhower oversaw the creation of the nuclear navy as well. The USS *Nautilus*, the world's first nuclear-powered submarine, was launched on January 21, 1954. First Lady Mamie Doud Eisenhower christened the boat. Interestingly, twenty-one years later in 1975, Mamie also christened the nuclear aircraft carrier USS *Dwight D. Eisenhower*, named in honor of her late husband.

As president, Ike also believed in the advantages of modern technology in energy. On December 8, 1953, in an address before the UN General Assembly, Eisenhower said:

> The United State knows that peaceful power from atomic energy is no dream of the future. That capability, already proved, is here—now— today. Who can doubt, if the entire body of the world's scientists and engineers had adequate amounts of fissionable material with which to test and develop their ideas, that this capability would rapidly be transformed into universal, efficient and economic usage.[12]

On his watch just four years later, in December 1957, the world's first full-scale nuclear power plant devoted exclusively to peacetime uses was operating in Shippingport, Pennsylvania.

Early in his administration, in March 1954, Eisenhower signed an executive order strengthening the scientific programs of the federal government. He noted in his statement accompanying the order that in 1940 the federal government spent only about $100 million supporting research and development. Ike reported he was submitting a budget to Congress allocating over $2 billion for scientific research and development in fiscal year 1955; a twenty-fold increase. In addition, the president was concerned that, heretofore, more than 90 percent of federal government support of the sciences was going into applied research and development with very little focused on new research and discovery. His executive order instructed the National Science Foundation to reexamine these priorities, with a new emphasis on basic research.[13]

Eisenhower noted that in the past half-century, science had transformed every facet of society, from medicine to transportation and agriculture to industry. All that progress had been brought about through a combination of vision, initiative, business enterprise, a strong educational system, and the dedicated enthusiasm of the scientific community. The federal government provided more than half of the investment for research and development. Ike felt more should come from free enterprise. The National Science Foundation was charged with assisting the president by providing him with a continuing review of scientific progress and recommendations on improving it.[14]

In April 1956, Eisenhower created the Committee on Scientists and Engineers. Ike asked the committee to identify obstacles preventing the development of more highly qualified scientists and engineers in America. In his official statement announcing the committee's establishment, he said the US had a special responsibility as the world's leader in technology to ensure it was used for the good of all mankind. Ike felt this was a sacred mission requiring intensive efforts in all fields of learning. "We must nourish those basic roots of our traditions and culture which lie deep in the humanities and social sciences, and in our fundamental religious conception of the relation of man to his Maker."[15]

After two-and-a-half years of work, his committee of leading scholars and scientists sent a final report to the president that zeroed in on the American education system. The report said the groundwork must be laid in the grade schools, to create "an appreciation of the romance of science" and forestall the distorted impressions too many teenagers and adults seemed to have about scientists and other intellectuals. Ike's committee recommended science courses in the secondary schools become as universal as courses in civics and American history, and students with special aptitudes should be identified and stimulated by this coursework.[16]

In November 1957, the president spoke to the nation in a live radio and television address on the subject of "Science in National Security." While the preponderance of Ike's remarks did indeed speak of the foremost importance of technology in maintaining US national security, he also took the opportunity to get to the heart of the issue, as defined by his science and technology committee. Eisenhower told his fellow citizens that according to his "scientific friends," one of our nation's glaring deficiencies was the failure to give high enough priority to scientific education and the place of science in American national life. While money could buy modern weapons, science education required time, incentive, and skilled teachers. Ten months later, President Eisenhower was able to sign into law the National Defense Education Act of 1958, providing funding for university science programs and low-interest student loans for scientific/engineering majors in college. It was during this address to the nation that Eisenhower also announced the creation of the new White House office of Special Assistant to the President for Science and Technology.[17]

While Ike could be quite a visionary when it came to technology, he was not accurate in predicting the future practicality of at least one radical concept. In remarks made while presenting the Legion of Merit medal to the captain of the USS *Nautilus* in 1958 to recognize the boat's historic two-week cruise beneath the North Pole ice, the president made this observation:

> Under his [Commander W. R. Anderson's] intrepid leadership, *Nautilus* pioneered a submerged sea lane between the Eastern and Western hemispheres. This points the way for further exploration and possible use of this route by nuclear powered cargo submarines as a new commercial seaway between the major oceans of the world.[18]

President Eisenhower's farewell address, televised to the nation as he prepared to leave office in January 1961, is best remembered for his warning of the dangers of acquisition of power by the "military-industrial complex." Myriad books, dissertations, and articles have been written about Ike's prescient concern over this rise of misplaced power. Less known, however, are Eisenhower's words of wisdom in the same farewell speech regarding the threat to the future of scientific and technological discovery in America. Just a few paragraphs after the military-industrial complex warning, Ike shared his great concern that scientific research, which has been central to the technological revolution, was in danger of becoming too formalized, complex, and costly, due largely to its reliance on federal government funding. "The solitary inventor, tinkering in his shop, has been overshadowed by task forces of scientists." A government contract had become a substitute for intellectual curiosity. There was the additional danger that public policy could become, in fact, captive to a scientific-technological elite.[19]

It would be interesting to know Eisenhower's reaction to the contemporary technological achievements of someone like Elon Musk, who has assembled his own private-sector scientific and engineering elite to work on SpaceX and Tesla. Frugal Ike would no doubt appreciate that Musk is achieving radical technological advances in space exploration much cheaper and quicker by disregarding the military-industrial complex. Dr. George Kistiakowsky, Eisenhower's presidential assistant for science and technology in the White House, wrote in his published diary that when Ike was presented in 1960 with NASA's astronomical cost estimates for the project to land a man on the moon and Mars, "he was shocked and even talked about complete termination of the man-in-space programs."[20]

The director of advanced projects at SpaceX explained to a Musk biographer the reason they can build a space capsule about ten to thirty times cheaper than other companies: "We build almost everything in-house. That is why the costs have come down." Several people at the National Aeronautics and Space Administration (NASA) have referred dismissively to the SpaceX engineers as "the guys in the garage." The Musk team may not be the missing "solitary inventor tinkering in his shop," so lamented by Ike in his farewell address, but Musk's creative engineers are not far off. On a return flight to the US from Moscow after failing in his effort to purchase less expensive surplus rockets from Russia, Musk suddenly turned around in his seat on the plane heading home and said to his staff, "Hey guys, I think we can build this rocket ourselves."[21] Ike would have cheered them on.

Under the Eisenhower administration, the US was a key participant in an international scientific program called the International Geophysical Year (IGY). The worldwide event lasted eighteen months, running from July 1957 to December 1958. There are few people familiar with IGY and that is not surprising. Americans are more likely to remember the 1982 hit song by Steely Dan entitled "I.G.Y. (What a Beautiful World)" and not realize its tribute to the great scientific experiment that took place a quarter century earlier. IGY was indeed a serious endeavor of scientific discovery undertaken by sixty-seven participating nations, including the erstwhile Cold War adversaries, the US and Soviet Union. For eighteen months the world's scientific community was able to focus on learning more about the Earth and its atmosphere. Under Eisenhower's direction the US space program was refocused from the development of missiles to launching Earth satellites to further scientific understanding as part of IGY.[22] It was the first American satellite, Explorer I, that made one of the most important discoveries of the International Geophysical Year: the Van Allen radiation belts.[23] IGY also had special focus on Antarctica, and Eisenhower pushed for a treaty banning any military activity on the ice-covered continent, which was signed in 1959. The Antarctica Treaty remains in effect today and still bars military activity and preserves the Antarctic as a nuclear-free zone.

During a White House cabinet meeting in February 1954, Ike's secretary of defense, Charles E. Wilson, once dared to profess an inability to get some information the president wanted quickly about personnel in the

Pentagon. An angry Eisenhower retorted, "Don't tell me you can't do it in Defense. I invented the system. You can ask for fat, bald-headed majors and they'll come tumbling out of the IBM machines."[24]

In the aftermath of the Soviet launch of Sputnik in October 1957, President Eisenhower acted quickly to reassure Americans that our nation was not falling behind in the new space race. In a radio and television address to the nation on November 7, Ike reminded his fellow citizens of the myriad technological achievements our nation had made and that the US was not behind the Soviets. He took this occasion to announce the creation of a new office, the White House Special Assistant to the President for Science and Technology. The president of Massachusetts Institute of Technology (MIT), Dr. James R. Killian, was the new presidential science advisor. It is significant that this White House advisory office created decades ago by President Eisenhower continues to this very day. In that speech to the nation in 1957, Ike stressed that science is about much more than merely national defense: "The peaceful contributions of science—to healing, to enriching life, to freeing the spirit—these are the most important products of the conquest of nature's secrets. And the spiritual powers of a nation—its underlying religious faith, its self-reliance, its capacity for intelligence sacrifice—these are the most important stones in any defense structure."[25]

President Eisenhower admired the scientific community. He found scientists very inspiring and respected their ideas, their culture, their values, and their importance to the country. He strived to surround himself with the nation's best scientific minds. Ike was the first president to host a formal White House dinner to specifically single out the scientific and engineering communities as his guests of honor. Presidents have more often honored artists and musicians at these banquets. Prominent American scientists who served on various panels and special committees were referend to by Eisenhower as "my scientists." One of these men was Detlev W. Bronk, president of the National Academy of Sciences, who observed that "Ike liked to think of himself as one of us."[26]

In a truly historic action, in February 1958, President Eisenhower created the Advanced Research Projects Agency (ARPA) in the Department of Defense. Its purpose was to do "high-risk, high-gain, and far-out" basic research, and this posture was enthusiastically embraced by the nation's scientists and research universities.[27] Ike had given the scientific community free rein to work on futuristic projects.

On his deathbed, Eisenhower did not focus on D-Day or his military career. Ike talked about "my scientists," who he said were one of the few groups that he encountered in Washington who seemed to be there to help the country and not help themselves.[28]

Presidential Science Advisor Dr. Killian noted that one of things scientists quickly discovered about President Eisenhower was "his curiosity in all things relating to science and technology." Science Advisory Committee meetings in the West Wing were "a free-for-all discussion." Killian added that he and other scientists who had the opportunity to advise several presidents felt the "informal and easy relationship" with Eisenhower was truly unique. Killian added:

> In these meetings we never went to him without his getting caught up enthusiastically in some problem we presented in our always carefully prepared agenda. But we never came out of one of those meetings without having an agenda of new things to do that Ike proposed during the course of the discussion. This kind of relationship with the President continued throughout his presidency, and was a memorable experience for all who participated in it.[29]

When the former president died on March 28, 1969, his scientists in the Advanced Research Projects Agency were finalizing the development of a system-wide networking of computers that became the internet. It was completed just a few months after his passing. Looking back, a *Forbes* magazine writer observed poetically, "Like the archetypal prophet, Dwight D. Eisenhower would die just short of the promised land."[30]

Granted, Ike may not exactly be the "father of the information superhighway" the way he is of the US Interstate Highway System. But if Eisenhower—a true believer in science and technology—had not consolidated basic research into the single Pentagon manager, ARPA, as he did from the Oval Office, that agency's crowning achievement, known as the internet, might not have happened as quickly as it did. He intervened at exactly the right moment of the computer's narrative arc.[31]

So, if not the actual inventor, we may certainly call Ike the godfather of the internet.

CHAPTER TWENTY

IKE THE WORDSMITH
"HE REALLY SHOULD HAVE BEEN AN EDITOR!"

"I read in the works of authors strange to me: Plato, and Tacitus of the Roman nation, and in historical and philosophical writers among the moderns, including Nietzsche."
—*Dwight D. Eisenhower,* At Ease

"My room was across the hall and while all the rest of us were cramming like mad, I'd see Ike with his feet on the desk, reading a magazine." That's how one West Point classmate remembered Cadet Eisenhower forty years later. Colonel Clifford R. Jones went further in describing Ike: "He was one of the most popular guys at the Point. Despite all his escapades he had no difficulty with classwork."[1] One perfect example involves his writing skills at this early age.

Cadet Dwight D. Eisenhower excelled in his English class as a plebe at the military academy. All 212 members of Ike's first-year class took the required course and one of the regular assignments was a two-page composition every week. While most cadets fretted and spent hours working on their written essay, Eisenhower was different. The day the class paper was due, Ike would return to his barracks room from lunch in the cadet dining hall and, as was his usual practice, immediately take a short nap. Remember the West Point yearbook teased that Ike "roars homage at the shrine of Morpheus on every possible occasion." (Morpheus was the Greek/Roman god of dreams.) After the snooze, Ike would get up refreshed, sit at his desk, and quickly write out his assignment that was due an hour or two later.

When the interim marks for English class were posted, Eisenhower ranked in the top section of his entire first-year class. His classmates razzed Ike about "book worming his way to the top," and he responded to the teasing by stubbornly pledging not to study an English book outside of class for the remainder of the term. His grade in English naturally began to fall rapidly. One of his more famous classmates, General James Van Fleet, recalled later, "I don't know why he did it . . . but he finally hit the bottom of the class . . . he wouldn't crack a book until the class members released him from his pledge."[2] Eventually his worried fellow cadets freed Ike to study and he once again excelled. In fact, West Point records show his best grade in any course in his four years at the academy was in English. Eisenhower's final ranking was tenth out of 212 members in that class.[3] Young Ike was already an impressive writer before he left the military academy.

Why was Eisenhower such a good wordsmith? One reason was certainly his love of reading. His first great interest as a student in Abilene was ancient history, especially the Greek and Roman accounts. At home, these subjects were so engrossing to young Ike that he sometimes neglected other responsibilities. "My mother's annoyance at this indifference to the mundane chores of life and assigned homework grew until, despite her reverence for books, she took my volumes of history away and locked them in a closet." This worked for a while, but eventually he found the key to that closet and would sneak out the books when Mother went to town shopping or was out working in her flower garden. Eisenhower included a chapter entitled "The Key to the Closet" in his personal memoir *At Ease*, in which he confessed a "sort of fixation" on dates in ancient military history, or details about battles fought, and the names of the generals and leaders. Throughout the rest of his adult life, he would interrupt a conversation to correct a speaker who was off even one year on the actual date or put aside a book if the author were less than scrupulous about chronology.[4]

This general theory about the benefit to writers of being voracious readers was discussed in a blog on *Farnham Street* entitled "3 Famous Writers on the Relationship Between Reading and Writing." Author Stephen King said that the real importance of reading is that it creates an "ease and intimacy with the process of writing." Constant reading, King added, gives the writer "a growing knowledge of what has been done and what hasn't, what is trite and what is fresh, what works and what just lies there dying on the page." Ernest Hemingway said, "The only people for a serious writer to compete with are the dead that he knows are good. . . . If you've always wanted to read the classics but keep putting it off, try breaking the task into manageable chunks." And David Foster Wallace talks of using reading as a self-teaching tool by "paying attention to the way the sentences are put together, the clauses are joined, the way the sentences go to make up a paragraph." Wallace says, "You don't get a sense of the infinity of choices that were made in that text until you start trying to reproduce them."[5] That Eisenhower learned these valuable writing lessons is evident in appreciating what an excellent self-editor he was. Every Ike speech or important presidential statement in the holdings of the Eisenhower Library archives includes early drafts with the general's/president's pen-and-ink scratches between the lines and in the margins.

In 1926, Major Eisenhower was the top graduate from the US Army Command and General Staff College (CGSC) at Fort Leavenworth, Kansas. The ability to write well was a prerequisite for success in that demanding ten-month, graduate-level course. Prior to CGSC, he had published a professional article on the use of a new weapon—the tank—in US Army battle doctrine. By this time Ike was already known in the US Army as a good writer and, as a result, after completion of the course at Leavenworth in 1927, he was detailed to a new army agency called the American Battle Monuments Commission (ABMC). His charge with this temporary assignment was a most challenging task of writing a guide to all the World War I battlefields in Europe where American forces had fought. Additionally, he needed to complete the project within a mere six months. Eisenhower was recommended for this assignment by his mentor General Fox Conner, who had served in World War I as operations officer to General "Black Jack" Pershing, the commander of the American Expeditionary Force and who now served as chairman of the ABMC. Conner told Pershing he believed Ike to not only be gifted in writing and other intellectual skills, but that the young officer also had the energy and organizational talent necessary to distill the mass of accumulated material into a helpful guidebook.[6]

General Conner was proven correct in his assessment of Eisenhower's abilities, and Ike received kudos for his outstanding work after the 282-page guidebook was completed on time. When Eisenhower returned to his regular assignment, General Pershing sent a letter of commendation to the chief of infantry expressing his appreciation for the "splendid service" Ike had rendered during his temporary detail with the commission. Pershing wrote in part:

> In the discharge of his duties, which were most difficult, and which were rendered even more difficult by reason of the short time available for their completion, he has shown superior ability not only in visualizing his work as a whole but in executing its many details in an efficient

and timely manner. What he has done was accomplished only by the exercise of unusual intelligence and constant devotion to duty.[7]

More revealing about Ike's writing skills is the fact that Pershing solicited Major Eisenhower's advice on his own writing project. General Pershing was working on his wartime memoir, destined to be a two-volume account taken from his diary. Eisenhower noted, forty years later in *At Ease*, that Pershing was cautious and slow in his writing habits. Pershing was having problems in accurately describing two of the major battles involving American soldiers in World War I: Saint Mihiel and the Argonne. He requested of Eisenhower, "Read the parts of the book that cover these two periods and let me know what you think." Ike quickly determined the heart of the issue was Pershing's insistence on approaching his memoir as a day-by-day recitation from his detailed diary. This destroyed the continuity of any major episode. As diary entries, "these battles could not have a beginning and a body and an end for the simple reason it had to be told in the form of Pershing's daily experiences, along with a score of other unrelated affairs coincident with it." After analyzing the draft chapters in question, Ike suggested to General Pershing that he abandon the diary form for just these two special chapters and instead tell the narrative of the battles as seen from his position as overall commander of the Allied Expeditionary Force. Pershing could still intersperse comments from the diary in these two chapters, showing where he was, what he was doing, and what he was thinking. Pershing liked the suggestion and asked Eisenhower to redraft the chapters, taking the approach he had recommended to the general.

Eisenhower spent considerable free time rewriting the two chapters on Saint Mihiel and the Argonne. Pershing seemed pleased when he read the new drafts but wanted to get a second opinion from another man he greatly respected, Colonel George C. Marshall. Ultimately, Pershing decided to stay with his original day-by-day diary approach for the entire book. Marshall had told him it would be a mistake to break up the format of the book right at the climax of the war. Privately, Marshall shared with Ike that his idea for making the suggested change was a good one, but knowing Pershing, Marshall thought the general would be happier if he stayed with the original theme.

Forty years later, in *At Ease*, Eisenhower looked back on his hours of labor spent rewriting the chapters of the Pershing memoir as "a futile expenditure of off duty time." After the two-volume memoir was published in 1931, Ike's opinion that Pershing had taken the wrong approach in the accounts of the major battles was reinforced by others. Several of Ike's army friends remarked it was not as interesting as they had hoped. They felt it was difficult to get the entire account of the war in mind from just the day-to-day movements of the commanding general. In a most diplomatic and gentle version of "I told you so," Eisenhower wrote, "Given my own work, I am probably no man to pass judgment on memoir writing but I still have to agree."[8] It should be noted, however, that Pershing was awarded the Pulitzer Prize for History in 1932 for *My Experiences in the World War: Volumes I and II.* Quite a prestigious award, but perhaps if Ike's version of the chapters on the major battles had been used, it may have been not only prizewinning but a more readable history.

In the 1930s Ike yearned for an assignment in the field, commanding infantry troops, but his well-known communication and organizational skills meant he was doomed to be chosen for staff positions in the War Department in Washington. General Douglas MacArthur became army chief of staff in 1932 and sought out Eisenhower to become his personal military assistant. Ike described the job as being MacArthur's "amanuensis" (i.e., a literary assistant) charged with drafting letters, reports, and statements for the general.[9] Once again, it was in part Ike's proven skill as a writer that led to this job. Eisenhower was not known for self-promotion, but he did tell his own White House speechwriter years later that General MacArthur had quite a reputation as "a silver-tongued speaker" when he was in the Philippines. Then Ike added, "Who do you think wrote those speeches? I did."[10]

His seven years serving with MacArthur in Washington, and later in the Philippines, were challenging and educational in many ways. "My duties were beginning to verge on the political." Gaining this political experience was no doubt useful preparation for Ike himself, who was destined in a mere four years to become Supreme Allied Commander in Europe in World War II, followed by serving as army chief of staff and NATO supreme commander.

In 1947, as Eisenhower's military career was ending, he wrote his wartime chief of staff, General Walter Bedell "Beetle" Smith, about his ideal retirement. Ike had already agreed to become president of Columbia University, the prestigious Ivy League institution, but that had not been his original hope. He wrote Beetle he had dreamed of being associated with a small, undergraduate college somewhere in the Virginia or Pennsylvania area, living quietly with Mamie in that kind of atmosphere. "Under such conditions I felt that I could write or not, just as I chose. I have given up all such dreams for the moment."[11] In the meantime, he had nevertheless found time to begin work on his first book.

Joseph Barnes, an editor at Simon & Schuster, shared an amazing fact concerning his experience working with Dwight D. Eisenhower in 1948 on *Crusade in Europe,* the supreme commander's book about his war years. Eisenhower dictated in a single session, without stopping, 5,000 words that required almost no editing. Barnes said he had never seen such a performance in his newspaper and book-publishing career.[12] When it appeared, critics regarded *Crusade in Europe* as one of the finest US military memoirs ever written. It was also a financial success for which Ike was paid over $600,000.[13]

McGeorge Bundy (1919–1996) was a Yale graduate and later a dean at Harvard University. He was a speechwriter for Thomas E. Dewey in the 1948 presidential campaign and, after Dewey's defeat, Bundy served a stint at the Council on Foreign Relations directing a task force on Marshall Plan aid to Europe. After his academic career, he went on to greater fame as national security advisor to both Presidents John F. Kennedy and Lyndon Baines Johnson from 1961 to 1966. While president of Columbia University, Eisenhower was a member of the Committee for the Marshall Plan and reviewed papers Bundy wrote for the task force. Bundy, obviously a very accomplished writer, remarked in an interview many years later that Eisenhower "marked them [Bundy's papers] with a soft pencil and persuaded me that he was one of the best editors I ever worked for."[14] Very unexpected praise from an Ivy League academic directed toward a graduate of West Point.

Ike was also well-informed about the distinct types of written discourse. In a recorded conversation in his office at Columbia University in 1950, Eisenhower hosted Roy Rutherford (1899–1975), a freelance writer from Ohio. Rutherford was the author of a book entitled *Boys Grown Tall,* describing American initiative as personified by biographical sketches of fifty-one highly successful Cleveland industrialists. In the conversation, Eisenhower compliments Rutherford's writing style and commends him for the "good job" he did showing what business had accomplished. Ike then proceeded to don his own mantle as a writer and explains how he was "raised" by generals in his military career—Fox Connor, George Moseley, Douglas MacArthur—and how they taught him to always take a logical approach to issues. Ike then gives Rutherford some author-to-author advice, saying, "The only thing I'm getting at, in expository or dialectic writing never make the basis of the story something that the carping critic can defeat you on."[15]

Gabriel Hauge was research director for Citizens for Eisenhower during the 1952 election campaign and then served in the White House as the President's Special Assistant for Economic Affairs. One time during the presidential campaign, after spending two hours alone with Ike going over speeches in detail, Hauge returned from his meeting with the candidate and told fellow campaign staffers he felt "beaten to a pulp." Hauge expressed exasperation that the general wasted endless time by "debating commas and tenses."[16] Yes indeed, Eisenhower was a well-known perfectionist when it came to writing.

One reason for this preciseness was later explained by William Ewald, who joined the White House staff in 1954 as a special assistant to President Eisenhower. Ike was not "unbuttoned" in his writing, said Ewald, "he just wasn't." Ewald had a keen eye for this tendency and understood. He had been on the English faculty at Harvard University for three years before joining the White House. He said Eisenhower was reserved in his writing and had a keen sense of the obligation of every office he held, whether it was as an officer in the army, a commanding general, or in the Oval Office. As president he had a special responsibility to the electorate.[17]

Eisenhower's personal secretary in the White House said of him, "He likes editing." Ann Whitman added, "He has many times said he really should have been an editor; he passionately edits his own dictation and when he has time, every draft submitted to him." Once, with pen in hand and looking over correspondence prepared for his signature, Eisenhower told her in great disgust, "the mark of a good executive, he supposed, was to learn to sign bad letters."[18] In an oral history interview, John McCone, chairman of the Atomic Energy Commission from 1958 to 1960, commented on his firsthand experience with President Eisenhower's very precise editorial skills, especially when it came to speechwriting. McCone said Ike liked to dramatize things. In one conversation with Ike about the issue of wasteful military spending, McCone shared the fact there was fifty years' worth of anchor chain stored in the Navy Yard in Washington, DC. "That just tickled him to death," said McCone, and Ike had exclaimed, "For Christ's sake!" It was just a fly speck in the military budget, but it dramatized what Eisenhower was talking about.[19]

Robert S. Kieve was a special assistant in the Eisenhower White House. He was a Harvard graduate who served as an information officer in an

American embassy abroad and then as a writer for CBS television before joining the administration's speechwriting staff. Kieve remarked on the public perception of President Eisenhower as a grandfatherly old man who had no concept of the English language, stemming no doubt from his occasionally confusing syntax in impromptu remarks. The impression of Ike was that he had no interest in the English language, no feeling for the precision of words, no capacity for determining when a sentence ended and when it began, and no knowledge of paragraphing or organization. Kieve, a White House wordsmith, said of Eisenhower, "In all of these things he had a greater capacity than anybody I've ever known." Ike was an "absolute pedant with the English language. Insufferable."[20]

In his 1978 oral history interview, Kieve noted that President Eisenhower inevitably edited any draft message or speech placed in front of him, and that he made the best changes editors can make. Namely, he would shorten and sharpen the draft document. Kieve then outlined some guidelines Eisenhower's writing staff quickly learned when writing for the boss:

- Do not use a poetic word when you can use a functional one instead.
- He had an enormous impatience for jargon. There was no jargon he hated worse than military jargon.
- Do not ever start two consecutive paragraphs with the vertical pronoun ("I").
- Never assume he knows something. When putting words in his mouth he must always be allowed to say "I understand that" or "I am told that." (Kieve noted that this was a mark of Ike's overall modesty and intellectual integrity.)
- Do not misuse the word "noble" in correspondence or speeches. That should never be attached to any enterprise whose scope is smaller than that of the Normandy landings.
- Be prepared. It did not matter if the letter or message was routine. If his name was going to be in the signature block, he was going to change it the way he wanted it to be.[21]

Arthur Larson was a special assistant in the White House and witnessed firsthand these strict guidelines. No one he had ever known was more conscientious than Eisenhower about their writing, whether as to content, clarity, correctness, or style. There was another important rule Larson quickly learned. During his first conference with the president about a speech, Ike stated, "Every speech must have a Q.E.D." This academic acronym stands for the Latin phrase *quod erat demonstrandum,* meaning "which was to be demonstrated." Ancient Greek mathematicians placed these letters at the conclusion of a logical problem indicating they had proven their answer. Eisenhower told Larson, "I don't want to give a speech just to hear my voice. I want to *say* something. The speech has got to have an idea—a Q.E.D."[22]

Gerald D. Morgan was another White House staffer very familiar with Eisenhower's writing abilities and style. Ike believed in brevity. In his succinct wire to General George Marshall after he had accepted the surrender of the Nazi forces in Reims, France, General Eisenhower said simply, "The mission of this Allied Force was fulfilled at 0241, local time, May 7th, 1945." A decade later, Morgan helped prepare Ike's State of the Union addresses to Congress. Eisenhower was very put out that the State of the Union message could not be made shorter. The White House speechwriters finally convinced him that it was impossible to trim it, and Ike finally resigned himself to the fact that this had to be a long oration.[23]

This personal drive for perfection in writing certainly carried over into Eisenhower's post-presidential years in the 1960s, when he was working on a two-volume history covering his eight years in the White House. William Ewald had rejoined Ike at the Gettysburg Farm to assist in his research and drafting of *Mandate for Change* and *Waging Peace*. Each time Ewald presented Eisenhower with the first rough draft of a chapter—the result of many hours of discussion and notetaking with the president—the work was far from finished. Ewald described what came next:

> Then he would do what he always did with any piece of paper, he would rework it and rework it and rework it, and change it and cross out, and write in and add, and so on. And then you ended up with what you would call the end of the beginning, I guess. It was a draft that was ready to be seen by the editors from Doubleday.[24]

As former president, Eisenhower received many invitations to speak from a wide variety of organizations. His response to Dr. Isidore S. Ravdin in January 1962 was indicative of his position on these myriad opportunities. Ike knew Dr. Ravdin very well—in fact, the doctor had been part of the medical team that performed heart bypass surgery on Eisenhower just six years earlier in 1956. Ike was asked to speak to a meeting of science writers in Phoenix about his views on the importance of research in the field of cancer treatment. He was assured his remarks need not be long, and, if Eisenhower preferred, Dr. Ravdin could have a portion of the speech written by "one of their people." The former president declined the speaking engagement because of his busy schedule in a warm personal letter with the salutation "Dear Rav." Ike said he was focused on his own writing projects and went on to explain that he insisted on preparing his own speeches or, inevitably, rewriting drafts prepared for him.

> Furthermore, it does no good to say that a part of the speech I am sup- posed to deliver would be prepared by someone else. I have never yet been able to bring myself to accept a "ghost" written talk without just as much work on my part as though I had started from scratch. And time of that kind I simply do not have, in view of my writing commitments.[25]

During his lifetime, Eisenhower was a diarist and wrote four well- received books and many articles, including a series of essays for *Reader's Digest*. The final product was always from his own hand, not ghostwritten. He passed his writing skills to his son John S. D. Eisenhower, who later served on the English faculty at the US Military Academy. This ability seems to be genetic; Ike's grandchildren have also authored books. In his early military career, Eisenhower was selected in large part for staff positions, not only for his leadership and initiative traits but for excellent writing skills. He could have become a great editor, if only a higher calling had not beckoned.

During the Dwight D. Eisenhower Centennial celebration in 1990, John S. D. Eisenhower gave his assessment of his father before a joint session of Congress, saying, "He made no pretense at intellectual bril- liance, but he was contemplative and literate." Understated, but very true.

CHAPTER TWENTY-ONE

IKE AND GOD
A COWORKER WITH THE ALMIGHTY

"I'm the most intensely religious man I know."
—*Dwight Eisenhower*

The evangelist Billy Graham said in *Time* magazine, "Eisenhower was the most religious president I have known." Reverend Graham knew each president from Dwight D. Eisenhower to Donald Trump. He did not name Jimmy Carter, as we might have expected Graham to say. High praise also came from the head of the Republic Steel company, who went as far as to proclaim Ike as "the only man since Christ who (could) bring peace to the world."[1] It may not have been quite walking on water, but was Ike indeed the most religious president in modern American history? This amazing assessment of Ike's religiosity could not have been anticipated when examining the earlier decades of his life.

Young Dwight was raised by his parents in the River Brethren faith, an offshoot sect of the Mennonites, religious refugees from Switzerland who settled in Pennsylvania in the 1770s. The devout River Brethren opposed war, alcohol, tobacco, and worldly pleasures. Eisenhower later in life enjoyed scotch whiskey, smoked cigarettes for almost thirty-five years, and was the commanding general of the greatest amphibious invasion in the history of global warfare. But did Ike at least avoid worldly pleasures? One out of four would not be too bad. But come to think if it, he enjoyed music, movies in the White House theater, was an avid card player, a fly fisherman, and a famous golfer. Let us just admit that some fundamental tenets of the River Brethren were short-lived in Dwight D. Eisenhower. The same applies to his brothers. As adults, all the Eisenhower boys were not particularly religious in the usual church-attending sense of that term. But while they reacted against religious dogma, the sons did keep lifelong personal beliefs about God and the moral tenets that their parents had given them.[2]

It is safe to say that Ike did not attend church services very often during his forty years in the military, and if he did, it would no doubt have been a non-denominational Protestant service at a base chapel. While serving in the Philippines in the 1930s, Lieutenant Colonel Eisenhower was rebuked on one occasion by his boss General Douglas MacArthur for never attending church. Ike replied, "I've gone to West Point Chapel so goddamn often, I'm never going inside a church again!"[3] We can infer that Ike was never much into church denominationalism or sectarianism. In fact, he was not baptized until the age of sixty-two, after his first presidential inauguration in January 1953, when he decided to quietly join Mamie's Presbyterian Church.

This in no way means Eisenhower was unfamiliar with scripture. Quite the contrary. Ike proudly boasted of having read the entire Bible twice as a youth. He said, "To read the Bible is to take a trip to a fair land, where the spirit is strengthened and faith renewed."[4] Ida Eisenhower allowed her sons to skip the so-called "begat chapters" in Genesis and 1 Chronicles. On Sunday afternoons in the Eisenhower family home in Abilene, the brothers would sit in a circle in the formal parlor and have Bible competition. They would read the Bible aloud until they made a pronunciation mistake and then had to pass the book to one of their brothers.[5] Ike knew and quoted scripture his entire life—as did all the brothers. The Eisenhower boys attended River Brethren Sunday School; however, one of Ike's classmates remembered that he "never seemed to pay any attention or take any interest in the lesson."[6]

Growing up in the Eisenhower home, prayer was central to daily religious practice. But prayers were requests for God's strength and blessing, not petitions for divine intervention. Decades later, General Eisenhower overlooked from a hilltop as the Allied armada departed Malta for their invasion of Sicily in July 1943, and he said a silent prayer. Ike believed there came a time when you had done all that you could in planning and preparation and the die is cast. Events were now in the hands of God—and there you had to leave them.[7] Ike felt the same way in reflecting on the Normandy invasion of June 6, 1944:

> If there is nothing else in my life to prove the existence of an almighty and merciful God, the events of the next twenty-four hours did it. This is what I found out about religion. It gives you courage to make the decision you must make in a crisis, and then the confidence to leave the result to higher power. Only by trust in one's self and trust in God can a man carrying responsibility find repose.[8]

One controversy about Ike and religion concerns his parents', especially his mother's, involvement with the Jehovah's Witnesses via the

Watchtower Society. Historic sources on this subject are sketchy and circular in nature, insofar as they tend to quote each other, which is never a very trustworthy indicator for historians. An exhaustive article appeared in *Kansas History* magazine in August 1998, entitled "Steeped in Religion: President Eisenhower and the Influence of the Jehovah's Witnesses." The author is Jerry Bergman, a biology professor at Northwest State Junior College in Archbold, Ohio. Bergman has a reputation as a rabid creationist, which may or may not add to his credibility in matters relating to religion. That said, *Kansas History* did publish the article, as it was certainly a topic of interest to their readership.

Family lore, as promoted by the sons of David and Ida Eisenhower, says their mother only became enamored with the Jehovah's Witnesses in her later years, as she was in decline. Ida herself said she became involved with the Watchtower in 1895 at age thirty-four (she lived another fifty years). Young Ike was no more than five years old in 1995. What drew her from the River Brethren background to become a follower of the Watchtower? Family tragedy is cited as the primary reason. Ike's baby brother Paul died from diphtheria at the age of ten months in May 1894. His parents found no solace among their own church members but were comforted by neighbors who happened to be Russellites, the forerunners of the Jehovah's Witnesses. The Russellite teaching promised death was merely sleep and that all those in the grave soon would be resurrected. The Eisenhower parents would see their son Paul again, as Christ's second coming was to happen in 1914, only nine years away. When that date came and went without the end times occurring, David Eisenhower became disillusioned and left the Jehovah's Witnesses, but Ida stayed and became even more involved.[9]

Upon the passing of Eisenhower's mother in 1946, the sons reportedly took steps to remove any references to the Jehovah's Witnesses from the household. According to Merle Miller, Ike's youngest brother, Dr. Milton Eisenhower, who was president of nearby Kansas State College in Manhattan, Kansas, bundled up a fifty-year collection of *Watchtower* magazine and got them out of the house and away from the eyes of reporters. He reportedly gave the embarrassing magazines to a neighbor, another Jehovah's Witness.[10]

The Eisenhower boys never totally denied David and Ida's connection to the Jehovah's Witnesses. While they may have disagreed with their parents on religious beliefs, the sons defended the strength of their convictions. General Eisenhower wrote his bother Arthur on May 19, 1943, from North Africa about a newspaper reporter's "expose" of how ironic it was that, at the same time the commanding general was fighting the Nazis, his mother was at home passing out *The Watchtower* on street corners promoting pacifism. An angry Ike wrote:

> Not long ago, I saw a clipping in which some reporter made a point of the fact that our dear old Mother likes to go to conventions of her beloved Jehovah's Witnesses. As far as I am concerned, her happiness in her religion means more to me than any damn wisecrack that a newspaper man can get publicized. I know full well that the government is not going to measure my service as a soldier by the religious beliefs of my mother. Moreover, the country has never had a more loyal citizen than she. Actually, the newspaper account indicated that the whole convention made a devil of a fuss over her, showing that even people who proclaim themselves pacifists at heart are not above getting on the publicity bandwagon, even if that publicity is generated out of a circumstance which they publicly deplore. Moreover, I doubt whether any of these people, with their academic or dogmatic hatred of war, detest it as much as I do.[11]

One thing is certain. Ida Eisenhower had a major influence on her boys when it came to religion. She had a deep interest in religion from her earliest years. It was written that as a schoolgirl growing up in Virginia, she once memorized 1,365 Bible verses in a mere six months. This was a fact proudly cited by her sons when remembering her.[12] No wonder Ike could quote scripture—it was in his genes.

There is a religious thread throughout General Eisenhower's famous D-Day message, a copy of which was given to the troops on the eve of the Normandy invasion of June 6, 1944. Note that he uses the term "Great Crusade" to describe the largest amphibious landing in history and the battle that would ensue. Ike's World War II memoir, published four years later in 1948, was titled *Crusade in Europe*. General Eisenhower reassured his men by saying "the prayers of liberty-loving people everywhere march with you" and closes his message by beseeching the blessing of Almighty God upon the great and noble undertaking. A crusade is defined as a military expedition under the banner of the cross. Perhaps General Eisenhower, in his mind at least, closed his D-Day message to the troops with a silent amen.

Soldiers, Sailors and Airmen of the Allied Expeditionary Force!

You are about to embark upon the Great Crusade, toward
which we have striven these many months.   The eyes of
the world are upon you. The hopes and prayers of liberty-
loving people everywhere march with you. In company with
our brave Allies and brothers-in-arms on other Fronts,
you will bring about the destruction of the German war
machine, the elimination of Nazi tyranny over the oppressed
peoples of Europe, and security for ourselves in a free
world.

Your task will not be an easy one.   Your enemy is well
trained, well equipped and battle-hardened.   He will
fight savagely.

But this is the year 1944 ! Much has happened since the
Nazi triumphs of 1940-41. The United Nations have inflicted upon the Germans great defeats, in open battle,
man-to-man.   Our air offensive has seriously reduced
their strength in the air and their capacity to wage
war on the ground.   Our Home Fronts have given us an
overwhelming superiority in weapons and munitions of
war, and placed at our disposal great reserves of trained
fighting men.   The tide has turned ! The free men of the
world are marching together to Victory !

I have full confidence in your courage, devotion to duty
and skill in battle.   We will accept nothing less than
full Victory !

Good Luck !   And let us all beseech the blessing of Almighty God upon this great and noble undertaking.

Dwight Eisenhower

Supreme Allied Commander General Eisenhower's historic D-Day message to the
soldiers, sailors, and airmen issued on the eve of the Normandy landings on
June 6, 1944. His closing words were, "let us beseech the blessing of Almighty God
upon this great and noble undertaking." (Courtesy Eisenhower Library)

Among the assigned wartime duties of Ike's orderly Sgt. Mickey Mc-Keogh was ensuring the general always had his lucky coins with him when he departed on his frequent inspection trips. "He never flew without them," Mickey said. Ike had a little zipper purse to hold the coins, which included a miraculous medal a little girl in Detroit had sent him in 1942 when he was still in England. The girl wrote General Eisenhower a letter saying she had adopted him as her soldier and prayed for him every day. Ike corresponded with her throughout the war, and he called her "my little godmother."[13]

In 1953, President Eisenhower told a luncheon board meeting of the National Council of Churches that being a soldier was not that different from a pastor's religious calling. In his view, military duty had called him to the same higher calling as "men of the cloth." Both soldier and pastor, Ike said, were "identical in our purposes, in our dedication of free government which means in some form or other a dedication to the dignity of man and, therefore, to the glory of God."[14]

Starting with the election of 1948, Eisenhower was urged by numerous influential people to run for president. Ike always demurred, indicating he was no politician, he was not really qualified, and he was not interested in the job. There is a Dictabelt recording of a candid conversation in his office at Columbia University on April 29, 1950, which reveals his strong feelings against seeking the presidency. Eisenhower responded to a visitor who was urging him to run for president, and Ike included a religious reference is his rejection of the idea:

> I think that anyone that definitely seeks to be president of the United States is the most egotistical so-and-so. . . . I don't understand how anybody could conceive that he would really be a worthy president. . . . The man I say ought to be president of the United States, I think, is at least St. Peter come back to earth.[15]

Eisenhower eventually relented and said yes to running for president—good news for America. After entering the White House, Eisenhower joined the Presbyterian Church in Washington, DC, in January 1953 and was baptized at the age of sixty-two. This was Mamie's church, and it was the first time Ike belonged to a particular denomination. For the remaining seventeen years of his life, when he did attend church, it was the Presbyterian Church in Washington, DC, or later in Gettysburg.

Eisenhower had to overcome his aversion to organized religion when he joined. He told his White House secretary that he "abhorred the trappings of the church as much as anyone" and believed that religion was a crutch for many. That did not mean he had any patience for atheists, whom he characterized as non-thinking persons.[16] Eisenhower once said jokingly, "An atheist is someone who can watch Southern Methodist University play Notre Dame in football and not care who wins."[17]

Ike was a strong believer in prayer. He felt it provided the spiritual equivalent of the Word and Sacrament offered by the mainline sacramental liturgical churches. In February 1953, the new president spoke to the first annual prayer breakfast. Eisenhower said, prayer is simply a necessity because it is an effort to get in touch with the Infinite. He went on to say that our prayers and supplications are imperfect because we are imperfect beings. Nevertheless, he urged us to continue praying because it is something that ties us all together.[18] On the occasion of his first lighting of the National Christmas Tree on December 24, 1953, Eisenhower said this about prayer:

> As religious faith is the foundation of free government, so is prayer an indispensable part of that faith . . . would it not be fitting for each of us to speak in prayer to the Father of all men and women on this earth, of whatever nation, and of every race and creed—to ask that He help us—and teach us—and strengthen us—and receive our thanks . . . with special thanks to God that the blood of those we love no longer spills on the battlefield abroad. May He receive the thanks of each of us for this, His greatest bounty—and our supplication that peace on earth may be with us, always.[19]

As Professor Jack Holl explained in *Religion and the American Presidency*, Eisenhower became a Presbyterian not for votes—he joined after his inauguration—but it was indeed still a political act. Ike felt his duty as president required membership and regular attendance at church to set a religious example and moral tone for the nation.[20] But religion had even broader meaning for him. Eisenhower told the Freedom Foundation in 1952, "Our form of government has no sense unless it is grounded in a deeply felt religious faith, and I don't care what it is." His civic religion encompassed all who believed in a God who helped mankind walk in dignity, without fear and safe from tyranny. It was a universal human brotherhood. Whatever America hoped to bring to pass in the world first had to happen in the heart of America.[21] One example of his inclusive perspective on religion can be found in a change the president made in his speechwriter's initial draft of his famous farewell address, given to a national television audience on January 17, 1961. Malcolm Moos had written about America's adventure in free government having as its basic purpose keeping the peace and enhancing liberty, dignity, and integrity among nations of the world and described it as the obligation of a "free and Christian people." Ike scratched out that last phrase and wrote "a free and religious people."[22]

Reverend Robert A. MacAskill, minister of the Gettysburg Presbyterian Church, was Ike's and Mamie's pastor during their retirement years in Gettysburg. In an oral history interview with the Eisenhower Presidential Library conducted in 1998, MacAskill gave his assessment of Ike and religion. He stated that Eisenhower had very strong faith in God. He also had a good knowledge of the Bible, especially the Old Testament, and particularly the "warring stories" as MacAskill called them. Eisenhower's faith was simple, direct, and uncomplicated. He believed in the sovereignty of God.[23] MacAskill noted that Eisenhower's attendance at military chapels liberated him from sectarianism or denominationalism. In somewhat of a contradiction, he also said that Ike saw the church as the "body of Christ." Perhaps this was a late revelation to Eisenhower of the reason for belonging to a church. Eisenhower also expected some practical benefit should derive from joining a particular denomination. He told MacAskill, "I come to church to get something out of the service."[24]

Eisenhower viewed his life as a partnership with God. He was a co-worker with the Almighty. This is reflected in the prayer he personally wrote and read as an introduction for his presidential inaugural address. Eisenhower may be the only president to open his inaugural speech by saying a prayer he had written himself for the occasion. Speaking to the crowd from the steps of the Capitol in January 1953, Ike asked God to help ensure he and his administration gave their full and complete dedication to the service of the people of America. He concluded by praying for God's help in seeing that "all may work for the good of our beloved country and Thy glory."

Almighty God, as we stand here at this moment my associates—my future associates in the Executive branch of Government join me in beseeching that Thou will make full and complete our dedication to the service of the people in this throng, and their fellow citizens everywhere. Give us, we pray, the power to discern clearly right from wrong, and allow all our words and actions to be governed thereby, and by the laws of this land. Especially we pray that our concern shall be for all the people regardless of station, race, or calling. May cooperation be permitted and be the mutual aim of those who, under the concepts of our Constitution, hold to differing political faiths; so that all may work for the good of our beloved country and Thy glory. Amen.[25]

Ike's actions as president spoke very loudly about the significant role played by religion in his life. In his inaugural address he proclaimed the need for strengthening our dedication and devotion to the precepts of our founding documents, a conscious renewal of faith in our country and in the watchfulness of a Divine Providence. He was the first president to appoint a special assistant for religion in the White House. Eisenhower also initiated an annual Presidential Prayer Breakfast in 1953, to be held each February. This eventually became the National Prayer Breakfast in 1970, and the religious event continues across the nation today. Open your wallet and take out any denomination of dollar bills. On the reverse side you will find the words "IN GOD WE TRUST." This religious motto was added to US currency during the Eisenhower administration. As president, he often had his cabinet meetings open with a prayer.[26]

Whenever Eisenhower started to philosophize, it invariably turned into a discussion heavy with religious overtones. Every major decision had moral implications for Ike, and he always strived to come down on the right side of the issue. Ann Whitman, his personal secretary at the White House, wrote her husband of her surprise at her boss's continual emphasis on religion, "I am amazed at the stress he always puts on spiritual values. That is to me the most unexpected facet of his personality." She never shared her observation with Eisenhower.[27]

In 1965, the former president agreed to be interviewed by Rev. Sherwood E. Wirt for an article in *Decision* magazine, published by the Billy Graham Evangelistic Association. Graham warned Rev. Wirt before the interview that "Eisenhower was inclined to be rather inarticulate on spiritual matters." Professor Jack Holl in *The Religious Journey of Dwight D. Eisenhower* concluded that what Graham meant more precisely was Ike was not inclined to confess that Jesus was his personal savior. Nor did Eisenhower claim to have been "born again" or offer other conversion testimony. This was bound to disappoint evangelicals.[28]

The interview with Ike resulted in a two-part article that eventually appeared in *Decision* magazine in July and August 1965. Wirt sent his finished draft of the article to Eisenhower for his review and approval. He

President Eisenhower is shown with Reverend Billy Graham in the Oval Office on May 10, 1957. The informal meeting lasted about 25 minutes just prior to the lunch hour and followed a busy morning for Ike who had a cabinet meeting and other official business earlier that day. This was one of several meetings of the two over the years and Graham later referred to Eisenhower as the most religious president of the twelve he had known, Ike through Trump. (Courtesy Eisenhower Library)

had obviously not succeeded in getting a satisfactory answer about Ike's views on Jesus in the original interview session and therefore included a request that the president provide some additional words to be included in the article: "Dear Mr. President: Could you add one thought here as to what Jesus Christ means to you personally. It would give just the note I think folks would like to hear."[29] Eisenhower responded to the request and sent Wirt the following statement:

It takes no brains to be an atheist. Any stupid person can deny the existence of a supernatural power because man's physical senses cannot detect it. But there cannot be ignored the influence of conscience, the respect we feel for moral law, the mystery of first life on what once must have been a molten mass, or the marvelous manner in which the universe moves about us on this earth. All of these [are] evidence of the handiwork of a beneficent Deity. For my part that Deity is the God of the Bible and of Christ His Son.[30]

This may not have been the emphatic recognition of Jesus that Reverend Wirt sought. However, he was able to conclude in his article that Eisenhower "had studied what he calls the astonishing influence of Jesus of Nazareth on human nature, history, forms of government, codes of jurisprudence and civilization in general, and came to the conclusion that, here was indeed more than a man."[31] Professor Holl echoed this assessment by adding Eisenhower believed Jesus "has meant more to civilization—western civilization certainly—than any other individual in history."[32] Wirt did receive definitive answers from Eisenhower in response to two questions. Ike responded that his favorite Bible verse was 2 Chronicles, 7:14, and his favorite hymn was "The Battle Hymn of the Republic."[33]

One of the clearest pieces of evidence about Eisenhower's religion is found in the unvarnished Dictabelt recordings of office conversations filed away in the archives at the Eisenhower Library. In one taped conversation in his office while president of Columbia University, he discussed the destructive nature of the atomic bomb with an unnamed administrator. Ike said, "You have no assurance in war that the right side wins the war, therefore it's stupid." But when asked if his political doctrine if he ever held higher office would be to oppose war, he responded, "Don't for a minute believe that my philosophy will incorporate a complete pacifistic approach." Then Ike proceeds to discuss the teachings of Christ in the New Testament about peace and the use of force. We do not hear the outcome of the discussion in the summary transcript of the conversation but can assume Eisenhower felt Christ gave his blessing to use the necessary weapons to fight a just war.[34] In another recorded conversation, he discussed with famous author John Gunther the importance of religion. Ike said, "Let's not forget the value of example, moral rectitude, honesty; all of the virtues that we think are included in the great religions."[35] These personal attributes of example, moral rectitude, and honesty are the very ones Eisenhower strived to maintain in both his personal and professional life.

There is one more poignant story to share. A very ill Eisenhower spent the last eleven months of his life (1968–1969) in the presidential suite in Ward Eight at the Walter Reed Medical Center, Bethesda, Maryland.

Grandson David Eisenhower visited him often and had many memorable conversations with his grandfather about politics and life, and Ike offered sage advice for twenty-year-old David. He was told, "Always take your job seriously, but never yourself." According to David, when Granddad was alone, he passed the time rereading many of his favorite boyhood books, including those by Arthur Conan Doyle, O. Henry, Rudyard Kipling, and Mark Twain. But there was more. David said of his grandfather, "To gird himself for the lonely and frightening moments at Walter Reed, he memorized the prayer of St. Francis of Assisi."[36]

Lord, make me an instrument of your peace.
Where there is hatred, let me sow love;
where there is injury, pardon;
where there is despair, hope;
where there is darkness, light;
where there is sadness, joy.
O Divine Master, grant that I may not so much seek to be consoled
   as to console;
to be understood as to understand;
to be loved as to love.
For it is in giving that we receive;
it is in pardoning that we are pardoned;
and it is in dying that we are born to eternal life.

A former soldier who did not attend church during most of his adult life and who was not baptized until he was sixty-two years of age . . . he was the most religious president Billy Graham knew? Ike himself concurred with Rev. Graham's view that, yes, he was the most religious president in recent history. Learning what we know about Eisenhower, one might well agree.

In September 1952, in the heat of his first presidential campaign, Ike wrote a personal and confidential letter to a professor he knew well at the Institute of Higher Studies in Princeton, New Jersey. Presidential candidate Eisenhower, ten weeks before the 1952 election, lamented the fact that there seemed no tangible way to bridge the chasm between making difficult political decisions based on moral values or choosing more practical solutions. He was obviously troubled by the compromises he had to make. Ike wrote, "In fact the farther I proceed in political life, the more

I believe that I, as an individual, should have striven to be worthy of the pulpit as an avenue of public service instead of the political podium."[37]

America was fortunate that Eisenhower served as Supreme Allied Commander in World War II and as our thirty-fourth president. No doubt, a Reverend Ike would have been a great man of the cloth. But fortunately for us, and the entire world, Dwight D. Eisenhower brought his spiritual values to the lofty positions he was destined to hold.

CHAPTER TWENTY-TWO

EISENHOWER ON AMERICA'S YOUTH
"I, FOR ONE, BELIEVE IN YOU"

"I am not here, of course, as one pretending to any expertise on questions of youth and children—except in the sense that, within their own families, all grandfathers are experts on these matters."
—*DDE opening address to White House Conference on Children and Youth, March 17, 1960*

Perhaps it was false modesty when President Eisenhower, in the above quote, professed no expertise on questions of youth and children in his opening address to the White House Conference on Children and Youth in 1960. Forty-five years earlier, as a West Point upper-class cadet, Ike was made the head football coach of the miliary academy's junior varsity (JV) team. Eisenhower was special. This was the first time the JV coach was a fellow cadet rather than a commissioned army officer. It was also the first time in years the underclass team had a winning season. Because of this early success at the academy, Ike developed an army-wide reputation and found himself given the additional duty of coach of the post football team with each new military assignment. Also, during World War I, Ike trained raw soldiers in the army's newest weapon system—the tank. Eisenhower may not have been an "expert" on children and youth, but he was very aware of what was necessary to mold teenagers into responsible young men capable of defending their nation.

In 1943, General Eisenhower wrote boyhood friend Swede Hazlett a private letter discussing the importance of the state of America's youth. Navy Commander Hazlett was disappointed about being denied sea duty during wartime and being assigned instead as an instructor for navy cadets at North Carolina State University. For a similar reason, Ike's youngest brother, Milton, had just assumed the presidency of Kansas State College and felt sorry about not contributing in a greater way to the war effort. Eisenhower shared with Swede what he had told Milton: "No man in the world has a more responsible job than those who are influencing the thinking of the younger generation, yet in school."

In his encouraging letter to Swede, sent from the war front in North Africa, Eisenhower listed the most important things he believed our nation needed to thoroughly inculcate the rising generation. As Ike had told college president Milton Eisenhower, we needed to teach the following "if we are to survive as a sturdy nation":[1]

- The obligations as well as the privileges of American citizenship.
- The virtue of old-fashioned patriotism.
- The need for a clean, honest approach to intricate problems.
- The necessity for earnest devotion to duty.

However, to Eisenhower it was about much more than simply patriotism and devotion to duty. As a military leader, he had long been concerned about the condition of draftees during World War II and the Korean War. The nature of work and recreation had changed in modern America since Ike's early life, and many of the young were growing overweight and out of shape. Later, as president, he received reports indicating that American boys and girls were physically unfit compared to the children of western Europe. Eisenhower then issued an executive order in 1956 establishing the President's Council on Youth Fitness. Ike felt that a comprehensive study of the status of youth fitness in America was a high priority. The executive order maintained that since the young were one of the nation's most valuable assets, it was imperative their fitness be improved and promoted to the greatest extent possible. Eisenhower called for a total reevaluation of all governmental and non-governmental programs and activities relating to the fitness of youth, in the interest of achieving and maintaining higher standards.[2] President John F. Kennedy continued this health initiative with his President's Council on Physical Fitness and Sports.

On May 1, 1962, former President Eisenhower returned to Abilene to speak at the dedication of his presidential library. He gave the usual thanks and recognition to the dignitaries and those individuals who had made his library a reality. Ike then gazed over at his boyhood home, sitting on its original site less than one hundred yards from the library steps where he stood to give his dedication speech. He noted that this very day was the hundredth anniversary of his mother's birth. "I think that all of her sons—indeed, all of her close relatives—would, today, like to think that she knows they still revere her teachings, her strength." Eisenhower followed this tribute by acknowledging to his audience that the twentieth century was "the greatest, most marvelous period for the development of scientific thought, accomplishment, industrial improvement, and every kind of advance that we can conceivably think of for the betterment of standards of living and for the material benefits of all our people." But Ike then asked the crowd to indulge him for a moment while he contemplated with them whether these changes—which, when properly used were certainly for the good of mankind—had marked a similar advance in our ideals, our aspirations, and the morale of our country—indeed, the nation's very soul. He posed the following questions to his audience:[3]

> We venerate the pioneers who fought droughts and floods, isolation and Indians, to come to Kansas and westward to settle into their homes, to till the soil, and raise their families. We think of their sturdiness, their self-reliance, their faith in their God. We think of their glorious pride in America.
>
> Now, I wonder if some of those people could come back today and see us doing a "twist" instead of a minuet, whether they would be particularly struck by the beauty of that dance. Now, I have no objection to the "twist," as such, but it does represent some kind of change in our standards. When we see movies and the stage, and books and periodicals, using vulgarity, sensuality—indeed, downright filth—to sell their wares, do you think that America has advanced morally as we have materially? When we see our very art forms so changed that we seem to have forgotten the works of Michelangelo and Leonardo da Vinci, and speak in the present in terms of a piece of canvas that looks like a broken down tin lizzie, loaded with paint, has been driven over it, is this improvement? What has happened to our concept of beauty and decency and morality?[4]

The original draft of the speech is on deposit in the post-presidential papers of President Eisenhower's library. The draft version was even stronger than the final speech, containing Ike's initial thoughts as dictated to a secretary for typing:

> Will the records in this Library tell the story of the beginning of moral decline like that of Rome and the beginning of a new dark age? Or will that story be one of strengthening of spirit and soul of the individual and therefore of the nation as it prepares to meet the trials and tests— and of these there are many—that lie ahead.
>
> Our nation is strong and a mighty influence for good in the world, but no one can deny the indications or existence of trends and practices,

which if long continued, could well spell an alarming weakness in our fiber, leading, if history has any validity, to disaster.

We have been through some 30 years of experience in so called "progressive education." Is there any connection between this theory of "everybody passes to the next grade without any test of merit" and the alarming and wide-spread increase in juvenile delinquency? Has the abandonment of the "hickory stick" softened the child's compulsion to do his duty?[5]

The *New York Times* covered the dedication speech at the new Eisenhower Library, reporting that the former president spoke with some nostalgia of the nation's traditions. The *Times* said Ike was making the point that the nation's spiritual and patriotic development had lagged scientific, industrial, and material accomplishments. But Eisenhower, ever the optimist about his country, told the crowd that America today was just as strong as it needed to be and was still the strongest nation in the world. "She will never be defeated or damaged seriously by anyone from the outside," Ike said. "Only Americans can ever hurt America."[6]

On a lighter note, in 1967 Ike spoke at granddaughter Anne's twelfth-grade graduation at Shipley School in Bryn Mawr, Pennsylvania. At the conclusion of his commencement address, he startled Anne and delighted the audience of female prep school students with his very Victorian view of the miniskirts that were coming into fashion around the country. No doubt with a grin, he said, "Remember, ankles are always neat, but knees are always knobby."[7] At West Point, some fifty years earlier, Ike had been demoted in cadet rank from sergeant to private for dancing improperly with a daughter of one of the professors—the couple whirled so fast her ankles showed, and perhaps even her knees. It was his second offense. Cadet Eisenhower had learned this lesson the hard way.[8]

Volume two of Eisenhower's account of his presidential administration, *Waging Peace, 1956–61*, was published in 1965. Near the end of this 740-page book was a closing chapter entitled "Afterthoughts." Ike reflected on issues ranging from the Cold War, White House reorganization, and term limits for elected officials. In the last pages of this chapter, Eisenhower says, because of his deep concern, he could not avoid addressing another profound question: "Will a great self-governing people such as ours . . . continue to practice, in affluence, the pioneering virtues and be guided by the moral values that in leaner times brought us, by the middle of the twentieth century, to an unparalleled pinnacle of power?"

Ike feared there were signs in America of a weakening of moral courage, determination, self-reliance, and the ambition to excel. He singled out the media for bringing our citizens sickening and depressing accounts of deliberate lawlessness, arrogant selfishness, disloyalty, laxity in conduct, and "all kinds of downright wickedness." To Eisenhower, Americans had lost some of their capacity for honesty and righteous indignation. He concluded by saying that the real question becomes, "Am I doing my duty as a citizen?" If every decent person in the nation would arouse their own conscience, help elect lawmakers of courage and integrity to public office, and support "vocally and morally" the police force and teachers, there could be change. Soon the numerous newspaper accounts of crime, neglect, and delinquency would decline. "And each of us would once again stand straight and proud; proud of himself, his children, and the community in which he lives."[9]

Eisenhower had serious qualms about America's youth. But even in his twilight years, Ike remained as always the cheerleader and coach, encouraging his team to complete its mission. On June 5, 1966, Eisenhower spoke to the 1,871 graduates of Kansas State University, including this author. The Associated Press headline the next day was "The Finest Generation Hailed by Eisenhower." Ike did indeed tell us students, "This is the finest generation this country has produced." General Eisenhower had of course led "the Greatest Generation" of Americans in his crusade in Europe during World War II, but he told us we were the "finest." Ike believed his statement was correct, "in spite of kooks and beatniks that were receiving lots of space." These types were getting coverage on television and in the press and Ike said, "I urge you not to let this disturb you or distort your own views." According to Eisenhower, every citizen had a duty to his country.[10] I was being commissioned a second lieutenant in the US Air Force the very next day through the Reserve Officer Training Program. My views on duty to my country were in little danger of being distorted by the beatniks and kooks. In the speech there was one final admonition from the old general. He confessed that his generation and even those who were younger had grown pessimistic and lethargic. He urged members of the graduating class of 1966 to take strong action. "Get a long hairpin or needle," Ike said, and then ask your elders, "What are you doing to help the United States?"[11]

Eisenhower never gave up on the younger generation. His mindset was the ever-positive "we can do this!" He maintained this same determined attitude as Supreme Allied Commander when he cajoled and motivated his subordinate field commanders during emergency planning for the Allied counter-offensive during the Battle of the Bulge in December 1944. Things looked very bleak for the Allies after the initial success of the surprise German attack that had reached far into Belgium. Undaunted, Eisenhower told Generals Bradley, Patton, and Devers, "The present situation is to be regarded as one of opportunity for us and not of disaster. There will be only cheerful faces at this conference table."[12] Ike was proven correct and the tide of battle turned in January 1945 with an Allied victory.

Susan Eisenhower had a revealing conclusion about her grandfather. After observing him in person, reading the voluminous Eisenhower scholarship, and examining the challenging issues Ike had to confront, she realized there was a "curious factor" in successfully providing consequential leadership. A leader must be authentic, as those who you are leading would spot a phony eventually. That said, leadership requires not just command of one's inner self, but also a level of acting. Susan noted, "One cannot imagine that Ike was optimistic all the time, but he understood, perhaps better than anyone else, pessimism's corrosive impact and the negativity it can produce in an organization and those associated with it."[13] In his leadership role, Dwight D. Eisenhower always strived to wear his game face.

In his later years, Ike had legitimate concerns about the direction of society, but as he had famously said, "Only Americans can hurt America." He was confident his nation would not allow that to happen. In a 1966 *Reader's Digest* article entitled "Thoughts for Young Americans," Eisenhower admitted young readers might be thinking to themselves, "Well, your generation certainly has made a mess of the world. Do you expect us to do better?" Ike always smiled when he heard this cliché, as he thought to himself, "We said it to our parents and teachers when I was young." According to Eisenhower, the proper answer to the accusation from the young was to confess, "My generation and the generations of the past have *not* done as well as they should." But then he would tell them, "And we do expect you to do better."

In his article, the former president gave specific advice to the up-and-coming generation. He told them to do their homework and not to be used by the sworn enemies of their country. "Be sure your idealism is for the right ideals." He also urged the young to develop their moral courage. Passive disapproval of bad and immoral behavior was not sufficient. Ike acknowledged it was not easy to stand up to a group intent on doing wrong. But speaking from his years of experience, he said moral courage did have its rewards. "It is essential to self-respect, and its practice brings satisfactions that will continue through all the years that lie ahead of you." And finally, Eisenhower told the young to know the obligations of their citizenship. "Democracy's most treasured possession is the vote." Ike said it was not only their privilege, but their duty to inform themselves about candidates and issues, and to then exercise their franchise once they became eligible to vote.

Eisenhower concluded his essay on "Thoughts for Young Americans" by reminding the youth of their wonderful opportunity and formidable responsibility to make the world a better place:

> The world will soon be yours, to do with as you can. I would urge that you approach your task with boldness and hope and the joy of challenge in your hearts—and with dedication to freedom and human dignity. For this is the only route to peace with justice. Good luck, then, and may the Lord go with you![14]

And he closed by saying, "I, for one, believe in you."

CHAPTER TWENTY-THREE

FINDING COMMON GROUND IN PUBLIC CONVERSATIONS

"I began to elaborate the idea of a truly national assembly where
we could mobilize . . . experts from every walk of life . . . (to)
examine the larger problems, find common ground of
agreements about answers, and arrive at working conclusions."
—*Dwight D. Eisenhower*, At Ease

There is only one problem I can see with the magnificent larger-than-life statue of Dwight D. Eisenhower that sits in the center of the Eisenhower Presidential Library grounds. Not the sculpture itself; it is indeed wonderful. In fact, the artist received the highest praise from the former president's own son at the 1985 dedication. From the speaker's podium, John S. D. Eisenhower looked at the statue over his shoulder and said, "I am not an expert on many things, but I am one on likenesses of my father. This is a good one."

The Ike statue is not the issue; rather, it is the six-foot-high pedestal on which it rests. The marble base is very attractive and, quite appropriately, has five sides reflecting the symbology of Eisenhower's five-star military rank. Each side panel of the pedestal is adorned with an emblem and accompanying title of an important position Eisenhower held during his fifty years of service to his nation—well, not quite each panel.

The bronze statue of Dwight D. Eisenhower, created by Robert L. Dean Jr., was presented to the Eisenhower Presidential Library and Museum by the Harry and Edith Darby Foundation. Unique among statues at presidential libraries, the Abilene monument very appropriately depicts Eisenhower in military uniform wearing his familiar World War II "Ike Jacket." The Georgia granite base has quotations from Eisenhower's illustrious tenure as president of the United States, supreme commander of the Allied Expeditionary Forces during World War II, general of the army, Supreme Allied Commander Europe (NATO), and chief of staff of the US Army. Note that four of the five panels on the pentagon-shaped pedestal depict important positions he held. There is one anomaly, however, and that is the panel for general of the army, which is a five-star rank (awarded to nine other generals and admirals during World War II). General of the army is not an office or command held; it is a rank.

As deputy director of the Eisenhower Presidential Library in 1984, when plans for the statue were being formulated, I was included among those asked to provide suggestions for what was to be depicted on the five sides of the pedestal. Rather than the generic general of the army rank—a rank which Eisenhower obviously held during all three military positions already deemed to be included on the base of the sculpture—I suggested the fifth panel should recognize Ike's "other presidency," namely his lesser-known but uniquely important role as president of Columbia University in New York City (1948–1953). My recommendation was not included in the final design for the statue base, and this was an opportunity missed to demonstrate one more facet of the Eisenhower legacy. Most Americans are unaware Ike was in very good company among eight other US presidents who also led universities as president, chancellor, or rector: namely, Washington, Jefferson, Madison, Tyler, Fillmore, Buchanan, Garfield, and Wilson. This is one more example of the underappreciation of the complexity of Dwight D. Eisenhower.

There is a common joke often cited when speaking of Ike's invitation to serve as president of Columbia University. Namely that the search committee at Columbia must have made a mistake and ended up talking to the wrong Eisenhower. Ike even enjoyed repeating the story in moments of self-deprecation. In his own memoir, *At Ease*, Ike wrote, "When a committee from the Board of Trustees of Columbia University asked me to consider becoming President of that great institution, I said that they were talking to the wrong Eisenhower." His brother Dr. Milton Eisenhower was indeed the academic in the family. He was president at Kansas State University (1943–1950) and would later serve as president of Pennsylvania State University (1950–1956) and Johns Hopkins University (1956–1967, 1972–1973). However, in *At Ease*, Ike went on to say perhaps he did have something to offer the academic world:

Without any disparagement to Milton the committee, of which Thomas Watson Sr. was chairman, countered that I had a broad, varied experience in dealing with human beings and human problems, a fundamental concern of the university; that I knew at firsthand many areas of the earth and their peoples; that my interest in training young Americans and my wish to spend the rest of my life in such work offset my lack of formal preparation.[1]

Eisenhower noted that during World War II, soldiers had often asked him why they were fighting and for what were they fighting. In 1950, he told a luncheon of Columbia University associates that the solders at times indicated a bitterness toward "certain parts of the economy at home."[2] Why should they put their lives on the line for big business and industry or finance? Ike explained:

> Democracy owes its soldiers at least this much: a sound and inspiring reason why they have to go to battle. I felt there was something wrong with an educational system that hadn't met that deficiency.... That gave me the courage to go into education.[3]

When Ike returned from the war, he believed America was in danger because of two reasons. The first was the more obvious threat from communism abroad. But secondly, in his opinion there was a failure "to remember that the basic values of democracy were won only through sacrifice and to recognize the dangers of indifference and ignorance." Believing that educational institutions needed to assume immediate leadership in studying, explaining, and perpetuating the American system, Eisenhower had accepted Columbia's presidency.[4]

Ike believed that the faculty of Columbia University was a tremendous asset capable of taking the lead in studying and analyzing the national viewpoint on the vast social, political, and economic problems thrust upon America after World War II. He felt the university's role needed to expand beyond the campus classrooms and scholarly conferences. Eisenhower, collaborating with Philip Young, dean of the Graduate School of Business, began to conceptualize the idea as a truly national assembly. The new assembly would not only mobilize Columbia's educational and intellectual resources but also bring in other experts from every walk of life to discuss and reflect on issues and together try to find common ground. In a December 1949 speech at the Waldorf Astoria Hotel, Eisenhower made a passing reference to the resistance his concept was receiving from some corners of the more traditional faculty members who viewed Columbia as a strictly academic institution. He joked, "Maybe we like caviar and champagne when we ought to be out working on beer and hot dogs." By late 1949, Ike had arrived at a name for his new creation; a name which highlighted its broader mission: the American Assembly.[5] The next major step occurred when William Averell Harriman became interested in the concept and offered his family home, Arden House, with surrounding acreage on the Hudson River north of New York City. It became known as the Harriman Campus of Columbia University and still serves as the home of the American Assembly.[6]

Most Americans, Eisenhower believed, went about their duties as citizens without the opportunity to thoroughly explore all the facts and factors involved in the problems of democracy. The American Assembly could bring together "all segments of our people" to study the issues to hopefully develop some truths and observations about challenges facing society. Business leaders, workers and labor leaders, professionals, and political figures from both parties would study and discuss the issues. Ike, ever the realist, wrote, "The Columbia Conference plan offers no complete answer, but it will be an effective start."[7]

It must be noted that the concept of an American Assembly had its practical importance for the university. The trustees and many distinguished alumni gave the project enthusiastic support. Dean Young said:

> The American Assembly will bring to Columbia the type of recognition that will lead to financial support in a wide variety of fields. . . . Under this program, Columbia, as a great university, has an unparalleled opportunity to exercise her leadership for the good of the country.[8]

On its website today, the American Assembly describes its aim as fostering "public conversations that lead to more just, equitable, and democratic societies." The forum has strived to do this for over seventy years by bringing research to bear on public problems, thereby creating added resources for public understanding that hopefully strengthen the trust and deliberation that help make democracy work.

In 1954, President Eisenhower traveled from the White House back to New York City to honor Columbia University on the institution's 200th anniversary. In his banquet address to a gathering of former colleagues and distinguished alumni, Ike once again stressed the importance for democracy of open dialogue. His prescient remarks were in many ways a reiteration of the role he envisioned for the American Assembly:

> May we never confuse honest dissent with disloyal subversion. Without exhaustive debate—even heated debate—of ideas and programs, free government would weaken and wither. But if we allow ourselves to be persuaded that every individual or party that takes issue with our own

convictions is necessarily wicked or treasonous—then indeed we are approaching the end of freedom's road. We must unitedly and intelligently support the principles of Americanism.[9]

The following are a few examples of the varied topics examined in open dialogue by the American Assembly since its inception in 1950:

- *A Workable Government: The US Constitution*
- *Matters of Faith: Religion in American Public Life*
- *The Performing Arts and American Society*
- *Building Advocacy for Middle Neighborhoods: Stabilizing Neighborhoods "On the Edge" between Growth and Decline*
- *Searching for the Uncommon Common Ground: Building a More United America*
- *Energy Conservation and Public Policy*
- *Seminar on Trust and Mistrust of Science and Experts*

In looking back at his tenure as president of Columbia, Eisenhower explained that the university was a concentration of outstanding characters and superior intellect. Every day, he encountered men and women who were "brilliant in their talk" and "profound in their thoughts." Ike, the career military officer, acknowledged the great benefit of his time on the campus, saying, "They immensely broadened my horizons."[10] In his memoir, Eisenhower reflected on the significance of his creation of the American Assembly: "Throughout the years, its influence, although difficult to measure, has been far reaching beyond my dreams of almost two decades ago. Much of the time I think its beginnings were my principal success as University President."[11]

During the year-long celebration of the Dwight D. Eisenhower Centennial in 1990, the American Assembly was quite appropriately recognized as one of the "Eisenhower legacy" organizations.[12] The assembly is still going strong today. In retrospect it seems that Ike would have been very pleased if his role as a university president had been included among the five-star panels on the base of the magnificent edifice that sits in the center of the Eisenhower Presidential Library grounds.

CHAPTER TWENTY-FOUR

ABILENE HONORS IKE
BEING A HOMETOWN HERO HAS
ITS LIMITATIONS

"A prophet is not without honor except in his native place."
Mark 6:4

Don't get me wrong. Dwight D. Eisenhower is honored in Abilene, Kansas. The citizenry is proud to live in the hometown of a World War II hero, former US president, and world-famous figure. American flags and five-star logo banners adorn the streetlight poles up and down Abilene's main north-south and east-west avenues. The beautiful twenty-two-acre Eisenhower Presidential Library and Museum complex on the south end of town is a treasure promoted to travelers by the convention and visitors bureau, with billboards all along Interstate 70 encouraging them to take exit 275 to learn more about Abilene's famous native son. I like Ike. You like Ike. And certainly, Abilene likes Ike. But over the years there have been episodes of wavering about the extent of this adoration.

Ike Eisenhower himself would not have been surprised about this limit on adulation. In an October 1942 letter penned to Mamie from London during World War II, he shared the joy he felt upon learning he had been selected for honorary membership in his hometown's prestigious Abilene Rotary Club. "The town may be only 4000—but it's my town, and I was d- - - happy to know they'd thought of such a thing." [Note Ike's self-censoring of profanity in his letter home.] General Eisenhower had just recently received his third star and been appointed as commander of the European Theater of Operations. He was now nationally known, if not a world-famous figure. Ike heard that a local radio broadcaster had made a flowery speech about Ike at halftime of the Abilene High School football game. He told his wife, "So apparently (for the time being) I'm the home town boy that made good in the big city." Ike then continued with a revealing observation in his letter to Mamie:

Sometimes I wonder what a lot of people—who now suddenly remember they knew me when—would say if a big reverse came to me. Possibly they'd not even wonder whether it was my fault, but would say

"I told you so!" However, I do not mean to be cynical, I'm quite overwhelmed to know how many people have taken the trouble to send me a cheery and encouraging word! But manifestly not all of them can be completely sincere, else they would have written some of their nice words before my name got in the newspapers.[1]

Eisenhower's hometown of Abilene was established in 1861 on the east side of the crossing of Armistead Creek. The small creek was named for US Army Captain Lewis Addison Armistead, who served at nearby Fort Riley and other posts along the Smoky Hill River in Kansas from 1855–1858. The creek's original name was short-lived, however, as the town changed it after the Civil War began and Armistead joined the Confederate States Army. Armistead Creek became Mud Creek, the name it still bears today. It is not certain if the new name was an intentional insult to Armistead as he took off his blue uniform and donned the gray. But it seems possible. In 1861, the citizens of Abilene were part of the brand new free state of Kansas, which joined the Union in January 1861, a mere two and a half months before Fort Sumter was shelled and the Civil War began. Lewis Armistead rose to the rank of brigadier general in the Confederate Army and died a hero of the South on July 5, 1863, from wounds received during the Battle of Gettysburg.

Ironically, Dwight D. Eisenhower was the winner in a more recent move in the ongoing effort to erase certain names from American history. On October 27, 2023, Fort Gordon near Augusta, Georgia, was renamed Fort Eisenhower. John B. Gordon may have served as a US senator and governor of Georgia in the years after the Civil War, but prior to those roles he was a general in the Confederate Army. The US Army press release announcing the new name cited Eisenhower's admiration for the Augusta area and noted that Ike found solace throughout his presidential years during his many visits to the community.

Mud Creek runs north and south, just east of Abilene's city park. The park dates from 1906, but many of the current structures were built by the Works Progress Administration (WPA) during the 1930s using Kansas native limestone. The impressive stone structures include a large municipal swimming pool and the rodeo stadium. The Central Kansas Free Fair takes place in the park. The city park was renamed Eisenhower Park in 1944 in honor of Ike at the height of his wartime fame. Quite appropriately, eight years later the stadium in Eisenhower Park was where Ike announced his candidacy for the presidency in June 1952.

Other than the Eisenhower Presidential Library, Eisenhower Park is the most visible community tribute to Abilene's famous native son. It is indeed a wonderful park and, in addition to the stadium and swimming pool, today the park includes the fairgrounds, a band shell, a large playground, basketball courts, a community garden, baseball diamonds, a beautiful rose garden, and even a skateboarding park. In 2002 the park was entered officially in the National Register of Historic Places. Abilene's registration application submitted to the National Park Service still cited the original name as Abilene City Park Historic District. On the line indicating "other name," it showed Eisenhower Park.

Twenty years after the city park was named for Eisenhower, Abilene declined an opportunity to further honor Ike. In the fall of 1962, construction began on a new elementary school on the north side of town. During the preceding campaign for the bond election to fund the construction, the naming of the future school was discussed. It was commonly understood and agreed upon (but without official action taken by the school board), that when completed it would become Eisenhower Elementary School in honor of Abilene's hometown hero, who by then had just left the White House. A tragic event intervened when President John F. Kennedy was assassinated on November 22, 1963. The matter of naming the future school came up for discussion again, and with understandable reason. The three existing elementary schools in Abilene all bore the names of martyred presidents—Lincoln Elementary, Garfield Elementary, and McKinley Elementary. Had a precedent been set? Historical research reveals that these buildings had not been so identified immediately upon opening but were renamed later. The board of education decided to delay the permanent naming of the new school under construction to permit any possible political implications to lessen and allow the matter to be decided later in an unemotional manner. Therefore, when the school opened its doors to K-6 students on August 31, 1964, it was known as Northside Elementary School.[2]

At a parent-teacher association meeting in February 1965, halfway through the first school year at Northside, a motion was made by one PTA member that a poll of the members present be taken concerning their opinion regarding the permanent name for the school. The motion was passed almost unanimously, and a secret ballot of those attending was duly taken. When the votes were counted it was forty-six for Kennedy and thirty-nine for Eisenhower. The clerk of the Abilene School Board passed the tally on to the board of education for their information, with the caveat that the vote result was merely an unofficial expression of those present at the school parents meeting, since the item had not been on the regular PTA agenda.³ The board took it under advisement. Some four months later, at the Abilene Board of Education meeting of July 6, 1965, the Northside Elementary School was officially accepted by the school board from the several contractors responsible for its construction. It was now school district property. At this same meeting, the board renamed Northside as Kennedy Elementary School.⁴

Today, one can be thankful that this chance to honor Eisenhower was voted down in 1965, as an even better opportunity arrived five decades later. In 2015, Garfield Elementary School was closed. The beautiful old structure had been built in 1942 and could not be brought up to modern code. The Garfield students were moved several blocks west into a brand-new, state-of-the-art school building named Eisenhower Upper Elementary. While Kennedy School is now almost 60 years old and showing its age, the modern Eisenhower School will be a shining monument to Ike for many years to come.

There have been other naming honors bestowed on Ike by the city over recent years. The Little Ike Park was constructed in the Eisenhower Centennial Year of 1990. In 1999 a statue of Eisenhower as a youth was added as the park's focal point. The mini-park lies in the middle of the town on a street corner and is a small, but very nice, green addition to the downtown area. In 2012, the historic Abilene City Building was renamed the Dwight D. Eisenhower Building. I suspect this decision by the city commission was, at least in part, making amends for the controversy surrounding a failed renaming opportunity that caused much dissension in Abilene the prior year. This was the "Buckeye Avenue Episode."

In 2011, the Eisenhower Foundation's Abilene Council proposed another way to honor the former president. Some three hundred signatures were collected on a petition to rename Abilene's primary north-south street for Ike. The thinking was that if the city were to make this simple change, the tens of thousands of visitors to the community would now exit Interstate-70 directly onto "Eisenhower Avenue" rather than a street bearing the name of a tree from the state of Ohio. It seemed only logical that changing Buckeye Avenue to Eisenhower Avenue would be effective in promoting the town on highway billboards and in tourism brochures. Supporters of the change said the renaming could help city businesses. During Presidents Day sales, for example, the already successful car dealership would be able to advertise in their out-of-town media ads, "visit us on Eisenhower Avenue just one block off I-70!" Indeed, over the years, outside community development consultants had always advised the city commission and the convention and visitors bureau to make the connection to Ike even stronger by such a move. Buckeye Avenue was already patriotically adorned with American flags on every other light pole all along its entire two mile stretch each year from Memorial Day to Ike's birthday in October. Addition of the Eisenhower name to the avenue would be a no brainer, right? Not so fast!

Immediately after the proposed name change was introduced for consideration by the Abilene City Commission, the same elected community leaders began receiving phone calls and email messages against the proposed Eisenhower Avenue. The growing opposition group created a "Save Buckeye" page on Facebook. Letters to the editor in the *Abilene Reflector-Chronicle* complained about the unnecessary burden the name change would cause the many residents and businesses on Buckeye Avenue, not to mention the additional costs in signage for the city in making the change.

One writer noted that there were many historic homes, businesses and churches on Buckeye Avenue and asked, "Should we bury this history with a street name?" The renaming proposal was called a short-sighted promotion campaign and nothing more than a short-term gimmick. In a constructive conclusion, this same writer suggested the focus be instead on promoting Kansas Highway 15 as "Eisenhower Memorial Highway," a designation that had already been bestowed a few years earlier by the state. Buckeye Avenue was only the name of the two-to-three-mile section of Kansas Highway 15 as it ran through the town of Abilene.[5] It should be noted that the Buckeye name dated from the late 1800s, many decades before the official state highway. It was the dirt road that went north out of Abilene toward a small township known as the Buckeye Community, established by settlers from Ohio around 1870.

Surprised by the opposition, the Abilene city commission formally solicited comments from the public to be sent in by letter or email about the proposed change, and indeed many responses were received from the community.[6] One Buckeye resident said, "I can't help but think a humble man, like Mr. Eisenhower, would object to such an imposition on residents, businesses, and tax payers." Most of the comments did concern the belief that the name change would result in an unnecessary financial burden to those affected. More than one former resident mourned the nostalgic loss that would result as they fondly remembered their teenage

A photo of the compromise signage now used on Buckeye Avenue, Abilene's main thoroughfare. At each intersection, the blue Eisenhower Memorial Highway sign is affixed atop the existing green colored Buckeye sign.

years "cruising Buckeye," aimlessly driving up and down the main drag on Friday and Saturday nights as all their high school classmates did. "Cruising the Ike" was not an appealing option to them.

Another individual stated, "We already have plenty of the President's name in the town. . . . We have named enough things after our great president. Thank you." Still another noted that Abilene had existed long before Eisenhower and should therefore not just capitalize and promote that name. This same writer took the opportunity to lament the fact Abilene did not have a decent Farmer's Market. Rather than name another thing after Ike, she wrote, "We have farmers, so promote the produce and attract people to the area." The sarcasm award goes to the citizen who said there were already enough things named for Ike, but if the town insisted on moving forward with this idea, why not simply "change the city name from Abilene, Kansas to Eisenhower, Kansas!"[7]

In the end, "Buckeye Wins!" was the headline in the *Abilene Reflector-Chronicle's* July 12, 2011, edition. In reaction to the uproar, the Eisenhower Foundation withdrew its request of the city commission to formally rename the main avenue in the town. Instead, there would be compromise signage. At each cross intersection, the Buckeye Avenue sign would remain and above it would be a new decorative sign stating "Eisenhower Memorial Highway." While the Eisenhower Foundation felt strongly about promoting the legacy of Abilene's most famous citizen, the organization did not want to do it at the cost of dividing the community.[8]

There might have been yet another honor for Eisenhower if the *Monocle* magazine's tongue in cheek suggestion had been given any serious consideration. In a 1960 article, the humor magazine argued, "Forget any Eisenhower statue!" Rather build a golf course in Abilene, Kansas. Eisenhower's detractors had long complained that he spent entirely too much time on the links during his eight years in the White House. Indeed, golf was the president's favorite pastime, and he was reported to have played some eight hundred rounds while serving as chief executive. Momentous presidential decisions had been made on the tee box during the years 1953 to 1960. The *Monocle* even offered a solution for the funding of the proposed golf course. Caddies from across the nation could retrieve lost balls from the roughs and water hazards on their course and the recovered balls could be sold as a fund raiser. Each hole on the Eisenhower Golf Course could be named for one of Ike's policies. Some suggestions were "Liberation," "Cost of Living," and "Peace and Prosperity."[9] This humorous proposal never got off the ground.

So, there are indeed many ways the Eisenhower name is honored today in Ike's Abilene. There is a city park, the city government building, an elementary school, a memorial highway, and most of all a very impressive presidential library with its fifteen-foot Eisenhower statue on its grounds. It is very apparent to every visitor that the community "Still Likes Ike." But the record shows there were occasional limitations on expressing pride in the greatest of hometown heroes. In the historic town of Abilene, history matters; even non-Eisenhower history.

But let us end on a positive note. In June of 2024, Abilene celebrated its hometown hero one more time by unveiling the *Guinness Book of World Records'* "World's Largest I Like Ike Button" in a permanent sculpture located in the downtown area for all townsfolk and visitors to see.

The author is shown visiting the World's Largest I LIKE IKE button in downtown Abilene. The button was unveiled in Eisenhower's hometown in June of 2024. The six foot in diameter sculpture was created by a local metal artist and is now another community attraction. The red, white, and blue sculpture is a giant replica of Eisenhower's 1952 presidential campaign button recognized as one of the most iconic campaign slogans in presidential politics.

CHAPTER TWENTY-FIVE

THE PRESCIENT EISENHOWER

"A degree of socialization will prevail in America. . . . How I pray that when the above sentence is read 35 years hence, it will be something to ridicule."
—*Dwight D. Eisenhower, 1965*

In 1965, the retired president scribbled in his own handwriting several predictions for thirty-five years hence, in the year 2000. These notes are found on lined sheets of yellow tablet paper in a folder entitled "DDE Drafts," located in his post-presidential files at the Eisenhower Presidential Library. Note that Ike accidentally skipped number three, had two number twelves, and the last prediction was unfinished. His estimations of the future were spot on in many cases. He was an "optimistic realist," if that is a valid term. And right or wrong, his predictions are nonetheless very interesting. The following are Eisenhower's exact handwritten words:

1. Because of increasing medical knowledge life expectancy will go up and population with it. This increase will be somewhat offset by smaller families. Population will be about 340,000,000.
2. There will be either a new monetary system jointly designed by the major trading nations or a new price of gold—not less than $70 per ounce.
3. ~~Red China will~~
4. Red China will still be a menace but the U.S.S.R. will then be oriented toward the West to the extent that China will be powerless to challenge the remainder of the world. Under democratic institutions there will be no dictators.
5. Africa will have advanced some degree of industrialization but will be far behind the rest of the world in education, economic and military strengths, and in unity.
6. The North Atlantic Community will comprise a United States of Europe and the U.S.A., with strong economic ties with Japan. It is likely that the entire British Commonwealth, the United States of Europe, Japan and the North American continent will form a

strongly Federated grouping with a common currency and a single foreign policy and security arrangements. (Russia might be a member.)

Latin America will have achieved some unification, higher levels of education, and partial industrialization—but a true middle-class will not have emerged.

7. A degree of socialization will prevail in America, with railways, electrical communications and a number of basic industries under government ownership. (How I pray that when the above sentence is read 35 years hence, it will be something to ridicule.) The individual will still enjoy a measurable degree of personal freedom, but wages and prices will be regulated, taxes on higher income will be at least 90% and death taxes will be particularly confiscatory.

8. Scientifically, no predictions of today will equal fact in the Year 2000. Radio and television broadcasts will be world-wide; city transportation systems will be exclusively public. They will feature mono-rail and subway systems with buses and taxi cabs. A private automobile will not be permitted in the big cities, while the pedestrian traffic will be on a different level from the vehicular.

9. Airways will use jet planes exclusively, but only a few (largely trans-oceanic and flying from isolated airfields) will be faster than sound, because of noise.

Space exploration will be common to the extent new launchings, even new programs will command little attention. However, travel by missile or satellite will not be attempted, because of cost, except as a stunt.

10. Individuals will have miniature (walkie-talkies) which, carried in a pocket will provide instant communications with selected individuals up to distances of a mile.

11. All buildings in the business section (of) cities will be constructed without windows. Heating and air conditioning systems, perfectly controlling temperatures and humidity will be installed as a common practice.

12. Water will be plentiful because of desalinization and power likewise because of success in the economical use of atomic fuel.

13. The big problems in America will be crime.[1]

Eisenhower's predictions about America's future were quite optimistic when it came to technological advances and nuclear power. The "miniature walkie-talkies" he envisioned became today's cell phones. Ike was always the "internationalist," even in his predictions for the future. He was positive about the continuation of close ties between the European Union, the British Commonwealth, and the United States, and he even imagined a common currency. He thought Russia might even be included among the new union of nations. On the other hand, he was certainly concerned that America could be headed in the direction of socialization. Eisenhower was less optimistic about the economic progress that would be achieved in South America, and especially in Africa.

It is unfortunate that Ike did not complete his final prediction about the "big problems" facing America on his 1965 list. The good news is that the former president wrote a series of essays published in *Reader's Digest* magazine from 1965 to 1968. One can surmise with some certainty what would have been included in Eisenhower's unfinished enumeration of major problems confronting the nation in number twelve of his predictions. Crime was the first and only concern listed as he began this unfinished prediction. What certainly could have followed was Ike's concern about growing juvenile delinquency and inner-city poverty.

Another troubling issue to Ike was his sense of a decline in patriotism, centered around the growing divide in the nation because of the Vietnam War. The need for political campaign finance reform was the topic of one of his 1968 essays, entitled "The Ticklish Problem of Political Fund-Raising and Spending." His last essay in *Reader's Digest* was published in April 1969, the month following his death, and was very prescient. It was simply entitled "We Must Avoid the Perils of Extremism." These essays likely cover some the significant issues he would have predicted in his unfinished final entry.

Eisenhower's many years of service to his nation, and to the wider world, reflected his great sense of duty. This higher cause did not, however, prevent him from questioning the reasons why things were done a certain way. Granddaughter Susan Eisenhower said he was not inclined toward groupthink: "In many ways, Eisenhower was a futurist, and he bristled at the conclusions people reached without reference to or consideration of changing circumstances that might soon make current thinking outdated."[2]

In his own words, President Dwight D. Eisenhower said at a press conference, "The world moves, and ideas that were good once are not always good."[3]

ACKNOWLEDGMENTS

It was my privilege to supervise the archives staff at the Eisenhower Library for two and a half decades. They were a group of professionals who were initiative-takers. You could tell they enjoyed their work and appreciated the good fortune they had to be at the presidential library bearing the name Dwight D. Eisenhower. The archives staff performed the daily reference service, the page-by-page processing and arrangement of manuscript collections, and document declassification. I benefited by overseeing the fruits of their outstanding work and this played a major role in my continuous learning about Ike and his legacy. Special thanks to my archives team: Jim Leyerzapf, David Haight, Dwight Strandberg, Tom Branigar, Herb Pankratz, Kathy Struss, Valoise Armstrong, Karen Rohrer, Rod Soubers, Barbara Constable, Linda Smith, Bonnie Mulanax, Michelle Kopfer, Hazel Stitt, Lois Baier, Deanna Kolling, Chalsea Millner, Darla Thompson, and Bob Paull.

The current staff at the Eisenhower Library has also been extremely helpful during my research for this book. I need to thank James Ginther, William Snyder, Kevin Bailey, Mary Burtzloff, Michelle Kopfer (again), and Nicole Beck for assisting in my continued search for original source material in the rich holdings of the library.

One of the greatest benefits of my time at the Eisenhower Library and Foundation was the privilege of becoming personally acquainted with the president's son, John S. D. Eisenhower, and Ike's four grandchildren, David, Anne, Susan, and Mary Jean, who has become a dear friend. They were and are certainly very impressive and accomplished individuals, but more importantly, they are amazingly kind and gracious. I thank them for their friendship and support over the years.

At the foundation's Eisenhower Legacy Gala in 2022, I told Susan Eisenhower of my work and distinctive approach to a book in progress about her grandfather. She was pleased to hear this news and encouraged me to continue writing and to publish. She also directed me to two lesser-known and very helpful monographs she thought I should consult and provided sound advice on one of the chapters. Thank you, Susan.

Elinor Haas served twenty-two years as a volunteer at the Eisenhower Library. In a task that took many hundreds of hours, she reviewed the one million–page Dwight D. Eisenhower's pre-presidential papers collection and transformed what was little more than a rudimentary file folder title list into an annotated finding aid for the collection, with detailed content descriptions for each folder. Elinor knew of my interest and along the way made a photocopy for me of every single document in Ike's pre-presidential papers that included mention of Kay Summersby.

Very special thanks goes to Michael MacCarthy-Morrogh (son of Seamus MacCarthy-Morrogh) in London, England, with whom I have exchanged several emails over the past twenty years. He is a historian and the nephew of Kay Summersby. Michael shared with me copies of his father's correspondence, legal documents, and photographs that make my chapter on the Ike-Kay relationship more authoritative. My personal library of monographs relating to Dwight D. Eisenhower is not inconsequential, totaling some sixty volumes. But it is not complete. There were other books I needed to see in pursuing this writing project. The Eisenhower Presidential Library has over 30,000 volumes in its printed materials collection, and I certainly consulted them. But, alas, they do not loan materials and one must schedule a visit to the research room in person to browse the book. That I did on several occasions, but an on-site visit did not always provide time to sufficiently peruse the book. A solution for me was the excellent Interlibrary Loan (ILL) service provided by the Abilene Public Library. If the volume in question was not already included in their own holdings, Laurie Ward, in charge of Interlibrary Loan, worked her magic to find it at a university library or another public library in Kansas. Even when I requested some obscure title, Ms. Ward rarely failed in her efforts to locate a copy for my work.

Sometimes Interlibrary Loan does not work. Case in point was my search for a copy of the out-of-print *Official Preppy Handbook* that was published in 1980. I could have purchased one on eBay but did not want to make that investment. My daughter Sandra told me she remembered having the book when she was in high school, but it is now long gone. I determined that the library at Emporia State University (ESU) had a copy, but it was not available for ILL. No worries. My grandson Joshua is a college student at ESU and checked the book out on my behalf, thereby earning the honorary title of research assistant. As a result, the chapter on Ike the Preppy is more thoroughly documented and even more entertaining.

Thanks to Mr. Doug Litts, research support librarian with the Archives and Special Collections at the US Military Academy Library. Mr. Litts guided me to their outstanding online sources for information on Eisenhower's grades and class standings for coursework in each of his four years at West Point. I was also able to see detailed descriptions for courses taken by cadets during Ike's time at the academy. This included a list of the assigned textbooks, helping me further demonstrate Eisenhower's early exposure to science and technology in the degree studies pursued by all cadets.

Thanks also to Ms. Lindsey Moen, Lead Public Services Librarian at the University of Iowa Special Collections and Archives. Ms. Moen secured for me hard-to-find copies of the Patriotic Tract Society publication that included anti-Eisenhower columns during the 1952 presidential election alleging Ike's Jewish ancestry.

Then there is Bruce Dale to thank. He passed along a trove of emails and other documents relating to the controversy surrounding the unsuccessful campaign to rename Buckeye Avenue for Eisenhower in Abilene, which is described in chapter 24. This helped flesh out an interesting episode.

I must give special kudos to Rebecca Whitehair Weidenhiller in Regensburg, Germany. She is the daughter of dear friends here in Abilene and my wife Inge's former student. A couple of years ago, Rebecca and I discovered we had something in common—namely, unfinished writing projects (her MA thesis and my book). What followed was the exchange of long-distance WhatsApp messages every couple of weeks from across the Atlantic, informing each other of the progress made. This proved to be a positive and powerful motivating force. The good news is that our pact worked, and we both met our mutually agreed upon deadlines.

I am indebted to Eisenhower scholars who read my draft manuscript and provided both encouragement and helpful suggestions to make it even better. They are Professor Michael Birkner at Gettysburg College; Dr. Daun van Ee, who was editor of the Eisenhower Papers Project at Johns Hopkins University; Susan Eisenhower, Ike's granddaughter and accomplished author; Professor Mary Stuckey, Pennsylvania State University; and Jim Newton, veteran journalist and author of *Eisenhower: The White House Years*.

I greatly appreciated the guidance and professionalism of the staff at the University Press of Kansas for their role in making this book a reality. Many thanks to senior editor David Congdon, Andrea Laws, Kelly Chrisman Jacques, Justin Henning, and the rest of the UPK team. Also special thanks to copy editor Nick Walther for his valuable work.

I want to acknowledge my parents, Kenneth and Natalie Teasley, who are now gone. They gave me a good upbringing, took me to live in exciting places as a military brat, instilled in me a desire to read about history when I was a teenager (especially military history), and provided support through my undergraduate college days. Thank you, Mom and Dad, I wish you could be here to receive a well-deserved copy of this book.

Our daughters, Sandra and Anja, have been along on this Eisenhower journey. They have lived in Germany, Washington, DC, Boston, and finally in Kansas (twice) as part of this saga. The good news is that the girls are now able to proudly claim that they graduated from Eisenhower's alma mater, Abilene High School. My wonderful grandchildren also deserve mention. These good troopers provide a lot of joy and have also pretended to never be bored while hearing (sometimes for the umpteenth time) another Eisenhower story or Ike quote from their grandfather. Thanks for listening patiently, Corinne, George, Joshua, Abigail, Anne, Francesca, Kenslie, and Ellie.

Finally, and most importantly, I want to thank my wife, Ingeborg Pauls Teasley. Throughout our marriage, she has been my strongest and loving supporter, best advisor, and a great motivator. She was my cheerleader as I worked on this writing project. Inge sees things from a different perspective and always provides sage advice. Her shared observations have made this a better book. I am blessed.

NOTES

CHAPTER 1. THE DWIGHT D. EISENHOWER PRESIDENTIAL LIBRARY IN ABILENE

1. Martin M. Teasley, "German Language Study at the Dwight D. Eisenhower Library," *Foreign Language Annals*, February 1987/Volume 20, 39–41.

2. Martin M. Teasley, "No Signs of Mid-Life Crisis: The Eisenhower Library at Thirty-something," *Government Information Quarterly*, 1995, 12, no. 1, 83–92.

CHAPTER 2. THE IKE NICKNAME

1. "Young Mr. Eisenhower," CBS film, 1966.

2. DDE to Benjamin Reese, September 6, 1943, in *The Papers of Dwight D. Eisenhower, Vol. 2: The War Years*, ed. Alfred Chandler (Johns Hopkins University Press, 1971), 1393–1394.

3. Alden Hatch, *General Ike: A Biography of Dwight D. Eisenhower* (Consolidated Book Publishers, 1944), 9.

4. Kenneth S. Davis, *General Eisenhower Soldier of Democracy: From Boyhood to Supreme Commander* (Doubleday, 1945), 14.

5. Stephen Ambrose, *Eisenhower: Soldier, General of the Army, President-Elect, 1890–1952* (Simon & Schuster, 1983), 28.

6. J. E. Lighter et al., eds., *Random House Historical Dictionary of American Slang* (Random House, October 1997).

7. Harold Wentworth and Stuart Berg Flexner, eds., *Dictionary of American Slang* (Thomas Y. Crowell Co., 1967), 279.

8. Eric Partridge, *A Dictionary of Slang and Unconventional English* (Macmillan Company, 1961), 420.

CHAPTER 3. IKE THE ATHLETE

1. Dwight D. Eisenhower, *At Ease: Stories I Tell to Friends* (Doubleday, 1967), 16.

2. "The Young Mr. Eisenhower," television interview film with DDE re: Abilene and West Point, CBS, 1966.

3. Mark E. Eberle, "Eisenhower, Wilson, and Professional Baseball in Kansas" (2017). *Monographs*. 1. http://scholars.fhsu.edu/all_monographs/1.

4. Dwight D. Eisenhower Post-Presidential Papers, Convenience File Series, Box 1, DDE Personals.

5. Carl Hodges, "As the Twig is Bent," *Esquire*, September 1944.

6. Ann C. Whitman to Kathryn P. Welsh, August 4, 1956, Eisenhower Papers as President, White House Central Files, Box 3, Folder 1-A 1956(2).

7. Eisenhower, *At Ease*, 16.

8. Merle Miller, *Ike the Soldier: As They Knew Him* (G. P. Putnam's Sons, 1987), 40.

9. Mack Teasley; "'The Kansas Cyclone'—Eisenhower the Athlete," *Kansas Sports Magazine*, 10, no. 1, August/September 1995.

10. Correspondence between the author and Dr. Michael Birkner regarding an oral history interview he conducted in Gettysburg, Pennsylvania, in 2024 with Gareth V. Biser.

11. Address to the Republican National Conference, June 7, 1957, in the Public Papers of the Presidents-Dwight D. Eisenhower 1957, Containing the Public Messages, Speeches, and Statements of the President (Office of the Federal Register, National Archives and Records Service), 456.

CHAPTER 4. "HAIL TO THE CHEF"

Epigraph: Amor Towles, *A Gentleman in Moscow* (Viking Press, 2016), 148.

1. Edward and Candace Russoli, *Ike the Cook: General, President, and Cook* (Benedettini Books, 1990), 15, 65.

2. Dwight D. Eisenhower, *At Ease: Stories I Tell to Friends* (Doubleday, 1967), 90–91.

3. Eisenhower, *At Ease*, 91.

4. David Eisenhower with Julie Nixon Eisenhower, *Going Home to Glory: A Memoir of Life with Dwight D. Eisenhower, 1961–1969* (Simon & Schuster, 2010), 63.

5. Eisenhower, *At Ease*, 92.

6. Russoli, *Ike the Cook*, 15–16.

7. Michael J. Mckeogh and Richard Lockridge, *Sgt. Mickey and General Ike* (G. P. Putnam's Sons, 1946), 13–14.

8. McKeogh and Lockridge, *Sgt. Mickey and General Ike*, 43–44.

9. John S. D. Eisenhower, *Strictly Personal* (Doubleday, 1974), 278.

10. Ambassador Gilbert A. Robinson, *Why I Like Ike* (International Publishers, 2012) (reissue), 36–37.

11. Russoli, *Ike the Cook*, 85.

12. Gary Shapiro, "Cooking Up Columbia's Culinary History," December 23, 2014, Columbia News, at news.columbia.edu.

13. Russoli, *Ike the Cook*, 39.

14. Recipe of Dwight D. Eisenhower for Vegetable Soup, as published in the *Marion Sentinel*, Linn County, Iowa.

15. Charlie Nardozzi, "Durable, Delectable Nasturtiums," National Gardening Association Learning Library, at garden.org.

16. Russoli, *Ike the Cook*, 89.

17. Russoli, *Ike the Cook*, 88.

18. Russoli, *Ike the Cook*, 78.

19. Russoli, *Ike the Cook*, 115.

20. Russoli, *Ike the Cook*, 83.

CHAPTER 5. THE FIRST PREPPY PRESIDENT

1. Lisa Birnbach, ed., *The Official Preppy Handbook* (Workman Publishing, 1980), 141.

2. Glenn Fowler, "Vincent Draddy, 83, an Innovator in Apparel Manufacturing, Dies," *New York Times*, July 10, 1990.

3. Emily Spivack, "The Story Behind the Lacoste Crocodile Shirt," *Smithsonian Magazine*, June 4, 2003.

4. "Alligator Shirts," Skooldays: Nostalgic & Vintage Memorabilia, undated online blurb.

5. Gift Files, White House Central Files, see cards for David Crystal and Vincent Draddy, 1956–1960, Eisenhower Presidential Library.

6. Eisenhower Records as President, White House Central Files, President's Personal File Series, Boxes 195–196, Eisenhower Presidential Library.

7. Birnbach, *The Official Preppy Handbook*, 19.

8. Birnbach, *The Official Preppy Handbook*, 156.

CHAPTER 6. OY VEY! IKE THE TERRIBLE SWEDISH JEW

1. Quentin Reynolds in Ambassador Gilbert A. Robinson, *Why I Like Ike* (International Publishers, 2012) (reissue), 16–17.

2. Dwight D. Eisenhower, *Crusade in Europe* (Doubleday, 1948), 108, 128.

3. Eisenhower, *Crusade*, 129.

4. Judah Nadich, *Eisenhower and the Jews* (Twayne Publishers, Inc., 1953), 13.

5. Nadich, *Eisenhower and the Jews*, 11.

6. *Federal Register*, 20FR 409, Wednesday, January 19, 1955.

7. "U.S. Presidential Elections: Jewish Voting Record (1916-Present)," The Jewish Virtual Library—a project of the American-Israeli Cooperative Enterprise (AICE).

8. Robert Griffith, *Ike's Letters to a Friend* (University of Kansas Press, 1984), 175.

9. Autopsy Protocol Dwight D. Eisenhower WRGH A-69-000, Box 9, Page 33, Medical Records of Dwight D. Eisenhower, 1911–69, US Army, Office of the Surgeon General, Eisenhower Presidential Library.

CHAPTER 7. IKE'S RUMORED BLACK ANCESTRY

1. Kaye Eisenhower Morgan, *The Eisenhower Legacy: A Tribute to Ida Stover Eisenhower and David Jacob Eisenhower* (Roesler Enterprises Publishing, 2005), 4.

2. *Insight* magazine, February 1, 1993, 27.

3. J. A. Rogers, *The Five Negro Presidents: According to What White People Said They Were* (Wesleyan University Press, 2014) (originally self-published in 1965), 13.

4. Auset BaKhufu, *The Six Black Presidents: Black Blood, White Masks* (PIK2 Publications, 1993), 235, 243.

5. BaKhufu, *Six Black Presidents*, 243.

6. BaKhufu, *Six Black Presidents*, 280–281.

CHAPTER 8. IKE THE PILOT

1. Dwight D. Eisenhower, "Fledgling at Fifty," six-page draft of a typed memoir, undated, written by DDE in the Philippines circa 1940, in Daniel D. Holt and James W. Leyerzapf, *Eisenhower: The Prewar Diaries and Selected Papers, 1905–1941* (Johns Hopkins University Press, 1998), 441–444.

2. Oral history interview with Brig. Gen. William L. Lee, USAF (Ret.), December 9, 1970, Eisenhower Presidential Library, 136–137.

3. Dwight D. Eisenhower, *At Ease: Stories I Tell to Friends* (Doubleday, 1967), 227.

4. Rebecca Grant, "Eisenhower, Master of Airpower" *Air & Space Forces Magazine*, January 1, 2000.

5. Dwight D. Eisenhower, *Crusade in Europe* (Doubleday, 1948), 452.

6. Special Message to the Congress Recommending the Establishment of a Federal Aviation Agency, June 13, 1958, in the Public Papers of the Presidents-Dwight D. Eisenhower 1958, Containing the Public Messages, Speeches, and Statements of the President (Office of the Federal Register, National Archives and Records Service), 466–467.

7. Dwight D. Eisenhower, *The White House Years: Mandate for Change, 1953–1956* (Doubleday, 1963), 453.

CHAPTER 9. "TAKE ME TO YOUR LEADER"

1. Letter from James M. Mixson to James Leyerzapf, archivist at the Dwight D. Eisenhower Library, February 13, 1995 (in possession of author).

2. The President's Appointments, Sunday, February 21, 1954, in Appointment Books, Dwight D. Eisenhower Presidential Library.

3. Robert H. Ferrell, ed., *The Diary of James C. Hagerty: Eisenhower in Mid-Course, 1954–1955* (Indiana University Press, 1983), 18.

4. The President's News Conference of December 15, 1954, in the Public Papers of the Presidents-Dwight D. Eisenhower 1954, Containing the Public Messages, Speeches, and Statements of the President (Office of the Federal Register, National Archives and Records Service), 1111–1112.

5. National Security Council Staff Papers, NSC Registry File, Box 3, folder "CIA

5(3), "CIA REPORT ON UFOs, Jan. 17, 1953," Dwight D. Eisenhower Presidential Library.

6. White House Central Files, General File, Box 1155, Folder GF145-F Science Earth-circling Satellites-Space Travel-Flyer Saucers Outer Space, "Special Report No. 14 (Analysis of Reports of Unidentified Aerial Objects) Project No. 1007," May 5, 1955, Dwight D. Eisenhower Presidential Library.

7. "Air Force Releases Study on Unidentified Aerial Objects," Office of Public Information, Department of Defense, Release No. 1053–55, October 25, 1955, Dwight D. Eisenhower Presidential Library.

8. Official website of the DoD All-domain Anomaly Resolution Office (AARO), aaro.mil.

9. Greg Eghigian, "In 2019, our Eyes Were on the Skies," *Air & Space Magazine*, February 2020.

10. Contactinthedesert.com.

11. Telegram from G. W. Van Tassel to the President, dated 4/6/54. Sent from Twenty-nine Palms, California. White House Central Files, Alpha File, Box 3197 "Vant." Dwight D. Eisenhower Presidential Library.

12. The Reference Report prepared on Majestic 12 or MJ-12 by the National Archives and Records Administration can be found at archives.gov/research/military /air-force/ufos.html.

CHAPTER 10. "OTHER LOSSES"

1. James Bacque, *Other Losses: An Investigation into the Mass Deaths of German Prisoners at the Hands of the French and Americans After World War II* (Stoddart Publishing Co., 1989), xix.

2. Bacque, *Other Losses*, 144–145.

3. Bacque, *Other Losses*, 30.

4. Günter Bischof and Stephen E. Ambrose, eds., *Eisenhower and the German POWs: Facts Against Falsehood* (Louisiana State University Press, 1992), 2.

5. Dwight D. Eisenhower, *Crusade in Europe* (Doubleday, 1948), 405, and "Translation from S.HA.E.F. News," April 10, 1945, in Eisenhower Pre-Presidential Papers, "Crusade in Europe Documents (1)," Box 137, Eisenhower Library.

6. Bischof and Ambrose, *Eisenhower and the German POWs*, 104, 111.

7. 189th Infantry Regiment S-3 Journal for June 1945, Box 1419, US Army Unit Records, 1940–1950, Eisenhower Library.

8. Cable, SHAEF to 12th Army Group, May 18, 1945, as cited in Earl F. Ziemke, Army Historical Series, "The U.S. Army in the Occupation of Germany, 1944–1946," Center of Military History, Washington, DC, 1975, 293.

9. Eisenhower, *Crusade in Europe*, 421–422.

10. Bischof and Ambrose, *Eisenhower and the German POWs*, 5–6.

11. Bischof and Ambrose, *Eisenhower and the German POWs*, 9–11, 57–60.

12. Bischof and Ambrose, *Eisenhower and the German POWs*, 22–23.

13. Rolf Steininger, "Some Reflections on the Maschke Commission," in Bischof and Ambrose, *Eisenhower and the German POWs*, 176.

14. Eisenhower, *Crusade in Europe*, 470.

15. John S. D. Eisenhower, *Dwight D. Eisenhower Letters to Mamie* (Doubleday, 1978), 209–210.

16. Dwight D. Eisenhower to Chief of Staff General George C. Marshal, May 25, 1943, Eisenhower Pre-Presidential Papers, and in Bacque, *Other Losses*, 21.

17. R. A. Winnaker (Historian, Office of the Secretary of Defense) to Prof. Alfred C. Chandler Jr. (The Eisenhower Project, The Johns Hopkins University), September 21, 1967 (copy in possession of the author).

18. Michael J. McKeogh. and Richard Lockridge, *Sgt. Mickey and General Ike* (G. P. Putnam's Sons, 1946) (reprint edition in 2016), 164.

19. Robert H. Ferrell, ed., *The Diary of James C. Hagerty: Eisenhower in Mid-Course, 1954–1955* (Indiana University Press, 1983), 175.

20. Stephen E. Ambrose, "Ike and the Disappearing Atrocities," *New York Times Book Review*, February 24, 1991.

21. Ambrose, "Ike and the Disappearing Atrocities."

22. Bacque, *Other Losses*, 32.

23. Eisenhower to Marshall, April 21, 1945, Pre-Presidential Papers, Eisenhower Library.

24. Bischof and Ambrose, *Eisenhower and the German POWs*, 23.

25. Albert E. Cowdrey, "A Question of Numbers," in Bischof and Ambrose, *Eisenhower and the German POWs*, 90.

26. Albert E. Cowdrey report to Chief of Military History, Department of the Army, "Subject: Deaths among German Prisoners of War in the Spring of 1945," September 14, 1989 (copy in possession of the author).

27. Ambrose, "Ike and the Disappearing Atrocities."

CHAPTER 11. KAY SUMMERSBY

1. Kay Summersby, *Eisenhower Was My Boss* (Prentice Hall, 1948), 6–7.

2. Kay Summersby Morgan, *Past Forgetting: My Love Affair with Dwight D. Eisenhower* (Simon & Schuster, 1975), 86.

3. Information on *Strathallan*, British troop transport, at uboat.net/allies/merchants/ship/2528.html.

4. Memorandum from Colonel R. R. Arnold to Commanding General—II Corps,

March 22, 1943, Pre-Presidential Papers of Dwight D. Eisenhower, Principal File, Box 112, Eisenhower Library.

5. Militaryhallofhonor.com, i.d. no. 199302, Col. Richard R. Arnold.

6. Summersby, *Eisenhower Was My Boss*, 132.

7. Summersby, *Eisenhower Was My Boss*, 174.

8. Morgan, *Past Forgetting*, 97.

9. Susan Eisenhower, *How Ike Led* (Thomas Dunne Books, 2020), 227.

10. Summersby, *Eisenhower Was My Boss*, 161.

11. Morgan, *Past Forgetting*, 107.

12. "Eisenhower is Cheered in London as He Returns for Tardy V-E Day," *New York Times*, May 16, 1945, 5.

13. Dwight D. Eisenhower to Kay Summersby, letter dated November 22, 1945, Eisenhower, Dwight D. Papers, Pre-Presidential, 1916–52, Principal File, Box 112, Eisenhower Library.

14. Dwight D. Eisenhower to Whom It May Concern, memo dated January 18, 1946, Dwight D. Eisenhower Papers, Pre-Presidential, 1916–52, Principal File, Box 112, Eisenhower Library.

15. Athan Theoharis, *From the Secret Files of J. Edgar Hoover* (Ivan R. Dee, Inc., 1991), 58, and "Bryant Confession Taken in Evidence by Federal Court," *Sausalito News*, 62, no. 23, June 5, 1947.

16. Dwight D. Eisenhower, *The Eisenhower Diaries* (W. W. Norton, 1981), December 2, 1947, 145.

17. Harry C. Butcher to Eisenhower, December 5, 1947, Dwight D. Eisenhower Papers, Pre-Presidential, 1916–52, Principal File, Box 16, Eisenhower Library.

18. Margaret Chase to Eisenhower, December 16, 1947, Dwight D. Eisenhower Papers, Pre-Presidential, 1916–52, Principal File, Box 22, Eisenhower Library.

19. Athan Theoharis, *From the Secret Files of J. Edgar Hoover.* (Ivan R. Dee, Inc, 1991), 58.

20. Capt. Harry Butcher to DDE, December 18, 1951, Eisenhower Pre-Presidential Papers, Principal File, folder "Butcher, Harry C. (1), Oct. 1951–June 1952," Box 16, Eisenhower Library.

21. Kay Summersby to Eisenhower, dated December 17, 1948, and Eisenhower to Kay Summersby, dated December 18, 1948, Dwight D. Eisenhower Papers, Pre-Presidential, 1916–52, Principal File, Box 112, Eisenhower Library.

22. Dwight D. Eisenhower to Captain Harry C. Butcher, December 26, 1945, in the Dwight D. Eisenhower Pre-Presidential Papers, Principal File, Box 16, Eisenhower Library.

23. Dwight D. Eisenhower to Kay Summersby, February 14, 1946, Dwight E. Eisenhower Pre-Presidential Papers, Principal File, Box 112, Eisenhower Library.

24. David Dempsey, review of *Eisenhower Was My Boss* entitled "Cinderella with Brass," *New York Times*, October 31, 1948, 16.

25. Dwight D. Eisenhower to George T. Bye, July 26, 1948, Eisenhower Pre-Presidential Papers, Secondary File, Box 16, Eisenhower Library.

26. Dwight D. Eisenhower to Harry Butcher, January 4, 1949, Dwight D. Eisenhower Pre-Presidential Papers, Principal File, Box 16, Eisenhower Library.

27. Eisenhower to Butcher, January 4, 1949.

28. Dwight D. Eisenhower cable to Office of US Military Governor, Berlin, Germany, September 17, 1946, Dwight D. Eisenhower Papers, Pre-Presidential, 1916–52, Principal File, Box 112, Eisenhower Library.

29. Memo from Kay Summersby to Sue Sarafian and Margaret Chick, September 30, 1945, in Pre-Presidential Papers of DDE, 1916–52, Principal File, "Kay Summersby," Box 112, Eisenhower Library.

30. John S. D. Eisenhower, *Strictly Personal* (Doubleday, 1974), 158.

31. Herbert Brownell (with John P. Burke), *Advising Ike: The Memoirs of Attorney General Herbert Brownell* (University Press of Kansas, 1993), 129.

32. Merle Miller, *Plain Speaking: An Oral History of Harry S. Truman* (Berkley Publishing Company, 1973).

33. Douglas R. Price, "The Truth About General Eisenhower's Alleged Affair During World War II," unpublished article dated 2012 in the author's possession.

34. Price, "The Truth About General Eisenhower."

35. Robert H. Ferrell and Francis H. Heller, "Plain Faking?" *American Heritage*, Volume 46, Issue 3, May/June 1995.

36. Ferrell and Heller, "Plain Faking?"

37. Dwight D. Eisenhower to George C. Marshall, June 4, 1945, Eisenhower Papers, Johns Hopkins University, Volume 6, 134.

38. George C. Marshall to Dwight D. Eisenhower, June 8, 1945, Eisenhower Pre-Presidential Papers, Eisenhower Library.

39. Merle Miller, *Ike the Soldier: As They Knew Him* (G. P. Putnam's Sons, 1987), 642.

40. Morgan, *Past Forgetting*, 7.

41. Morgan, *Past Forgetting*, 171–172.

42. Morgan, *Past Forgetting*, 16.

43. Morgan, *Past Forgetting*, 9.

44. Gil Troy, "With Ike, Rumors Were Steamer Than Facts," *Washington Post*, March 1, 1998.

45. Susan Eisenhower, *Mrs. Ike: Memories and Reflections on the Life of Mamie Eisenhower* (Farar, Straus and Giroux, 1996), 206.

46. Email message in possession of the author, dated March 28, 2002.

47. Morgan, *Past Forgetting*, 103.

48. Letter J. C. F. MacCarthy-Morrogh to Burlingham, Underwood & Lord, 25 Broadway, New York City, February 21, 1975, in possession of the author.

49. Letter from L. A. Robinson of Burlingham, Underwood & Lord to J. C. F. MacCarthy-Morrogh, March 4, 1975, in possession of the author.

50. Bob Considine, column entitled "To Kay Summersby from a close friend," King Features Syndicate in *Reading Eagle* (Reading, PA), January 30, 1975.

51. Considine, "To Kay Summersby."

52. Considine, "To Kay Summersby."

53. John S. D. Eisenhower, ed., and commentary, *Letters to Mamie by Dwight D. Eisenhower* (Doubleday, 1978), 7.

54. Eisenhower, *Letters to Mamie*, 7–8.

55. Eisenhower, *Letters to Mamie*, 11–12.

56. Susan Eisenhower, *Mrs. Ike: Memories and Reflections on the Life of Mamie Eisenhower* (Farar, Straus and Giroux, 1996), 205.

57. Jim Newton, *Eisenhower: The White House Years* (Doubleday, 2011), 22.

58. Eisenhower, *Letters to Mamie*, 28.

59. Eisenhower, *Letters to Mamie*, 32–33.

60. Eisenhower, *Letters to Mamie*, 35, 213, 249.

61. Eisenhower, *Letters to Mamie*, 137.

62. Eisenhower, *Letters to Mamie*, 75, 83.

63. Eisenhower, *Letters to Mamie*, 280.

64. Steve Neal, *The Eisenhowers* (University Press of Kansas, 1984), 178–179.

65. Eisenhower, *Mrs. Ike*, 206.

66. Peter Lyon, *Eisenhower: Portrait of the Hero* (Little, Brown and Company, 1974), 387.

67. Virgil Pinkley with James F. Scheer, *Eisenhower Declassified* (Fleming H. Revell Company, 1979), 363, 368.

68. Stephen E. Ambrose, *Eisenhower: Soldier, General of the Army, President Elect, 1890–1952* (Simon & Schuster, 1983), 245, 285.

69. Gary Wills, "Truman, Eisenhower and Kay Summersby," *New York Post*, August 18, 1997.

70. Geoffrey Perret, *Eisenhower* (Random House, 1999), 214.

71. Carlo D'Este, "The Myth of Ike and Kay Summersby," four-part series in *Armchair General* magazine, February/March/July/August 2013.

72. Pinkley and Scheer, *Eisenhower Declassified*, interview with Harry Butcher, 362.

73. Carlo D'Este, "The Myth of Ike and Kay Summersby—Part 4—Conclusion," in *Armchair General* magazine, August 4, 2013.

74. Lord Keith of Castleacre (Lt. Colonel Retired) to the Editor, *Washington Post*, July 5, 1997.

75. Pinkley and Scheer, *Eisenhower Declassified*, 362–364.

76. David Eisenhower, *Eisenhower at War 1943–1945* (Random House,1986), 198.

77. Telephone conversation, the author with Mrs. Anthea Saxe, May 2, 2002.

78. Oral History (OH-517) interview with Sue Sarafian Jehl, February 13, 1991, Dwight D. Eisenhower Presidential Library.

79. Robert J. Donovan, *Confidential Secretary: Ann Whitman's 20 Years with Eisenhower and Rockefeller* (F. F. Dutton, 1988), 14.

80. Oral history interview with Ann Whitman, Dwight D. Eisenhower Presidential Library, February 15, 1991, 25–26.

81. Cathy Ritchie, "Book Review: Loving Eleanor, by Susan Wittig Albert," *Rainbow Round Table Book and Media Reviews*, August 2016.

82. Susan Wittig Albert, *The General's Women* (Gale Cengage Learning, 2017), 4, 626.

83. Susan Eisenhower, "Hardly an Affair," *Washington Post*, June 22, 1997.

84. Morgan, *Past Forgetting*, 192.

85. Michael MacCarthy-Morrogh, "Kay Summersby – Helping Ike Win the War," in Skibbereen Historical Journal, Volume 16, 2020.

86. Virgil Pinkley letter to John S. D. Eisenhower, June 17, 1977.

87. Eisenhower, *Eisenhower at War*, 198.

88. Summersby, *Eisenhower Was My Boss*, 288–289.

CHAPTER 12. THE PROFANE IKE

1. Herbert S. Parmet, *Eisenhower and the American Crusades* (Macmillan Company, 1972), 176. Note that Parmet credits a "confidential source" with this information. Nevertheless, it is a great quote that fits the narrative about Eisenhower and has now entered the lore.

2. John S. D. Eisenhower, *Dwight D. Eisenhower Letters to Mamie* (Doubleday, 1978), 241.

3. Michael J. McKeogh and Richard Lockridge, *Sgt. Mickey and General Ike* (G. P. Putnam's Sons, 1946), 51.

4. Sue Sarafian Jehl oral history interview, February 13, 1991, Eisenhower Library, 39.

5. Kay Summersby, *Eisenhower Was My Boss* (Prentice Hall, 1948), 21.

6. Kay Summersby Morgan, *Past Forgetting: My Love Affair with Dwight D. Eisenhower* (Simon & Schuster, 1975), 251.

7. Ann Whitman oral history interview, Eisenhower Presidential Library, February 15, 1991, 6.

8. Frederick N. Rasmussen, "Douglas R. Price, Historian and Former Aide to President Eisenhower, Dies," *Baltimore Sun*, March 4, 2016.

9. Dictabelt EL-T-IBM-264, May 19, 1950, Columbia University, New York City, Eisenhower Library.

10. Dictabelt EL-IMB-139-1, January 4, 1955, Oval Office, The White House, Washington, DC, Eisenhower Library.

11. DDE letter to Swede Hazlett, February 26, 1958, in *Ike's Letters to a Friend, 1941–1958*, edited by Robert Griffith, 200.

12. Dictabelt EL-IBM-141-2, January 7, 1955, Oval Office, The White House, Washington, DC, Eisenhower Library.

13. John S. D. Eisenhower, *Strictly Personal: A Memoir* (Doubleday, 1974), 8.

14. Catherine M. Lewis, *Don't Ask What I Shot: How Eisenhower's Love of Golf Helped Shape 1950s America* (McGraw Hill, 2007), 28, 66.

15. Eisenhower to Arthur S. Nevins, August 31, 1954, White House Central Files, Eisenhower Library.

16. Peter Andrews, "Ike and the Gang," *Golf Digest*, April 1993, 164, as cited in Catherine M. Lewis, *Don't Ask What I Shot: How Eisenhower's Love of Golf Helped Shape 1950s America* (McGraw Hill, 2007), 28.

17. Dwight D. Eisenhower, *At Ease: Stories I Tell to Friends* (Doubleday, 1967), 88–89.

18. Tristin Hooper, "Are Swears Becoming So Common, They Aren't Even Profanity Anymore? F— That!" *National Post*, April 11, 2014.

CHAPTER 13. "DWIGHT VAN GOGH"

1. Sister Wendy Beckett, "President Eisenhower the Painter," *White House History, No. 21* (The White House Historical Association, Washington, DC, 2007).

2. Kenneth S. Davis, "Eisenhower, The Man as Painter," in *The Eisenhower College Collection: The Paintings of Dwight D. Eisenhower* (Nash Publishing, 1972), 147.

3. Beckett, *White House History*, and Dwight D. Eisenhower, *At Ease: Stories I Tell to Friends* (Doubleday, 1967), 340–341.

4. Dwight D. Eisenhower to Winston S. Churchill, September 21, 1950, Pre-Presidential Papers, 16–52, Box 22, folder "Churchill, W (2)," Eisenhower Library.

5. Susan Eisenhower, *How Ike Led: The Principles Behind Eisenhower's Biggest Decisions* (Dunne Books, 2020), 226–227.

6. Eisenhower, *At Ease*, 341.

7. Richard Cohen, "A Visit with the Real Dwight D. Eisenhower," *Washington Post*, April 9, 2012, as cited in Susan Eisenhower, *How Ike Led*, 224.

8. "Art By Eisenhower to be Shown Here," *New York Times*, February 14, 1967, 49.

9. Davis, "Eisenhower: The Man as Painter," 147–148.

10. DDE Eisenhower Library dedication speech, May 1, 1962, Post-Presidential Papers, 1961–1969, Speech Series, Box 2, Eisenhower Presidential Library.

11. Frieda Kay Fall, "The Painter Dwight D. Eisenhower: A Critical Look," in *The Eisenhower College Collection*, 156.

12. Eisenhower, *How Ike Led*, 224.

CHAPTER 14. IKE AND THE ATOMIC BOMB

1. Inaugural Address, January 20, 1953, in the Public Papers of the Presidents-Dwight D. Eisenhower 1953, Containing the Public Messages, Speeches, and Statements of the President (Office of the Federal Register, National Archives and Records Service), 2.

2. Dwight D. Eisenhower, *Crusade in Europe* (Doubleday, 1948), 443, 456.

3. Dwight D. Eisenhower, *Mandate for Change: The White House Years, 1953–1956* (Doubleday, 1963), 312–313.

4. Dwight D. Eisenhower Dwight D. to John J. McCloy, June 18, 1965, Post-Presidential Papers, Eisenhower Library.

5. Barton J. Berstein, "Ike and Hiroshima: Did He Oppose It?," *The Journal of Strategic Studies*, 10, no. 3 (September 1987): 377.

6. Berstein, "Ike and Hiroshima," 382.

7. Bernstein, "Ike and Hiroshima," 386.

8. Dwight D. Eisenhower, Columbia University Dictabelt Recordings, 1949–50, C. W. Boyer, February 28, 1950 (in the holdings of the Eisenhower Presidential Library). To listen to the Dictabelt visit the Miller Center Presidential Records, University of Virginia. (millercenter.org/search=bayer) (note: recording is filed under incorrect name).

9. Inaugural Address, January 20, 1953, in the Public Papers of the Presidents-Dwight D. Eisenhower 1953, Containing the Public Messages, Speeches, and Statements of the President (Office of the Federal Register, National Archives and Records Service), 2–3.

10. Eisenhower, *Mandate for Change*, 224.

11. Statement by the President After Reviewing the Case of Julius and Ethen Rosemberg, February 11, 1953, in the Public Papers of the Presidents-Dwight D. Eisenhower 1953, Containing the Public Messages, Speeches, and Statements of the President (Office of the Federal Register, National Archives and Records Service), 40–41.

12. Eisenhower, *Mandate for Change*, 225.

13. Eisenhower, *Mandate for Change*, 143.

14. Eisenhower, *Mandate for Change*, 144–145.

15. Address "The Chance for Peace" Delivered Before the American Society of Newspaper Editors, April 16, 1953, in the Public Papers of the Presidents-Dwight D. Eisenhower 1953, Containing the Public Messages, Speeches, and Statements of the

President (Office of the Federal Register, National Archives and Records Service), 179, 188.

16. Eisenhower, *Mandate for Change*, 181.

17. Evan Thomas, *Ike's Bluff: President Eisenhower's Secret Battle to Save the World* (Little, Brown and Company, 2012), 78, 98–99.

18. Robert Ferrell, *The Eisenhower Diaries* (W. W. Norton, 1981), 175–176.

19. Thomas, *Ike's Bluff*, 80.

20. Cited in frontispiece in Campbell Craig, *Destroying the Village: Eisenhower and Thermonuclear War* (Columbia University Press, 1998).

21. Memorandum regarding "Operation Candor," July 22, 1953, White Office, National Security Council Papers, PSB Central Files Series, Box 17, Eisenhower Library.

22. Eisenhower, *Mandate for Change*, 252.

23. Jack M. Hall and Roger M. Anders, *Atoms for Peace*, Milestone Documents in the National Archives, National Archives and Records Administration, Washington, DC, 1990, 5.

24. Address Before the General Assembly of the United Nations on Peaceful Uses of Atomic Energy, December 8, 1953, in the Public Papers of the Presidents-Dwight D. Eisenhower 1953, Containing the Public Messages, Speeches, and Statements of the President (Office of the Federal Register, National Archives and Records Service), 820.

25. Address Before the General Assembly of the United Nations on Peaceful Uses of Atomic Energy, December 8, 1953, in the Public Papers of the Presidents-Dwight D. Eisenhower 1953, Containing the Public Messages, Speeches, and Statements of the President (Office of the Federal Register, National Archives and Records Service), 822.

26. Memorandum of conference with the President, May 24, 1956, Whitman File, DDE Diaries, Eisenhower Library.

27. Thomas, *Ike's Bluff*, 103.

28. Ferrell, *The Eisenhower Diaries*, 261–262.

29. I. I. Rabi, *My Life and Times as a Physicist* (Claremont College, 1960), 27.

30. Rabi, *Life and Times as a Physicist*, 19.

31. Rabi, *Life and Times as a Physicist*, 28.

32. Holl and Anders, *Atoms for Peace*, 6–7.

33. World Nuclear Association (world-nuclear.org/information-library).

34. Rabi, *Life and Times as a Physicist*, 22.

35. Holl and Anders, *Atoms for Peace*, 8.

36. Nina Tannenwald, *The Nuclear Taboo: The United States and the Non-Use of Nuclear Weapons Since 1945* (Cambridge University Press, 2007), 140.

37. Tannenwald, *Nuclear Taboo*, 149.

38. Thomas, *Ike's Bluff*, 108.

39. Radio Address to the American People on the National Security and Its Costs, May 19, 1953, in the Public Papers of the Presidents-Dwight D. Eisenhower 1953, Containing the Public Messages, Speeches, and Statements of the President (Office of the Federal Register, National Archives and Records Service), 820.

40. William Safire, *The New Language of Politics: An Anecdotal Dictionary of Catchwords, Slogans, and Political Usage* (Random House, 1968), 34–35.

41. Jim Newton, *Eisenhower: The White House Years* (Doubleday, 2011), 267.

42. Robert Griffith, ed., *Ike's Letters to a Friend* (University Press of Kansas, 1984), 168–169.

43. Alex Roland, "The Grim Paraphernalia: Eisenhower and the Garrison State," in *Forging the Shield: Eisenhower and National Security for the 21st Century*, edited by Dennis Showalter (Imprint Publications, 2005), 21.

44. Dwight D. Eisenhower to General Alfred M. Gruenther, May 4, 1953, Gruenther Papers, Eisenhower Correspondence Series, 1941–78, Box 1, Eisenhower Library.

45. Eisenhower, *Mandate for Change*, 446.

46. The President's News Conference of March 16, 1955, in the Public Papers of the Presidents-Dwight D. Eisenhower 1955, Containing the Public Messages, Speeches, and Statements of the President (Office of the Federal Register, National Archives and Records Service), 333.

47. Memorandum of conference with the President, May 24, 1956, Whitman File, DDE Diaries, Eisenhower Library.

48. Susan Eisenhower, *How Ike Led: The Principles Behind Eisenhower's Biggest Decisions* (Thomas Dunne Books, 2020), 172.

49. Clayton D. Laurie, "The Invisible Hand of the New Look: Eisenhower and the CIA," in *Forging the Shield*, 98–99.

50. Eisenhower Post-Presidential Papers, 1961–1969, Secretaries Series, Box 1, DDE Drafts (3), Eisenhower Presidential Library.

51. Holl and Anders, *Atoms for Peace*, 10.

CHAPTER 15. MOVE OVER RICHARD NIXON!

1. D. Robert Jonovan, *Confidential Secretary: Ann Whitman's 20 Years with Eisenhower and Rockefeller* (E. P. Dutton, 1988), 3.

2. John C. Powers, "The History of Presidential Audio Recordings at the Archival Issues Surround Their Use," CIDS Paper, National Archives and Records Administration, July 12, 1996, as cited on the Miller Center website (millercenter.org).

3. Hugh Sidey, "Ike's Beautiful Bugged Desk," *Time* international edition,

September 6, 1982, as cited in William Doyle, *Inside the Oval Office: The White House Tapes from FDR to Clinton* (Kodansha International, 1999), 357.

4. Powers, "History of Presidential Audio Recordings."

5. Oral history interview with Ann C. Whitman, February 15, 1991, 4–5.

6. Powers, "History of Presidential Audio Recordings."

7. Recorded conversation of January 4, 1955, with Civil Aeronautics Board member Oswald Ryan, Tape 3, Eisenhower Library.

8. Oral history interview with Ann C. Whitman, 4–5.

9. Stephen E. Ambrose, *Eisenhower: The President* (Simon & Schuster, 1984), 203.

10. Dwight D. Eisenhower, *Crusade in Europe* (Doubleday, 1948), 38.

11. Evan Thomas, *Ike's Bluff: President Eisenhower's Secret Battle to Save the World* (Little, Brown and Company, 2012), 13.

12. Richard Nixon, *Six Crises* (Doubleday, 1962), 161.

CHAPTER 16. IKE THE CULTURAL WARRIOR

1. Ralph E. Becker, *Miracle on the Potomac: The Kennedy Center from the Beginning* (Bartleby Press, 1990), 2.

2. Annual Message to the Congress on the State of the Union, January 6, 1955, in the Public Papers of the Presidents-Dwight D. Eisenhower 1955, Containing the Public Messages, Speeches, and Statements of the President (Office of the Federal Register, National Archives and Records Service), 28–29.

3. Becker, *Miracle on the Potomac*, 10.

4. Becker, *Miracle on the Potomac*, 7.

5. Becker, *Miracle on the Potomac*, 42–43.

6. Michael J. McKeogh and Richard Lockridge, *Sgt. Mickey and General Ike* (G. P. Putnam's Sons, 1946), 72–73.

7. *Collier's Magazine*, January 31, 1953.

8. Dwight D. Eisenhower: Records as President, White House Central Files, 1953–1961, President's Personal File, Box 2, folder "PPF1-A 1954(2)1954."

9. Kay Summersby, *Eisenhower Was My Boss* (Prentice Hall, 1948), 214.

10. McKeogh and Lockridge, *Sgt. Mickey and General Ike*, 61–62.

11. Becker, *Miracle on the Potomac*, 10–11.

12. Dan Reifsnyder, "Who Knew These US Presidents Were Also Musicians?" Soundfly.com, February 19, 2018.

13. Becker, *Miracle on the Potomac*, 12, 15.

14. Becker, *Miracle on the Potomac*, 13.

15. Becker, *Miracle on the Potomac*, 10.

16. "NSC 5602/1—Basic National Security Policy," March 15, 1956, in the Records

of the White House Office of the Special Assistant for National Security Affairs, NSC Series, Policy Papers Subseries, Box 17, Eisenhower Presidential Library, pages 1, 15–16.

17. Remarks at the People-to-People Conference, September 11, 1956, in the Public Papers of the Presidents-Dwight D. Eisenhower 1956, Containing the Public Messages, Speeches, and Statements of the President (Office of the Federal Register, National Archives and Records Service), 751.

18. Becker, *Miracle on the Potomac*, 32.

19. Becker, *Miracle on the Potomac*, 30.

20. Becker, *Miracle on the Potomac*, 32.

21. Becker, *Miracle on the Potomac*, 61–72.

22. Becker, *Miracle on the Potomac*, 163–164.

23. Becker, *Miracle on the Potomac*, 163.

24. Becker, *Miracle on the Potomac*, 187–188.

25. The Report of the President's Commission on National Goals, The American Assembly, Columbia University, November 1960, 8.

CHAPTER 17. "DEPORTER IN CHIEF"

1. Robert H. Ferrell, ed., *The Diary of James C. Hagerty: Eisenhower in Mid-Course, 1954–1955* (W. W. Norton, 1981), 23.

2. Frank Tannenbaum, *The Struggle for Peace and Bread* (Alfred A. Knopf, 1950), 8, as cited in Juan Ramon Garcia, *Operation Wetback: The Mass Deportation of Mexican Undocumented Workers in 1954* (Greenwood Press, 1980), 3.

3. Author's note: I too have waded across the Rio Grande; however, the crossing occurred in south-central Colorado very close to the source of the famous river. This legal (and in retrospect unwise) crossing was done with a group of my backpacking buddies hiking near Ute Creek in September 1993. The river was ice cold, still fed from the snow melt of the Rockies, and the waist-deep water was fast moving. My back did not get wet, but my lower body was frigid in the deep water during the long, slow journey, where every step was slippery and treacherous along the boulder-strewn riverbed. If one of us had lost our forty-pound pack in the river, our planned weeklong hike would have had a premature ending for everyone. We were too cheap and unwilling to pay a toll of $10 per person to use a footbridge available from a private landowner just a few hundred yards up the river. It was the principle of the thing, but in retrospect not very smart. I recently read a US Forest Service advisory that states, "The main Ute Creek Trail begins with a difficult crossing of the Rio Grande River. Early summer crossings of the river at the trailhead should not be attempted." At least we were crossing in the late summer, and I can now say, "I too have waded across the Rio Grande."

4. Garcia, *Operation Wetback*, 40.

5. Garcia, *Operation Wetback*, 36.

6. Garcia, *Operation Wetback*, 39.

7. Garcia, *Operation Wetback*, 36.

8. Report on the "Wetback" and Bracero Programs dated January 26, 1955, in Dwight D. Eisenhower Papers as President of the United States, 1953–61 (Ann Whitman File), Cabinet Series, Box 4, Folder title "Cabinet Meeting Jan 18, 1955," Eisenhower Library.

9. Thomas Caloway Langham, "The Eisenhower Administration and Operation Wetback, 1953–56: A Case Study of the Development of a Federal Policy to Control Illegal Migration," PhD dissertation (1984), University of Texas, Eisenhower Library, 1.

10. Report on the "Wetback" and Bracero Programs dated January 26, 1955.

11. Report on the "Wetback" and Bracero Programs dated January 26, 1955.

12. Report on the "Wetback" and Bracero Programs dated January 26, 1955.

13. Report on the "Wetback" and Bracero Programs dated January 26, 1955.

14. Herbert Brownell, *Advising Ike: The Memoirs of Attorney General Herbert Brownell* (University Press of Kansas, 1993), 151.

15. Brownell, *Advising Ike*, 224.

16. Langham, "The Eisenhower Administration and Operation Wetback," 6–7.

17. DDE letter to Swede Hazlett, 20 July 1954, in Robert Griffith, ed., *Ike's Letters to A Friend, 1941–1956* (University Press of Kansas, 1984), 129.

18. Garcia, *Operation Wetback*, 225–227.

CHAPTER 18. IKE AND THE EMMY

1. Kathryn Cramer Brownell, "This is How Presidential Campaign Ads First Got on TV," Time.com, August 30, 2016.

2. Jonathan Glancey, "The Statuette Has a Rich, Rumour-filled History—But Was a Dog Really the First Winner," BBC.com, February 19, 2016.

3. "History of the Television Academy Television-The Beginning of Syd Cassyd's Dream," Academy website (emmys.com), November 17, 2020.

4. Bernard M. Shanley to George Murphy, March 1, 1955, White House Central Files, President's Personal File, folder PPF1-Q, Box 343, Eisenhower Library.

5. Memo on White House letterhead from "Ex. Sec. M" to Ann (Whitman), undated, White House Central Files, President's Personal File, folder PPF1-Q, Box 343, Eisenhower Library.

6. Brownell, "This is How Presidential Campaign Ads First Got on TV."

7. Martha Joint Kumar, "Presidential Press Conferences: Windows on the Presidency and Its Occupants," Heritage Lecture, US Department of State, May 16, 2011, as shown on the White House Historical Association website.

8. The President's News Conference of January 19, 1955, in the Public Papers of the Presidents-Dwight D. Eisenhower 1955, Containing the Public Messages, Speeches, and Statements of the President (Office of the Federal Register, National Archives and Records Service), 185.

9. Robert S. Kieve oral history interview, Eisenhower Presidential Library, 4/10/78, 14.

10. Dwight D. Eisenhower, *Mandate for Change: The White House Years, 1953–1956* (Doubleday, 1963), 478.

11. Evan Thomas, *Ike's Bluff: President Eisenhower's Secret Battle to Save the World* (Little, Brown and Company, 2012), 160–161.

12. James Hagerty oral history interview, Eisenhower Presidential Library, April 16, 1968, 464.

13. Arthur Larson, *Eisenhower: The President Nobody Knew* (Charles Scribner's Sons,1968), 14–15.

14. Robert H. Ferrell, ed., *The Diary of James C. Hagerty: Eisenhower in Mid-Course, 1954–1955* (W. W. Norton, 1981), 169.

CHAPTER 19. A NATURAL CURIOSITY

1. Remarks at the Fifth International Congress on Nutrition, September 1, 1960, in the Public Papers of the Presidents-Dwight D. Eisenhower 1960–61, Containing the Public Messages, Speeches, and Statements of the President (Office of the Federal Register, National Archives and Records Service), 668–670.

2. Dwight D. Eisenhower, *At Ease: Stories I Tell to Friends* (Doubleday, 1967), 103–104.

3. Reference the Official Registers of the Officers and Cadets, at usma.libguides .com/special-collections-archives/WestPointResources.

4. Eisenhower, *At Ease*, 117–118.

5. Eisenhower, *At Ease*, 172–173.

6. Daniel D. Holt and James W. Leyerzapf, *Eisenhower: The Prewar Diaries and Selected Papers, 1905–1941* (Johns Hopkins University Press, 1998), 28–35.

7. Eisenhower, *At Ease*, 173.

8. Carlo D'Este, *Eisenhower: A Soldier's Life* (Henry Holt, 2002), 245.

9. Aviation Flight Log Book, Bush, G. H. W., June 9, 1943–September 1945, at bush41library.tamu.edu/archives/selected-documents.

10. Individual Flight Record, Bush, George W., as of December 31, 1972 (copy in possession of the author).

11. Herman S. Wolk, "Ike and the Air Force," *Air Force Magazine*, April 1, 2006.

12. Address Before the General Assembly of the United Nations on Peaceful Use of Atomic Energy, New York City, December 8, 1953, in the Public Papers of the

Presidents-Dwight D. Eisenhower 1953, Containing the Public Messages, Speeches, and Statements of the President (Office of the Federal Register, National Archives and Records Service), 820.

13. Statement by the President Upon Signing Executive Order Strengthening the Scientific Programs of the Federal Government, March 17, 1954, in the Public Papers of the Presidents-Dwight D. Eisenhower 1954, Containing the Public Messages, Speeches, and Statements of the President (Office of the Federal Register, National Archives and Records Service), 335.

14. Statement by the President Upon Signing Executive Order Strengthening the Scientific Programs of the Federal Government, March 17, 1954, in the Public Papers of the Presidents-Dwight D. Eisenhower 1954, Containing the Public Messages, Speeches, and Statements of the President (Office of the Federal Register, National Archives and Records Service), 336.

15. Statement by the President on Establishing the National Committee for the Development of Scientists and Engineers, April 3, 1956, in the Public Papers of the Presidents-Dwight D. Eisenhower 1956, Containing the Public Messages, Speeches, and Statements of the President (Office of the Federal Register, National Archives and Records Service), 365.

16. US President's Committee on Scientists and Engineers, Records, 1956–58, Box 35, Folder "Committee PCSE—Final Report," Eisenhower Library, 37–38.

17. Radio and Television Address to the American People on Science in National Security, November 7, 1957, in the Public Papers of the Presidents-Dwight D. Eisenhower 1957, Containing the Public Messages, Speeches, and Statements of the President (Office of the Federal Register, National Archives and Records Service), 794–795.

18. Awards Presented to Commander Anderson and to Other Officers and the crew of the U.S.S. Nautilus, August 8, 1958, in the Public Papers of the Presidents-Dwight D. Eisenhower 1958, Containing the Public Messages, Speeches, and Statements of the President (Office of the Federal Register, National Archives and Records Service), 600.

19. Farewell Radio and Television Address to the American People, January 17, 1961, in the Public Papers of the Presidents-Dwight D. Eisenhower 1960–61, Containing the Public Messages, Speeches, and Statements of the President (Office of the Federal Register, National Archives and Records Service), 1038–1039.

20. George B. Kistiakowsky, *A Scientist in the White House: The Private Diary of President Eisenhower's Special Assistant for Science and Technology* (Harvard University Press, 1976), 409.

21. Aslee Vance, *Elon Musk: Tesla, SpaceX, and the Quest for a Fantastic Future* (HarperCollins, 2015), 107, 235–237.

22. Dwight D. Eisenhower, *Waging Peace: The White House Years* (Doubleday, 1965), 208.

23. APS News, October 2007 (Volume 16, Number 9), American Physical Society, College Park, MD.

24. Robert H. Ferrell, ed., *The Diary of James C. Hagerty: Eisenhower in Mid-Course, 1954–1955* (Indiana University Press, 1983), 15.

25. Radio and Television Address to the American People on Science in National Security, November 7, 1957, in the Public Papers of the Presidents-Dwight D. Eisenhower 1957, Containing the Public Messages, Speeches, and Statements of the President (Office of the Federal Register, National Archives and Records Service), 798–799.

26. Katie Hafner and Matthew Lyon, *Where Wizards Stay Up Late: The Origins of the Internet* (Simon & Schuster, 1996), 15–16.

27. Hafner and Lyon, *Where Wizards Stay Up Late*, 22.

28. Oral history interview with James R. Killian Jr., OH-216 (Columbia University Oral History Project), November 16, 1969, Eisenhower Library, 68.

29. Killian OH, 47–48.

30. Thomas Farnan, "How Dwight D. Eisenhower Invented the Internet—and the Desktop Computer," *Forbes*, September 2, 2014.

31. Farnan, "How Dwight D. Eisenhower Invented the Internet."

CHAPTER 20. IKE THE WORDSMITH

Epigraph: Dwight D. Eisenhower, *At Ease: Stories I Tell to Friends* (Doubleday, 1967), 187.

1. From Plebe to President: Ike as His Classmates Remember Him," *Collier's*, June 10, 1955, 92.

2. "From Plebe to President," 93.

3. Information from the Archives and Special Collection, US Military Academy Library.

4. Eisenhower, *At Ease*, 39.

5. "3 Famous Writers on the Relationship Between Reading and Writing," *Farnam Street* blog (undated).

6. Daniel D. Holt and James W. Leyerzapf, *Eisenhower: The Prewar Diaries and Selected Papers, 1905–1941* (Johns Hopkins University Press, 1998), 59.

7. Dwight D. Eisenhower Pre-Presidential Papers, Principal File, Box 92, Folder "PERSHING, John J.," Eisenhower Library.

8. Eisenhower, *At Ease*, 207–209.

9. Eisenhower, *At Ease*, 213.

10. Arthur Larson, *Eisenhower: The President Nobody Knew* (Charles Scribner's Sons, 1968), 145.

11. Kevin McCann, *Man from Abilene* (Doubleday, 1952), 161.

12. Eli Ginzberg and Henry Graff, "Two Who Liked Ike," *Columbia Magazine*, February 1985, 17.

13. David Pietrusza, *1948: Harry Truman's Improbable Victory and the Year That Transformed America* (Union Square Publishing, 2011), 201.

14. Gordon M. Goldstein, *Lessons in Disaster: George Bundy and the Path to War in Vietnam* (*New York Times Books*, 2008), 11.

15. Description of Dictabelt recorded conversation, DDE and Roy Rutherford, April 29, 1950, Columbia University, New York City, belt 2 of 2, in holdings of the Dwight D. Eisenhower Library.

16. Transcription of handwritten notes by Stephen Benedict, made during August 12 to September 2, 1952, while at Citizens for Eisenhower.

17. Oral history interview with William Ewald, OH487, December 16, 1977, in the holdings of the Eisenhower Presidential Library, 42.

18. Robert J. Donovan, *Confidential Secretary: Ann Whitman's 20 Years with Eisenhower and Rockefeller* (E. P. Dutton, 1988), 44.

19. Oral history interview with John McCone, OH396, August 26, 1976, in the holdings of the Eisenhower Presidential Library, 50.

20. Robert S. Kieve oral history interview, OH 411, April 10, 1978, Eisenhower Library, 8.

21. Kieve OH411, 8–11.

22. Larson, *Eisenhower*, 146.

23. Gerald D. Morgan oral history, OH223, 2 OF 3, April 29, 1968, Eisenhower Library, 83.

24. Ewald oral history OH487, 35.

25. Dr. I. S. Ravdin to DDE, December 18, 1961, and DDE to Ravdin, January 1, 1962, in 1962–1963 Signature File Series of DDE Post-Presidential Papers, Box 13, folder "Invitations Declined (IN-2)-Ra," Eisenhower Library.

CHAPTER 21. IKE AND GOD

Epigraph: Press conference at Columbia University, *New York Times*, May 4, 1948, as cited in Richard V. Pierard and Robert D. Linder, *Civil Religion and the Presidency* (Academic Books, 1988), 185, and cited by Jack M. Holl in "Dwight D. Eisenhower: Civil Religion and the Cold War," in Mark J. Rozell and Gleaves Whitney, eds., *Religion and the American Presidency* (Palgrave and MacMillan, 2007) , 119.

1. Ernest W. Lefever, "The Candidates Religious Views," *The Christian Century*, September 1956, p. 1072, as cited by Holl in "Dwight D. Eisenhower," 119.

2. Jerry Bergman, "President Eisenhower and the Influence of the Jehovah's Witnesses," *Kansas History*, 21, no. 3 (Autumn 1998): 163.

3. William Clark to Stewart Alsop, March 3, 1954, Alsop's Papers, Library of Congress, cited in Piers Brendon, *Ike: His Life and Times* (Harper & Row, 1986), 7.

4. David Eisenhower with Julie Nixon Eisenhower, *Going Home to Glory: A Memoir of Life with Dwight D. Eisenhower, 1961–1969* (Simon & Schuster, 2010), 192.

5. Dwight D. Eisenhower, *At Ease: Stories I Tell My Friends* (Doubleday, 1967), 82.

6. Bergman, "President Eisenhower and the Influence of the Jehovah's Witnesses," 151.

7. Pierard and Linder, *Civil Religion and the Presidency*, 193.

8. Pierard and Linder, *Civil Religion and the Presidency*, 193.

9. Bergman, "President Eisenhower and the Influence of the Jehovah's Witnesses," 155.

10. Bergman, "President Eisenhower and the Influence of the Jehovah's Witnesses," 160.

11. Dwight D. Eisenhower letter to Arthur Eisenhower, May 18, 1943, Pre-Presidential Papers of Dwight D. Eisenhower, Eisenhower Library.

12. Bergman, "President Eisenhower and the Influence of the Jehovah's Witnesses," 151.

13. Michael J. McKeogh and Richard Lockridge, *Sgt. Mickey and General Ike* (G. P. Putnam's Sons, 1946) (reprint edition in 2016), 85.

14. Remarks at a Luncheon Meeting of the General Board of the National Council of Churches, November 18, 1953, in the Public Papers of the Presidents-Dwight D. Eisenhower 1953, Containing the Public Messages, Speeches, and Statements of the President (Office of the Federal Register, National Archives and Records Service), 792.

15. Dwight D. Eisenhower quote, Dictabelt recording of a conversation in the office of president at Columbia University, April 29, 1950, Eisenhower Presidential Library.

16. Ann C. Whitman to E. S. Whitman, undated, Personal Papers of Ann C. Whitman, Box 1—"Correspondence, E. S. Whitman," Eisenhower Presidential Library, as cited by Holl in "Dwight D. Eisenhower: Civil Religion and the Cold War."

17. No official source found. Eisenhower quote on atheism cited by many quotation books and websites.

18. Remarks at the Dedicatory Prayer Breakfast of the International Christian Leadership, February 5, 1953, in the Public Papers of the Presidents-Dwight D. Eisenhower 1953, Containing the Public Messages, Speeches, and Statements of the President (Office of the Federal Register, National Archives and Records Service), 38.

19. Remarks Upon Lighting the National Community Christmas Tree, December 24, 1953, in the Public Papers of the Presidents-Dwight D. Eisenhower 1953, Containing the Public Messages, Speeches, and Statements of the President (Office of the Federal Register, National Archives and Records Service), 858–859.

20. Holl, "Dwight D. Eisenhower," 119.

21. *New York Times*, December 23, 1952, as cited in Pierard and Linder, *Civil Religion and the Presidency*, 16.

22. Jim Newton, *Eisenhower: The White House Years* (New York, Doubleday 2011), 340–341.

23. Rev. Robert A. MacAskill, Reverend Robert A., oral history interview 1998 OH532, Dwight D. Eisenhower Presidential Library, 19.

24. MacAskill OH532, 8.

25. Inaugural Address, January 20, 1953, in the Public Papers of the Presidents-Dwight D. Eisenhower 1953, Containing the Public Messages, Speeches, and Statements of the President (Office of the Federal Register, National Archives and Records Service), 1.

26. Holl, "Dwight D. Eisenhower," 120.

27. Robert J. Donovan, *Confidential Secretary: Ann Whitman's 20 Years with Eisenhower and Rockefeller* (E. P. Dutton, 1988), 7–8.

28. Jack Holl, *The Religious Journey of Dwight D. Eisenhower: Duty, God, and Country* (William B. Eerdmans Publishing Company, 2021), 300.

29. DDE Post-Presidential Paper, 1965 Principal File, Box 16, Folder "PU-1 Publications-Accepted (Forewords, etc.)," Eisenhower Library.

30. Original handwritten copy in DDE Post-Presidential Papers, 1965 Principal File, Box 16 in folder: "PU-1 Publications-Accepted (Forewords, Etc.)(9)" and cited in Holl, *The Religious Journey of Dwight D. Eisenhower*, 305.

31. *Decision* magazine, July 1965.

32. Holl, *The Religious Journey of Dwight D. Eisenhower*, 300–301.

33. Memorandum for Record from the Office of Dwight D. Eisenhower, Palm Desert, CA, March 23, DDE Post Presidential Papers, 1965 Principal File, Box 2, Eisenhower Library.

34. Dwight D. Eisenhower quote, Dictabelt recording of a conversation in the office of president at Columbia University, April 29, 1950.

35. Dwight D. Eisenhower quote, Dictabelt recording of a conversation in the office of president at Columbia University, April 29, 1950.

36. Eisenhower, *Going Home to Glory*, 252–253.

37. Dwight D. Eisenhower letter to Dr. Edward Mead Earle, September 2, 1952, in John S. D. Eisenhower, *Strictly Personal* (Doubleday, 1974), 393–394.

CHAPTER 22. EISENHOWER ON AMERICA'S YOUTH

1. Robert Griffith, ed., *Ike's Letters to a Friend, 1941–1956* (University Press of Kansas, 1984), 20.

2. Executive Order 10673, Fitness of American Youth, issued July 16, 1956.

3. Post-Presidential Papers of Dwight D. Eisenhower, Speech Series, Box 2, Eisenhower Presidential Library.

4. Post-Presidential Papers of Dwight D. Eisenhower, Speech Series, Box 2. Eisenhower Presidential Library,

5. Post-Presidential Papers of Dwight D. Eisenhower, Speech Series, Box 2, Eisenhower Presidential Library.

6. *New York Times*, May 2, 1962, 1, 40.

7. David Eisenhower with Julie Nixon Eisenhower, *Going Home to Glory: A Memoir of Life with Dwight D. Eisenhower, 1961–1969* (New York: Simon & Schuster, 2010), 181.

8. Dwight D. Eisenhower, *At Ease: Stories I Tell to Friends* (Doubleday, 1967), 9.

9. Eisenhower, *Waging Peace 1956–61*, 655–656.

10. *New York Times*, June 6, 1966, 47, and *K-Stater Magazine*, July 1966.

11. *New York Times*, June 6, 1966, 47.

12. Eisenhower, Dwight D, *Crusade in Europe* (Doubleday, 1948), 350.

13. Susan Eisenhower, *How Ike Led: The Principles Behind Eisenhower's Biggest Decisions* (Thomas Dunne Books, 2020), 227.

14. Dwight D. Eisenhower, "Thoughts for Young Americans," *Reader's Digest*, April 1966, included in "The Eisenhower Essays," 57.

CHAPTER 23. FINDING COMMON GROUND IN PUBLIC CONVERSATIONS

1. Dwight D. Eisenhower, *At Ease: Stories I Tell to Friends* (Doubleday, 1967), 336.

2. Travis Beal Jacobs, *Dwight D. Eisenhower and the Founding of the American Assembly* (The American Assembly, 2004), 37.

3. Jacobs, *Dwight D. Eisenhower and the Founding of the American Assembly*, 37–38.

4. Jacobs, *Dwight D. Eisenhower and the Founding of the American Assembly*, 33.

5. Eisenhower, *At Ease*, 349–350.

6. Eisenhower, *At Ease*, 350.

7. Jacobs, *Dwight D. Eisenhower and the Founding of the American Assembly*, 33.

8. Jacobs, *Dwight D. Eisenhower and the Founding of the American Assembly*, 35.

9. "Address at the Columbia University National Bicentennial Dinner," New York City, May 31, 1954, in Public Papers of the Presidents—Eisenhower 1954, Containing the Public Messages, Speeches, and Statements of the President (Office of the Federal Register, National Archives and Records Service), 524.

10. Eisenhower, *At Ease*, 344.

11. Eisenhower, *At Ease*, 350.

12. Eisenhower legacy organizations recognized by the Eisenhower Memorial Commission in 1990: The American Assembly, The Eisenhower Foundation and

Presidential Library, People to People International, the Eisenhower Institute at Gettysburg College, and the Eisenhower Fellowships.

CHAPTER 24. ABILENE HONORS IKE

1. John S. D. Eisenhower, *Letters to Mamie* (Doubleday, 1978), letter of October 27, 1942, 49.

2. "Official Now . . . Kennedy School on North Side," *Abilene Reflector-Chronicle*, July 7, 1965.

3. Minutes of Abilene Board of Education, April 5, 1965.

4. *Abilene Reflector-Chronicle*, July 7, 1965.

5. *Abilene Reflector-Chronicle*, July 1, 2011.

6. *Abilene Reflector-Chronicle*, July 6, 2011.

7. Copies of email messages sent by members of the public to the Abilene City Commissioners, July 2011, in the possession of the author.

8. *Abilene Reflector-Chronicle*, July 12, 2011.

9. Catherine M. Lewis, *Don't Ask What I Shot: How Eisenhower's Love of Golf Helped Shape 1950s America* (McGraw Hill, 2007), 186–187.

CHAPTER 25. THE PRESCIENT EISENHOWER

1. Dwight D. Eisenhower Post-Presidential Papers, Secretary's Series, Box 1, Folder "DDE Drafts," 3.

2. "The Eisenhower Essays," *Reader's Digest*, a reprint collection of fourteen articles that appeared in *Reader's Digest* between 1963 and 1969.

2. Susan Eisenhower, *How Ike Led: The Principles Behind Eisenhower's Biggest Decisions* (Dunne Books, 2020), 72.

3. The President's News Conference of August 31, 1956, in the Public Papers of the Presidents-Dwight D. Eisenhower 1956, Containing the Public Messages, Speeches, and Statements of the President (Office of the Federal Register, National Archives and Records Service), 723.

BIBLIOGRAPHY

Adams, Sherman. *First-Hand Report: The Story of the Eisenhower Administration*. New York: Harper Brothers, 1961.

Albert, Susan Wittig. *The General's Women*. Farming Hills, MI: Gale Cengage Learning, 2017.

Ambrose, Stephen E. *Eisenhower: The President*. New York: Simon & Schuster, 1984.

Ambrose, Stephen E. *Eisenhower: Soldier, General of the Army, President-Elect, 1890–1952*. New York: Simon and Schuster, 1983.

Ambrose, Stephen E. "Ike and the Disappearing Atrocities." *New York Times Book Review*, February 24, 1991.

Bacque, James. *Other Losses: An Investigation into the Mass deaths of German Prisoners at the Hands of the French and Americans After World War II*. Toronto, Canada: Stoddart Publishing, 1989.

BaKhufu, Auset. *The Six Black Presidents: Black Blood, White Masks, USA*. Washington, DC: PIK2 Publications, 1993.

Bergman, Jerry. "President Eisenhower and the Influence of the Jehovah's Witnesses." *Kansas History* 21, no. 3 (Autumn 1998).

Birnbach, Lisa, ed. *The Official Preppy Handbook*. New York: Workman Publishing, 1980.

Bischof, Günter. *Eisenhower and the German POWs: Facts Against Falsehood*. Baton Rouge: Louisiana State University Press, 1992.

Brownell, Herbert (with John P. Burke). *Advising Ike: The Memoirs of Attorney General Herbert Brownell*. Lawrence: University Press of Kansas, 1993.

Butcher, Harry C. *My Three Years with Eisenhower*. New York: Simon & Schuster, 1946.

Craig, Campbell. *Destroying the Village: Eisenhower and Thermonuclear War*. New York: Columbia University Press, 1998.

Davis, Kenneth S. *General Eisenhower Soldier of Democracy: From Boyhood to Supreme Commander*. Garden City, NY: Doubleday, 1945.

D'Este, Carlo. *Eisenhower: A Soldier's Life*. New York: Henry Holt, 2002.

Donovan, Robert J. *Confidential Secretary: Ann Whitman's 20 Years with Eisenhower and Rockefeller*. New York: E. P. Dutton, 1988.

Doyle, William. *Inside the Oval Office: The White House Tapes from FDR to Clinton*. New York: Kodansha International, 1999.

Eberle, Mark E. "Eisenhower, Wilson, and Professional Baseball in Kansas" (2017). *Monographs*. http://scholars.fhsu.edu/all_monographs/1.

Eisenhower, David. *Eisenhower at War, 1943–1945.* New York: Random House, 1986.

Eisenhower, David, and Julie Nixon Eisenhower. *Going Home to Glory: A Memoir of Life with Dwight D. Eisenhower, 1961–1969.* New York: Simon & Schuster, 2010.

Eisenhower, Dwight D. *At Ease: Stories I Tell to Friends.* New York: Doubleday, 1967.

Eisenhower, Dwight D. *Crusade in Europe.* New York: Doubleday, 1948.

Eisenhower, Dwight D. Letter to Arthur Eisenhower, May 18, 1943, Pre-Presidential Papers of Dwight D. Eisenhower, Eisenhower Presidential Library, Abilene, KS.

Eisenhower, Dwight D. "Thoughts for Young Americans," The Eisenhower Essays. *Reader's Digest,* 1966.

Eisenhower, Dwight D. *The White House Years: Mandate for Change, 1953–1956.* Garden City, NY: Doubleday, 1963.

Eisenhower, Dwight D. *The White House Years: Waging Peace, 1956–1961.* Garden City, NY: Doubleday, 1965.

Eisenhower, John S. D. *Dwight D. Eisenhower Letters to Mamie.* New York: Doubleday, 1978.

Eisenhower, John S. D. *Strictly Personal.* Garden City, NY: Doubleday, 1974.

Eisenhower, Susan. *How Ike Led: The Principles Behind Eisenhower's Biggest Decisions.* New York: Thomas Dunne Books, 2020.

Eisenhower, Susan. *Mrs. Ike: Memories and Reflections on the Life of Mamie Eisenhower.* New York: Farar, Straus and Giroux, 1996.

Farnan, Thomas. "How Dwight D. Eisenhower Invented the Internet—and the Desktop Computer." *Forbes,* September 2, 2014.

Ferrell, Robert H., ed. *The Diary of James C. Hagerty: Eisenhower in Mid-Course, 1954–1955.* Bloomington: Indiana University Press, 1983.

Ferrell, Robert H., ed. *The Eisenhower Diaries.* New York: W. W. Norton, 1981.

Garcia, Juan Ramon. *Operation Wetback: The Mass Deportation of Mexican Undocumented Workers in 1954.* Westport, CT: Greenwood Press, 1980.

Goldstein, Gordon M. *Lessons in Disaster: George Bundy and the Path to War in Vietnam.* New York: Times Books, 2008.

Griffith, Robert, ed. *Ike's Letters to a Friend, 1941–1956.* Lawrence: University Press of Kansas, 1984.

Hafner, Katie, and Matthew Lyon. *Where Wizards Stay Up Late: The Origins of the Internet.* New York: Simon & Schuster, 1996.

Hatch, Alden. *General Ike: A Biography of Dwight D. Eisenhower.* Chicago: Consolidated Book Publishers, 1944.

Holl, Jack M. "Dwight D. Eisenhower: Civil Religion and the Cold War," in *Religion and the American Presidency,* eds. Mark J. Rozell and Cleaves Whitney. Palgrave, NY: MacMillan, 2007.

Holl, Jack M. *The Religious Journey of Dwight D. Eisenhower: Duty, God, and Country.* Grand Rapids, MI: William B. Eerdmans Publishing Company, 2021.

Holl, Jack M., and Roger M. Anders. *Atoms for Peace.* Milestone Documents in the National Archives, National Archives and Records Administration, Washington, DC. 1990.

Holt, Daniel D., and James W. Leyerzapf. *Eisenhower: The Prewar Diaries and Selected Papers, 1905–1941.* Baltimore, MD: Johns Hopkins University Press, 1998.

Kistiakowsky, George B. *A Scientist at the White House: The Private Diary of President Eisenhower's Special Assistant for Science and Technology.* Cambridge, MA: Harvard University Press, 1976.

Langham, Thomas Caloway. "The Eisenhower Administration and Operation Wetback, 1953–56: A Case Study of the Development of a Federal Policy to Control Illegal Migration." PhD dissertation, University of Texas, in the Eisenhower Presidential Library, 1984.

Larson, Arthur. *Eisenhower: The President Nobody Knew.* New York: Charles Scribner's Sons, 1968.

Lewis, Catherine M. *Don't Ask What I Shot: How Eisenhower's Love of Golf Helped Shape 1950s America.* New York: McGraw Hill, 2007.

Lighter, J. E. (ed.), et al. *Random House Historical Dictionary of American Slang.* New York: Random House, 1997.

MacCarthy-Morrogh, Michael, "Kay Summersby – Helping Ike Win the War," in *Skibbereen Historical Journal,* Volume 16, 2020.

MacManus, James. *Ike and Kay.* New York: Overlook Duckworth, 2018.

McCann, Kevin. *Man From Abilene.* Garden City, NY: Doubleday, 1952.

McKeogh, Michael J., and Richard Lockridge. *Sgt Mickey And General Ike.* New York: G. P. Putnam's Sons, 1946 (reprint edition in 2016).

Miller, Merle. *Ike the Soldier: As They Knew Him.* New York: G. P. Putnam's Sons, 1987.

Miller, Merle. *Plain Speaking: An Oral History of Harry S. Truman.* New York: Berkley Publishing Company, 1973.

Morgan, Kay Summersby. *Past Forgetting: My Love Affair with Dwight D. Eisenhower.* New York: Simon & Schuster, 1975.

Neal, Steve. *The Eisenhowers.* Lawrence: University of Kansas Press, 1978.

Newton, Jim. *Eisenhower: The White House Years.* New York: Doubleday, 2011.

Nixon, Richard. *Six Crises.* New York: Doubleday, 1962.

Papers of Dwight D. Eisenhower. Johns Hopkins University Press.

Parmet, Herbert S. *Eisenhower and the American Crusades.* New York: Macmillan Company, 1972.

Perret, Geoffrey. *Eisenhower*. New York: Random House, 1999.

Pierard, Richard, and Robert Linder. *Civil Religion and the Presidency*. Grand Rapids, MI: Academic Books, 1988.

Pietrusza, David. *1948: Harry Truman's Improbable Victory and the Year that Transformed America*. New York: Union Square Publishing, 2011.

Pinkley, Virgil, with James F. Scheer. *Eisenhower Declassified*. Old Tappan, NJ: Fleming H. Revell Company, 1979.

Public Papers of the Presidents of the United States: Dwight D. Eisenhower 1953–1961. Washington, DC, Government Printing Office.

Rabi, I. I. *My Life and Times as a Physicist*. Claremont, CA: Claremont College, 1960.

Robinson, Ambassador Gilbert A. *Why I Like Ike*. McLean, VA: International Publishers, 2012 (reissue).

Rogers, J. A. *The Five Negro Presidents: According to What White People Said They Were*. Middletown, CT: Wesleyan University Press 2014 (originally self-published in 1965).

Russoli, Edward and Candace. *Ike the Cook: General, President, and Cook*. Allentown, PA: Benedettini Books, 1990.

Safire, William. *The New Language of Politics: An Anecdotal Dictionary of Catchwords, Slogans, and Political Usage*. New York: Random House, 1968.

Showalter, Dennis E. ed. *Forging the Shield: Eisenhower and National Security for the 21st Century*. Chicago: Imprint Publications, 2005.

Summersby, Kay. *Eisenhower Was My Boss*. New York: Prentice Hall, 1948.

Tannenwald, Nina. *The Nuclear Taboo: The United States and the Non-Use of Nuclear Weapons Since 1945*. New York: Cambridge University Press, 2007.

Teasley, Mack. "The Kansas Cyclone—Eisenhower the Athlete." *Kansas Sports* 10, no. 1 (August/September 1995).

Teasley, Martin M. "German Language Study at the Dwight D. Eisenhower Library." *Foreign Language Annals*, February 1987/Volume 20.

Teasley, Martin M. "No Signs of Mid-Life Crisis: The Eisenhower Library at Thirtysomething." *Government Information Quarterly*, 1995, Volume 12, Number 1.

Theoharis, Athan. *From the Secret Files of J. Edgar Hoover*. Chicago: Ivan R. Dee, Inc, 1991.

Thomas, Evan. *Ike's Bluff: President Eisenhower's Secret Battle to Save the World*. New York: Little, Brown and Company, 2012

Towles, Amor. *A Gentleman in Moscow*. New York: Viking Press, 2016.

Troy, Gil. "With Ike, Rumors Were Steamer Than Facts." *Washington Post*, March 1, 1998.

Vance, Ashlee. *Elon Musk: Tesla, SpaceX, and the Quest for a Fantastic Future*. New York: Ecco, 2015.

INDEX

Page numbers in italics represent photos.

www.ingramcontent.com/pod-product-compliance
Lightning Source LLC
Chambersburg PA
CBHW020605270326
41927CB00005B/186